EXPLORE AUSTRALIA'S WILDERNESS

TWELVE UNIQUE ADVENTURES

Written and Photographed by Leigh Hemmings

ANGUS
& ROBERTSON

A division of HarperCollins*Publishers*

To Charles Murray (1912–1983)
who always disputed the indisputable

AN ANGUS & ROBERTSON BOOK

First published in Australia in 1990 by
Collins/Angus & Robertson Publishers Australia

Collins/Angus & Robertson Publishers Australia
Unit 4, Eden Park, 31 Waterloo Road, North Ryde
NSW 2113, Australia

William Collins Publishers Ltd
31 View Road, Glenfield, Auckland 10, New Zealand

Angus & Robertson (UK)
16 Golden Square, London WIR 4BN, United Kingdom

Copyright © Leigh Hemmings 1990

National Library of Australia
Cataloguing-in-Publication data:

Hemmings, Leigh.
Explore Australia's wilderness.

Includes index.
ISBN 0 207 16447 9.

1. Outdoor recreation — Australia — Guide-books.
2. Wilderness areas — Australia — Guide-books.
2. Australia — Description and travel — 1976-
Guide-books. I. Title.

Typeset in 12.5/14pt Bembo by Post Typesetters, Queensland
Printed in Hong Kong

5 4 3 2 1
95 94 93 92 91 90

CONTENTS

INTRODUCTION

The preservation of wilderness has traditionally been given low priority. The Australian wilderness has been cleared, mined, eroded, grazed, trampled, since the arrival of Europeans. You only have to consider the flooding of Tasmania's Lake Pedder, the concreting of stretches of Queensland's coastline, the clear felling of vast tracts of northern New South Wales rainforests, the creation of dustbowl wastelands in Western Australia's Kimberley and the degradation of the Victorian Alps to realise that this process has been widespread. Given that harsh reality, few people would disagree that preserving the remaining fragments of wilderness is one of our greatest conservation challenges. Yet with so much already destroyed, and so little remaining, some people retain open hostility to wilderness preservation.

In defining wilderness I roughly follow the Australian Conservation Foundation's definition: 'a large tract of primitive country with its lands and waters and its native plant and animal life substantially unmodified by humans and their works'. Preservation of Australia's remaining wilderness is an attainable challenge. The dedication of thousands of individuals has resulted in protection of the Great Barrier Reef, the Franklin River, Kosciusko and Kakadu, just to name a few. Wilderness is ours in the sense that we must agitate, promote and legislate for its protection, but it is the world's in the sense that it is part of a rapidly vanishing commodity on a global scale.

In writing *Explore Australia's Wilderness*, I have attempted to share my love of the wilderness and to present a range of non-destructive means of access to its areas. In doing so I hope to debunk the myth that all conservationists want to simply 'lock-up' wilderness. Managing these areas is a complex, expensive, time-consuming task, but unless the wilderness is a last resort sanctuary for the preservation of near-extinct species, it is irresponsible for environmental authorities to deny people access to it. All access has some impact, but provided wilderness is not regarded as an outdoor gym, or a wasteland awaiting 'improvement', then impact can be minimal. Exploring wilderness requires understanding — a will to move softly through the landscape like a native animal.

Keeping an untouched piece of nature wild is not difficult. Walking on a primitive beach between the high and low tide marks ensures that tracks will last only a few hours. Just like orange peel, toilet paper doesn't belong in the wilderness. If you carry it in, then carry it out. Burying just means it is dug up later and trying to set fire to used toilet paper just makes for more bushfires.

Writing a book that seeks to encourage enjoyment of wilderness areas places me in a quandary. Publicity often increases people's desire to experience a wilderness area and greater use increases pressure on its resources. At the same time, publicity can alert people to the value of wilderness, as shown by the snowballing force behind struggles to protect the Great Barrier Reef, Cooloola National Park and the Franklin River.

In writing this book I have tried to strike a balance between low impact access and the maintenance of wilderness values. Unequivocally, motorised vehicles, aircraft, mining, forestry and development have no place in a wilderness. Restricted airspace above the area should also be an integral part of wilderness preservation.

Explore Australia's Wilderness arose from many years of magazine and newspaper adventure travel writing, tens of thousands of photographs, and hundreds of trips into wild and beautiful locations throughout Australia. The twelve areas featured are personal favourites as are the types of adventure travel within them.

I've written *Explore Australia's Wilderness* as a resource book as well as a book simply to be enjoyed. The historical connections place each activity in an Australian and international context. The experience section follows trips I have done through the chosen wilderness areas. Sometimes, things will go awry between planning stages and actually achieving the objective; for example, the Jagungal trip described here was my second attempt to set cross-country skis on that mountain — the first ended in a two-day tent-bound blizzard! However, each of the activities outlined is well within the means of anyone who has some flexibility of mind and body. (As you may judge from the photograph on the inside back cover I am hardly a super-strong 'macho'!)

The location guides that follow each experience are not meant to be exhaustive texts on every living creature in a specific area; rather they are intended to give you a general idea of the area and the flora and fauna you are most likely to encounter. The basics are designed to give down to earth information to make your trip more enjoyable and to ensure that, within the framework of sensible packing and carrying, exploring wilderness can be enjoyable *and* pain-free. Once you have embarked on a wilderness adventure, try to match it with a change in habits. Leave the soap behind, just rinse off the day's dirt, and keep the streams pristine. Adopt the sun as your timekeeper, but try to be up before it reveals the earth each day. And rediscover (with sunscreen on the delicate parts) what it means to be an unclothed mammal.

I fervently hope that twenty generations from now when this book is dusty and dog-eared, the featured areas will still be wilderness and can be enjoyed in the same way that I have experienced them. When you are reading or exploring wilderness areas in the near future, remember that they were preserved only because dedicated conservationists peacefully and persistently argued against their destruction. Often derided for their actions, they continue to use meagre resources against powerful opponents. If you are not already a member of a conservation group, I urge you to join one today.

LEIGH HEMMINGS

RAFTING

If ever a word gives birth to ideas of escape and adventure it is "raft". Making a device to float, jumping aboard, pushing off and letting wind, waves, tide or river current do the rest has a seductive quality of pure abandonment. Romance aside, the beginnings of rafting are centred in the practicality of safely crossing fast rivers or broad stretches of estuary.

The earliest aid to floating recorded in Australia was the Aborigine's use of single logs. It puzzled the first European explorers to come across abandoned logs lying on the sides of river banks — until, that is, they saw the locals using the logs as floating aids to cross from one shore to the other. My favourite report is one from late last century of a four metre pandanus log being used by a group in the following way: leader holds log with left hand and swims with right, number two rests right hand on leader and swims with left, number three grasps number two with left hand and swims with right and so on down the line. For a rest, they alternate positions with the leader and, on pausing, all cling to the log.

In Australia the chronology of constructed water craft which peaks at ocean-going, double outrigger sailing canoes, began humbly with rafts of bark. Bark rafts were perhaps one of the first throw-away consumer items with an extremely short shelf life. Aborigines made them quickly to solve an immediate crossing problem or as a temporary platform for a spot of spear fishing. Their advantage over single logs was that the platform kept hunters out of cold or shark-overrun waters. Once used however, the bark rafts became water-logged and sank.

The search for a longer term stable platform resulted in the

□ OPPOSITE *The Franklin River bubbles untamed and undammed after a peaceful struggle by conservationists throughout Australia to protect it.*

development of a peculiar craft, the triangular raft. There's a recently made one permanently aground in the Derby library, Western Australia, and it looks just like the one pictured by W.E. Roth in 1910. Essentially the triangular raft is vee-shaped and made of saplings with their butts at one end — tied together fore and aft with a cross brace. According to Roth "... over the wider portion of the raft is placed a bundle of dried grass, upon which the traveller squats and paddles...". Later developments produced a double layer of logs making the craft more stable and more durable.

Rafting today contains echoes of the past. On a rafting trip a group becomes a tightly-knit clan journeying through a wild uninhabited place, in much the same compact way as early nomadic people roamed the earth. Basic elements of earth, fire and water which are paid scant attention in an urban environment gain a rare prominence. The river is generally a friend carrying the clan gently, but at times it is a thing to be feared. At day's end a fire provides warmth, renewed life and laughter, and mother earth offers protection in caves, caverns and river banks above the river's reach just as it has done for more than 40,000 years of habitation in Australia. And perhaps just as it will for the next one hundred millenniums. With careful management and minimal impact camping, rafters can leave the environment as they find it.

Although white water rafting is full-on adventure travel, new-chum rafters come from all walks of life, and range in age from early twenties to late sixties. It's an incredible buzz to float down a fast flowing stream aboard a rolling, diving, weaving rubber raft, but there's more mental courage required than sheer brawn. In fact, too much brawn and not enough pulling to the bank to inspect the next rapid gets people into trouble.

Flat and folded, a modern raft resembles the left-over skin of an elephant. It is only when all hands enthusiastically work the air pumps that life is wheezed into it. Then it takes on a new shape — bulbous, bouncy and ready to float. Going rafting with a good adventure travel operator requires little more than that you turn up, struggle into a wetsuit, don a life jacket and helmet and clasp hold of your paddle. The operator takes care of all the logistics involved in getting to and from the river while you bring along a sense of adventure, some fitness and the ability to swim — self-guided trips require much more planning and packing.

On-shore and on-board paddling lessons help to make things clear for first timers. For a trip in inflatable kayaks the guides conduct an on-water demonstration of some of the techniques for safe white-water travel. Inflatable kayaks may look a little ungainly but it is remarkable just what fancy feats you can get them to perform. Tucking in behind the eddy of a large rock while seeing and feeling the water rage past is great, as is powering through giant pressure waves created by fast water moving over an uneven bottom.

Most magical of the manoeuvres is the ferry glide. This sounds weird, but it is really a sneaky way of getting across a swift current without a capsize or a rock-wrapping drama. By paddling upstream with the bow pointed slightly towards your destination bank, the kayak, canoe or raft simply "glides" across the stream.

Aboard a large multi-person raft and under the direction of an experienced guide, beginners learn paddling and control. A few basic strokes combined with clear instructions, and a supposedly lumbering raft is made to perform.

Following a call from the guide of "forward hard left, back hard right", the paddlers on the left hand side begin to paddle with strong forward strokes and the paddlers on the right hand side start paddling with strong reverse strokes — in response the raft spins like a top. Other calls from an experienced river guide can position the raft exactly for rapid running — well, most of the time. Being uncontrolled in a heart-in-the-mouth white water rapid, then going over backwards or sideways is lots of fun. Even capsizes are good fun, especially after the event when everyone is back on board.

Tackling any big water gives a heady rush of apprehension mixed with enthusiasm. On entering the vee-shaped pattern at the top of the rapid, the raft is held for a brief moment in limbo — committed yet moving ever so gently. Your attention is then turned to shallow rocks as they flick past. Big dips and swirls and pressure waves are sufficient to up end both cargo and

☐ Able to bend and bounce, it is easy to see why inflatable canoes are known as on-water dodgems.

passengers, but most of the time they will shoot the raft clear at the bottom like a surfer blown out of a tube.

During any rafting trip someone is likely to be whipped out of the raft and bobbed along in the water. If they are protected by a helmet, life jacket, wetsuit and wetsuit booties, an unplanned swim is pretty safe.

□ *Sometimes, especially if the weather is kind, it can be fun to try running a rapid without a raft!*

Despite this, at the start of the trip to be told what to do "when" you fall out does little to instil confidence. However, if you do fall out of the raft, face downstream and keep your feet up in front of you. This avoids the possibility of catching your feet on a submerged rock and being dragged under by the force of the stream. Amazingly, running a rapid without a raft is really enjoyable and if the river water isn't too much like melted ice you will probably walk upstream at lunchtime stops and jump in and bob downstream through the white water.

Just as rock climbers name their routes, most big rapids on recognised rafting rivers have had names bestowed on them by the rafters who first explored the river. Some are descriptive titles reflecting the geography or a state of mind. Take for example the Sidewinder, Boulder Brace, Nasty Notch and the Pig Trough.

Because food and safety equipment are of paramount importance and since everything must be carried aboard the rafts, space for personal gear is tight. You are given either a waterproof river bag or a small drum. Into this, ten days or more of clothes, a sleeping bag, sneakers, and personal bits and pieces must be stuffed. Prior to departure it takes about five attempts at stripping out the non-essentials to shoehorn all your gear into a river bag. But packing on cold wet mornings beside a river is a diabolical task. There is nothing so frustrating as to have struggled everything in and fought with cramping fingers to get the lid closed, only to discover you have forgotten your only dry towel!

Each day's rafting ends with the group moving all its gear up the river bank to that night's campsite. And this involves an enthusiastic session of bucket-brigading. Even if some people have had a couple of unscheduled dips in icy water, by the time the gear is unpacked, tents are erected and firewood is collected everyone is well warmed and getting fitter each day.

With the chores done something very special follows: releasing your wet body from a clammy wetsuit and soggy socks. Ah, the joy of it all. This can be followed by an even greater delight — reopening a river bag after a day of dunkings to discover camp clothes still warm and dry. Last century, travellers made do with salt messpork and flourcakes baked in a frying pan with a pannikin of tea sweetened with brown sugar; today, rafters travel in gourmet style. Settle in front of the fire with a glass of wine in hand and watch in salivating anticipation as dinner nears completion.

Rafting down the Franklin River is one of Australia's great adventures.

RAFTING THE FRANKLIN RIVER

We assemble beside a swiftly flowing stream (the Collingwood) and I'm damn sure everyone's nervous, I certainly am. From what I've read of this white water journey through Tasmanian wilderness, rafting the Franklin River can be anything from frantic to fantastic. Last night's briefing did plenty to fill me in on the specifics, but not much to calm nerves.

Rasping cries fill the air as our two leaden grey rafts slowly inflate. They are transformed. We take on new roles as river rafters by the simple act of donning wet suit, rubber booties, helmet and life vest, although we are hardly seasoned river rafters: in us, image and reality are two vastly different things though for the guides they are one — all bronzed strength and fitness, they ooze confidence.

Perhaps a little of this confidence rubs off, for I climb aboard, even though I still have a heavy load of misgivings, grasp a paddle and try to wear a look of eager anticipation. However there is no time for the real concerns as the river grabs hold of the raft and sweeps us headlong into this adventure. In a big backwashing pool of dark sluggish water, paddling lessons capture my attention. I begin to learn the process of transforming a guide's call into appropriate paddle action. In doing

Powering through a sizeable rapid on the Franklin River gets the adrenalin flowing.

so I find that what looks like a cumbersome immobile raft with a resolute mind of its own is indeed that, but that with a team paddling approach even the stubbornest of rafts can be made to perform.

Collingwood water mingles with Franklin water a little while later and it feels like we have really begun. The Franklin River is actually born many kilometres away, high in the Cheyne Range. And this river does seem to possess life. Unlike cowered waterways at the whim of dam controllers, the Franklin is more akin to a wild animal — tough, free, unpredictable and periodically dangerous. Fittingly for a wild creature, it traipses through pure wilderness, not degraded landscape.

The first-day rapids are fun, and while rougher rapids may follow, by nightfall my energy is completely expended from accumulated tension, excitement and physical exertion. It's a just reward to be off the river and wrapped in a sleeping bag ensconced on an inflated lilo under the protection of a natural cavern. Coming from an urbanised lifestyle it's a shock to bunk down in a cave, but sleep comes quickly.

Awakening to a call of "coffee's on" in Angel Rain Cavern, I gaze out through a gossamer mist to the river below. It is like being nestled behind a delicate waterfall. Less delicate is the river-created fall at Log Jam, which has us all out of the raft and struggling — lumbering full-of-gear grey monsters over and past obstructions. The rapid Nasty Notch demands everything be removed from the rafts and repacked before it allows us to experience the turbulent madness of Descension Gorge and then finally to enter a deep peaceful haven, the Irenabyss, where the Franklin enjoys life at a calmer pace.

Overnight awakenings are greeted by rain splattering on the tarp, yet I emerge to a morning warmed by a new sun glow and breakfast under a deep blue sky. Today, I'm sure, will be sunshine and warmth, so of course by the time we are loading the rafts heavy rain is being lashed down by a driving icy gale. Tasmanian weather is a fickle beast — like the river in a way. In the first of a couple of days of trouble-free rafting we come upon a section called the Crankle where water is persuaded to travel to every point of the compass over a very short distance.

By the second of these idyllic days a touch of complacency is creeping in, even though the rapids seem to be getting larger at each bend of the river. Peak excitement for me comes when a dipping, swirling run turns into a big, gut-wrenching drop punctuated by a full stop mid-stream collision with an immense boulder. I'm propelled from the raft like a popped cork and then proceed to bob along. A river-level view is not pleasant — lots of bewildering confused water coupled with what seem to me to be fast moving rocks. Becoming a human pancake between granite and neoprene is to be avoided at all costs so I gyrate to a position up-side of the raft and snatch the safety ropes. A numb mind makes reboarding a bit confusing, but as I am trying to hoist my waterlogged body up, the nicest, most comforting large hand grabs the base of my life jacket and forward rolls me into the bilges. Even wet and cold it's nice to be back.

Through a campsite in an ancient

☐ Just after I took this photograph the raft hit a rock and I was ejected into the rapid — the camera was waterproof. Unharmed, I was soon back on board.

rainforest at the foot of the rugged Engineer Range peals the most incongruous sound — a 5.20 am wrist watch alarm. Its jarring reminder of that other world is necessary in this wilderness for today we face the Great Ravine. If rafting the Franklin can be viewed as taking part in a living symphony, then the terrifying rapids of the Great Ravine are its truly awe-inspiring crescendo. Nothing that has come before has prepared me for this place. The intimidating sight of water attempting to pulverise solid rock by its sheer volume is accompanied by a deafening head-numbing roar which seems to vibrate through me like some primeval force. Suddenly it seems the Franklin is in a paranoid rush to escape to the sea and nothing can impede its progress. Little wonder rafters have died here.

Above each leviathan rapid we land and survey scenes of immense, unharnessed power. Names like the Churn, Coruscades, the Forceit, Side Winder, Thunderush and the Cauldron come to violent life and I share the reverence of those rafters who have come before. Only an experienced eye and a cool nerve can determine which of these gargantuan rapids we will attempt with thin, air-filled neoprene and frail bodies, and those which we must find laborious ways around on foot. Portaging is time consuming and energy sapping but it keeps us safe from the clutches of the river — river running is fast and tantalising.

Each time a decision is made to run a section I can't believe what I'm hearing. The water looks so enormous. Back in the raft I listen intently to the words of the guide, trying to memorise how we are to attempt the unattemptable. In this calm before the storm the raft is stable, hardly moving. Yet I discover that once we have slipped through the smooth water vee at the rapid's

☐ FOLLOWING PAGE The Franklin River begins life high in the Cheyne Range and travels 125 kilometres before joining the Gordon River.

beginning and dived into the rapid proper, we are in the clutches of something powerful. Our cumbersome weighty rafts dance, shake, fly and plunge — driven at lightning speed through water and air. On board it's like being trapped in some sort of gigantic washing machine — on the heavy cycle.

It seems only a second or two after starting into each mad maelstrom white-water world that a raft scooped empty of excess water is dumped full to the gunwales. This transforms an air-filled raft into a leaden water carrier which responds to our frantic efforts with the greatest of reluctance.

Attaining the sanctity of calmer water, I am elated with a heady exhilaration born of tempting fate, and getting away with it. We look at each other in amazement.

The exuberance which has hyped us all is tempered by concern as we watch the second raft run the same gauntlet, but our reservations are soon extinguished by the sight of the next rapid; and the next, and the next. Awash, afloat, submerged and refloated, the challenges queue up until the essence of the day becomes a struggle where our sole aim is to make it beyond the nearest obstacle. And in the midst of everything it begins to hail. Hail becomes rain which, as the sun returns, converts our river-scape into a world of gloss and steam.

Deliverance Reach, the name says it all. We glide into a river bank of time-smoothed boulders and gritty sand. Gear out, tarp erected and immediately two of our group fall asleep only a few metres above the river. By now the Franklin is the constant theme of our lives so its

close proximity does nothing but caress us.

Our reward for passing the Great Ravine is a day of magical rafting: lots of rapids interspersed with energy-restoring calmer water. We run Ol' Three Tiers, Ganymede's Pool and the Trojans. Ahead is Newland Cascades and a two-night rest stop, but in between is the Pig Trough. This horror was named way back in 1840 by government surveyor James Calder's track cutters during an epic journey when they laboured for thirty-one weeks to cut a track from Lake St Clair to the Gordon River. Lining one of the rafts through the first part of Pig Trough we delicately negotiate a walk on deadly slimed rocks, then rejoin the river and do a madcap ferry glide only metres above an ugly drop. Raft two has a mind of its own, casting asunder one of its crew then jamming. Tonnes of water bury it (and our gear) and refuse to give it back. Eventually ten humans overcome one river and we can bounce happily through the cascades.

Soft dawn light filters into our multi-level cavern just above the river and I can see other caterpillar-curled dwellers intent on sleeping in. I'm too excited to stay immobile. As we've been travelling down the river, in the back of my mind has been a poster that was used with marvellous effect during the long campaign to save the Franklin. Having our day off the river just downstream from Rock Island Bend where the photograph for the poster was taken means I am able to see the island for myself. An upstream scramble takes me to the spot where wilderness photographer Peter Dombrovskis must have been

☐ *A moment of drama at Pig Trough as guide Steve Prothero jumps aboard a stuck raft to try to free it.*

standing to create his beautifully crafted image. Rock Island Bend in reality has even more majesty than the poster portrays and I am unable to comprehend why anyone would even contemplate drowning this river.

The delicate loveliness of Shower Cliff Cavern detours us next morning and it seems the nature of the river is changing. Jane River enters just past Little Fall and we are now rafting a Franklin comprised of long languid pools and occasional rapids. Rhythmical paddling takes us to Mantree Creek Camp, a patch of rainforest where tree ferns intermingle with huge fronds to form a jade canopy. Nearer to earth the local leeches greet our arrival with delight.

From what is a primeval forest we paddle even further back in time to Kutikina Cave. We enter this place silently for it has been estimated that the cave contains over ten million artifacts. Kutikina (which means spirit) is believed to be the southernmost occupation point of Ice-Age humans. As a group of fascinated visitors we are keen that the evidence remains unaltered.

Our last night river-bound is spent on Shingle Island, an island where burnished stones seem to vibrate tenderly with the passing water. Post-breakfast paddling is a quiet affair tinged with sadness. As the Franklin River loses its identity and is intermingled with the Gordon, we too lose our identities as river rafters.

LOCATION GUIDE

Tasmania's largest river system is the Gordon and one of its major tributaries is the Franklin River. Named after the governor of Tasmania by surveyor James Calder in 1839, the Franklin begins life high in the Cheyne Range sliding down 1,400 metres in its 125 kilometres journey to join the Gordon River. Calder while on a preliminary survey for a later exploration by Governor Franklin, came upon what he called "a large and furious torrent". Franklin's extraordinary journey in 1842 was made partially on a huon pine twin log raft named Eleanor Isabella and the party included a number of convicts whose job it was to carry Lady Jane Franklin in her chair. In reality this adventurous lady shared the joy of slogging over mountain passes, wading through the mush and trying to sleep on beds of ferns during long wet cold nights. The chair can still be seen in the Tasmanian Museum, Hobart. Huon pine was the catalyst for later exploration and exploitation by the piners who achieved incredible feats hauling punts up river to fell the giant trees. Winter floods carried the fallen timber downstream where it was claimed and milled. Stumps which can still be seen today document their progress upstream.

Bushwalkers, canoeists and rafters came to share the beauty that remained. In 1958, the marvellous wilderness photographer Oleg Truchanas solo kayaked the Gordon (he drowned in 1972). The Franklin repelled John Hawkins and John Dean's 1951 attempt to canoe it with 250 kilograms of food and equipment in two army disposal kayaks. Years later they returned and were again defeated after one canoe was jammed under a three metre waterfall and broken in halves. Joined by Trevor Newland and Henry Crocker, they finally made a successful trip in 1958. It took nineteen days for the first rafting trip (Hansen-Keelhoff) in 1971 and many rubber duckie rafters and commercial trips have followed.

After years of undamaging enjoyment, a period of madness centred on the Franklin beginning in 1979. What conservationist Bob Brown saw as "a wild and wondrous thing" was planned by the Tasmanian Hydro Electricity Commission (HEC) to be placed at the bottom of a sterile reservoir. Brown had first rafted the Franklin in 1976; he fell in love with it and named many of its features. Amid great uproar the HEC had flooded Lake Pedder, one of the most magical places in Tasmania, then set out to do the same thing to the Franklin River. Such was the overwhelming response that it brought an environmental question to the forefront of federal politics (a place it has retained ever since).

Also out of previous conservation debates came, in 1976, the formation of the Tasmanian Wilderness Society (now known as the Wilderness Society). What developed was a grinding, all-consuming, but peaceful struggle, involving the Society, the Australian Conservation Foundation and a good percentage of the Australian public. More than 3,000 people took part in the actual blockade, with over 1,400 of them being arrested under special trespass laws enacted by the state government of Robin Grey, but the support for saving the Franklin was overwhelming

□ OPPOSITE *Rock Island Bend has always been a symbol of the spirit of the Franklin: wild and untouched.*

12

and nationwide. In December 1982, the Franklin and Lower Gordon Wild Rivers, Cradle Mountain–Lake St Clair, and the South West national parks were placed on the World Heritage List. This enabled the newly elected Federal Government which was led by Bob Hawke, to stop the dam. The government's decision was upheld by the High Court of Australia in July 1983.

The Lower Gordon Scenic Reserve was decreed in 1908 and it was declared and named the Franklin-Lower Gordon Wild Rivers National Park of 195,200 in 1981, but later had 14,125 hectares revoked for the HEC.

Precambrian metamorphic rock forms the precipitous quartzite mountain ranges through which the Franklin has etched its way for countless years, producing the highly polished rock faces so loved by wilderness photographers. The region has a plethora of limestone caves created by water eating into rock formed more than 400 million years ago. Glacial features such as horns, cirques and moraines abound and it is believed that the Franklin once carried melting glacier ice.

The rediscovery of the Kutikina (in 1981) and Deenareena (1985) caves beside the Franklin River, along with radiocarbon dating, indicate that Aboriginal occupation began between 13,000 to 20,000 years ago. For archaeologists, the hearths, fires, charcoal bones, stone implements, flaked chips and hammer stone are clear evidence of almost 5,000 years of continual occupation. So far, Kutikina has produced 40,000 stone artifacts and almost 250,000 bone fragments and so provides a mountain of reasons to preserve the region.

In 1937 and 1938 confirmed Thylacine (Tasmanian tiger) tracks were discovered in the region, but after many expeditions, most scientific opinion leads to the conclusion that the tiger is extinct. It is important that in the future none of the currently resident animals go the same way. Though they are not often seen by river rafters, Tasmanian devils, brushtail and ringtail possums, pademelons, Bennet's wallabies, wombats, echidnas and marsupial mice are resident in the Franklin-Lower Gordon Wild Rivers National Park. Quiet river rafters are more likely to see water rats and platypuses enjoying life in the wilderness. And to be lunch for a leech.

Overhead is the domain of the wedgetail eagle and goshawk, but swallows and tree martins are constant close river companions. Rosellas, honeyeaters, thornbills, cormorants and grey fantails are also often seen. You may have an occasional uplifting sighting of azure kingfishers flitting along the river. Because of the reduction of the orange-bellied parrot's winter habitat in Victoria's saltmarsh, the Royal Australasian Ornithologists' Union is concerned for the survival of this endangered bird which breeds only in south west Tasmania.

Where the river begins, the most striking flora are sub-alpine cushion plants and pineapple grass. At lower altitudes are tall alpine ash, king william pine and deciduous beech. The surviving huon pines (up to 2,500 years old) are surrounded by the moss-camouflaged skeletons of those that were logged many years ago. Within the riverine rainforest are sassafras, leatherwood, horizontal scrub and tree ferns, along with a marvellous array of mosses, fungi and lichens.

FUTURE PROBLEMS

Few dangers could compare to that of the area being drowned sixty metres below the surface of an HEC impoundment and, as ridiculous as it may seem, there are still politicians who would wish this to occur. May they never come to power.

THE BASICS

Depending on the length of trip and the grade of the river, craft can be big stable gregarious rafts carrying four or more adventurers, smaller single and two person inflatable canoes (called white water dodgems because of their delightful ability to bounce off river obstacles) or single person cheap rubber duckies (usually with a very short lifespan). Inflatable canoes and rubber duckies are powered by double ended paddles (a suggested design can be found in the Wilderness Society's "Notes for Franklin River Rafters").

Rapids are caused by a drop and/or a turn in the river which can result either in nicely spaced waves down a gentle slope, or in confusing eddies and cross currents. White-water rapids are graded from one to six. This grading roughly describes the degree of difficulty from easy rocky races, to dips and swirls which are just plain fun, through to life threatening monsters which cannot be rafted by anyone.

Ideally you are trying to choose a line through the rapid which is parallel with the current — side on or backwards is not necessarily a great position to be in. Where there's a rapid above your ability there are two choices, lining and portaging. Lining is simply getting out of the raft, tying a line to it and guiding the empty raft through. Portaging is getting out, unpacking and carrying the raft and the gear around the rapid. On a low portage the raft is unpacked and all the gear is carried across the rocks beside the rapid then the unladen raft is either lined through the rapid or struggled around the rocks. Once you reach a safe area below the major obstacle everything is repacked before pushing on. High portage is where it is impossible to simply walk around the rapid — sometimes due to the presence of sheer-sided gorges. The only way past is for every piece of equipment, including the deflated raft, to be carried over often steep goat tracks leading up and around the rapid. Regrettably it can sometimes take three hours to make a downstream gain of 600 metres. A day of high portages is a real mongrel.

River levels dictate portages and following heavy rain, a wild river can rise with incredible speed. Dead eels have been found on branches of trees ten metres above normal river level. Overnight a docile river stream becomes a raging sea of gigantic pressure waves. Rafting through sections of sheer sided ravines is too dangerous, so the only option is to stay put at camp and wait. The waiting can sometimes stretch into numerous days. Fortunately it's the likelihood of getting marooned which is used as justification for carrying mountains of delicious food.

Dangers

Rafting can be terminal as a number of unfortunate accidents over the past few years have proved. Minimising that danger is a matter of being conservative and not being foolhardy, and portaging all rapids that are beyond your skill level. Stopper rocks at the foot of sudden drops can create a situation like a tumble action washing machine, recycling anything that gets trapped — including you if the rocks are big enough. Experienced rafters suggest approaching one as strongly as possible and keeping paddling until you are through. Out of the raft and in the rapid, the cardinal rule is to face downstream keeping your feet

up. Once out of the raft there's always a chance of being crushed against rocks, jammed between rock and raft, trapped under water or caught by a log jam. A panic free attitude and the correct gear (particularly helmet and lifejacket) will help to minimise damage.

Exposure and exhaustion go hand in hand. Dunkings and frightening swims, icy winds on wet clothing, long portages and paddling fatigue all contribute to a lowering of enjoyment and can lead to life threatening situations. Keeping warm is vital so don't wear cotton, instead go for a mix of wool or fibrepile, thermal underwear, wet suit and booties.

☐ *Languid image of a fast flowing river.*

☐ OPPOSITE *Lunching on the river stones, as the Franklin roars in the background.*

RAFTING THE FRANKLIN RIVER — LUXURY CHECK LIST

Body Protection

Canoeing style buoyancy vest
Long john style wetsuit
Wetsuit booties
Woollen socks
Lifa underwear
Long sleeved woollen shirt
T shirts
Helmet
Visor (worn under helmet)
Tracksuit/woollen pants for night
Sneakers — quick dry nylon uppers with good
  grip for slippery rocks
Change of woollen socks
Bathers
Dry woollen sweater
Gore-Tex waterproof full length jacket with
  hood (e.g. J & H Cats & Dogs)
100 per cent UV protection sunglasses with
  retaining strap
Sunscreen
Rid insect repellent
Moisturiser cream (river water dries skin)

Accommodation

Tarpaulin & poles (caves & caverns can be used
  on the trip)
4-season Karrimat, Thermarest or Lilo mattress
Candle/reading torch (spare long life batteries)
Sleeping bag winter rated (e.g. J & H Winterlite
  or a synthetic fill if you are not sure the bag will
  be kept perfectly dry)
Silk inner sheet

Getting There

Air to Hobart, bus to Collingwood River bridge
Pick up in Gordon River by one of day boats out
  of Strahan
Rafting Permit Tasmanian National Parks and
  Wildlife Service, Hobart

Transport

Raft, as good as you (or group) can afford
Paddles & spare
15 m of 6 mm rope
Tie down straps or webbing
Raft repair kit & air pump
Home brewing barrels
Silva type compass
Plastic pealess whistle
Franklin & Olga 1:100,000 Tasmaps
Waterproof self-sealing inner bags
Extra waterproof pack liners
Smaller waterproof stuff sacks for clothing

Camping

Emergency matches (in self-sealing plastic bags)
Candle lantern & spare candles
Swiss army knife
Cup, bowl, eating utensils
Trangia stove (with kettle)
Metholated Spirits (in more than one container)
Aluminium billy (for fire)
Toasting fork
Food (worked out for each day & placed in self-
  sealing bags)
Lots of fresh vegetables
Toiletries — but don't use soap in the river
Toilet paper & trowel — carry used paper out
Waterbottles or waterbag

Recreation

Backpack — for day trips, or for emergency walk
  out
Slater, Slater & Slater, *Field Guide to Australian
Birds*, Lansdowne Rigby, Willoughby, NSW,
1986
Kirkpatrick & Backhouse, *A Guide to Tasmanian
Native Trees*
Camera bodies in very waterproof container
Amphibious camera e.g. Nikonos (with flotation
  strap)
Lenses, wide (18 or 24 mm) & medium (35 to 85
  mm for fellow rafter shots)
Strong torch & flash unit for nocturnal visitors
Sturdy tripod — for use on land
Slow & fast speed film
Notebook & pen

Further Reading

Davidson, D.S., "Chronology of Australian
  Watercraft", *Polynesian Society Journal*, Vol 44,
  March, June, September and December 1935,
  Department of Anthropology, University of
  Pennsylvania, New Plymouth, New Zealand.
Duncan, F. & Brown, B., *Notes for Franklin River
  Rafters and Bushwalkers*, The Wilderness Society,
  Hobart, 1982

TREKKING

To "hike" is an old English dialect word which, though it now means to walk for pleasure, originally meant to proceed in a stricken or laborious manner — perhaps a definition much closer to the truth. "Walk", according to Gerald Donaldson, came into being around 1,000 AD by way of the Old English "wealcian" which meant to roll or toss, and incorporated bits of the Middle Dutch and German word "walken" which meant to knead, beat, or press.

Our way of describing the activity may have come from Europe but to see truly smooth energy-efficient walkers we must look at barefoot hunters and gatherers: they're movements embody all the grace and smoothness that it is possible to put into walking.

Nomadic Aborigines combed this country's immense variety of landscape — from mountains to deserts, tropical rainforests to spinifex-strewn savanna — on travel-conditioned feet following songlines passed on both aurally around campfires and in rituals, and visually in sacred site paintings and carvings. Essentials, which sometimes included the smouldering glowing embers of that night's campfire, were carried in woven baskets and carved containers. Food was gathered and prepared as needed, shelter constructed when the conditions demanded, and clothing only worn when custom or the weather decreed. In Queensland many tribes walked to the Bunya mountains for a nut festival, and in New South Wales local tribes trekked into the Snowy Mountains for a time of feasts and social gatherings built around Bogong moths.

Initially the European's attitude to walking in Australia

□ OPPOSITE *The first ascent on the Overland Track in Cradle Mountain–Lake St Clair National Park.*

☐ *Waiting for the billy to boil.*

☐ OPPOSITE *Emerging from the mist are the cutting edges of Cradle Mountain. An Austrian, Gustav Weindorfer, was the prime force behind the preservation of Cradle Mountain–Lake St Clair National Park.*

was an indication of socio-economic status: you walked if that's all you could afford to do. It followed on from the early days in Europe where there was an almost constant stream of walkers: traders, dealers, messengers, preachers, friars and pilgrims. In Australia they were soon joined by prospectors who jumped ship and headed for hills of gold.

The romantic notion of walking for enjoyment of wild countryside took until about the middle of the eighteenth century to become widely accepted. Chasing, hunting and killing became repugnant and the first walking or "rambling" club was formed in England in 1879 by Leslie Stephen. Their outings became known as "Sunday Tramps" which may explain the popularity of the term tramping in New Zealand. In Australia, William Mogford Hamlet is credited with kicking things off in 1895 with the Warragamba Walking Club. According to their club magazine *With Swag and Billy* the club's objectives were to encourage road walking in the country carrying light, non-camping packs. For overnight accommodation, members booked into boarding houses and farmhouses — an English style of accommodation still favoured today.

In Australia between 1910 and 1930 recreational walkers were forced by the proliferation of motor vehicles to relinquish roads. This made national parks and crown land even more valuable for walking. The popularity of walking in the bush can be judged by the Mystery Hikes centred in Sydney during the late 1920s and early 1930s. A report in the *Sydney Morning Herald* of 25 July 1932 noted that eleven special trains were needed to carry the 8,092 people taking part in a Sunday Cowan to Brooklyn bush ramble, commencing after an open air church service. So popular was this activity that newspapers were full of fashion tips for women hikers and announced the latest invention of shirts and blouses with built-in rucksacks.

It seems that long distance walking has always been popular. Wordsworth is reported to have managed 296,000 kilometres in his eighty years and the great Japanese Haiku poet Basho walked for three years on a 2,400 kilometre journey. But you don't have to be famous to walk long distances. George Lockwood started a Fremantle to Sydney walk in 1946, and when he arrived, ninety-seven days and five pairs of shoes later, the only original piece of clothing left was his cap. Just over ten years later David Kwan completed an eighty-one week trip from London to Singapore which

covered fourteen countries and 29,600 kilometres. David averaged a creditable fifty-one kilometres a day, but Jesse Casteneda set a long distance record in 1976 by walking 227.409 kilometres in twenty-four hours.

There's a certain natural introspection in walking. Rousseau wrote that there was something about walking which stimulated and enlivened his thoughts, and both Coleridge and Wordsworth composed poetry aloud as they rambled over the hills of the Lake district in England.

A common thread amongst enthusiastic walkers is that while they developed individual walking styles each nonetheless contained similar essential flowing elements. Coleridge described his walking as meandering with a mazy motion, and the doyen of Australian walkers, Myles J. Dunphy, suggested "swing out the legs and stride, stride steady and lightly, rhythmically, fling the miles behind you".

Our 256 bones evolved for walking and doing it involves most of our 650 muscles.

Unfortunately, not everyone is blessed with a naturally smooth walking style and it is a trial to be cursed with a plonker who insists on lifting and slamming each foot down like a base drum, as a companion. Bush bashing takes on a new meaning with one of these masochists hard on your heels.

A gentle stride is one which is rhythmical and lithe, where feet are landed with almost dainty placement — no matter how large the individual or how heavy the load. Although a gentle stride takes time to develop, this is time well spent in that it decreases wear and tear on the body and the bush.

Essentially trekking now can mean walking with a light pack while guides, sometimes paid, struggle

☐ Trekking with a light pack enables people of all ages to explore and enjoy wilderness areas.

along ahead under monumental loads. It has been sarcastically described as being only for people who couldn't pitch a tent or light a fire to save their lives, but it's much more than that. Trekking is a wilderness recreation that is open for people of all ages and of differing levels of fitness and even for those shouldering some disability such as blindness.

In its easiest form trekking involves half or full day walks carrying lunch, wet weather gear, warm jumper and camera. Slightly more adventurous is a base camp trip, requiring one or two days pack-carrying (with sleeping bag and a change of clothes) to establish the base camp. The following days are spent enjoying day walks radiating from a campsite carrying minimum gear but with the advantage that the base camp is well within a wilderness area. Most adventurous trekking is a multi-day long distance walk where you carry a backpack (about ten kilograms of clothes and sleeping bag etc.) which, though presenting tougher challenges, also provides greater personal rewards.

At times going trekking seems to require some pretty major adjustments. Just turning over in a snug sleeping bag without strangling yourself, and learning to feel comfortable about squatting over a toilet hole, can prove daunting. Few people enjoy being cold and miserable, but that doesn't mean you shouldn't expect, or look forward to, wet days. In good wet weather gear (see page 39) rain is fun and with the right attitude you may even recapture that childhood love of splashing through puddles. In dense forest especially, a sheath of wetness

☐ *A helping hand from fellow trekkers. Carrying a pack raises your centre of gravity and the likelihood of a tumble.*

imparts a special radiance and exemplifies the life-giving nature of pure fresh water.

Unfortunately, while you stop and admire the scenery other opportunist creatures may make designs on your warm body. After discovering that you are being reduced to a meal of fresh blood by fat bloated leeches, you'd be a rare soul if you could keep to the conservation code of leaving all creatures unharmed.

Fewer people still are in love with life when they have just walked up a blister. The secret here of course is not to get one in the first place. So called wimps don't get blisters. Upon feeling a "hot spot" they immediately stop, take boots and socks off, then cover the rub point with moleskin (a thick pair of socks over a thin pair will help minimise rubbing). The toughies soldier on, creating blisters which eventually burst making these people real liabilities for the remainder of the group.

While blisters are avoidable, rough terrain is not. It can be murder on joints not used to the jarring, twisting motions, but you will make it even harder for yourself if you don't cultivate a habit of walking lightly and placing your feet carefully. However, even after the most careful of walking, trekking for many kilometres over a myriad of misshapen, jagged and precariously balanced rocks can become a bit of a nightmare. The best description of rocks I've ever read came from Andrew Giger who, after walking the very long Appalachian Trail in America, described them as "anvils of torture". He also made the valid point that you have to take care of your feet since there are no spares (see page 39).

With a backpack on your shoulders you trek rather than stroll. As ergonomically designed and beautifully crafted as modern backpacks are, they still take some getting used to. Correct fit and adjustment are vital (see page 38), and essentially, the pack should not slop about nor ride too much on either shoulders or hips. In some circumstances, such as when descending steep hills, you may want to ease the shoulder straps; and when crossing rivers it's a good idea to undo the waist strap.

Ascending hills with a pack is best achieved in no haste. In the Himalayas the guides' attitude to their trekkers is "if I can see you moving, then you are going too fast". Most mountain trekking in Australia is not as extreme, but one tip is to begin the climb at the same pace as you intend to finish it — slowly. Your body takes a while to adjust to the demands being placed on it so rushing an uphill until you are exhausted, then stopping and starting off again is ultimately much

harder and slower than beginning a little more slowly in the first place and not stopping until the crest. In the same way it is essential if walking in a group not to get too close to, and be balked by, the person in front.

Discover your own pace and take in the gradually emerging views below, without engaging in the confidence-destroying practice of looking up and being appalled at how far it is to the top.

Aside from excess weight and low levels of general fitness nothing saps energy faster than dehydration and low blood sugar levels. Always ensure you have clean fresh water available and make sure you keep drinking — waiting until you feel thirsty is too late. In hot conditions strip off excess layers before you

begin to sweat excessively. Nibbling a little scroggin (nuts, seeds, glucose) as you meander is a good way of maintaining an adequate supply of fuel. Keeping warm in cold conditions also reduces your body's demand for energy.

Even though there are times when trekking may seem to be little more than an accumulation of hardships, the good aspects generally outweigh the bad. Captain Robert Scott summed this up pretty well when he wrote in his journal, "What lots and lots I could tell you of this journey. How much better has it been than lounging in too great comfort at home".

The route of my chosen trekking experience is the Overland Track in Cradle Mountain–Lake St Clair National Park, Tasmania.

A Short Walk In The Cradle Of The Gods

An unlikely ensemble of trekkers share the cloying smoky intimacy of an old hut at the start of the Overland Track.

A lawyer from Perth chats confidently to a nurse from Sydney, while over at the fire a carpenter nearing retirement is learning about life from an upwardly mobile Melbourne executive. At least the guides look as though they belong slogging through the bush.

Even though the original Waldheim Chalet (built in 1912) burnt down years ago, the spirit of the park's mentor, Gustav Weindorfer, an Austrian who first came to the area in January 1909, is

☐ The Overland Track, in Cradle Mountain, Tasmania, is one of the most beautiful walks in Australia.

still about, infusing his love of the wilderness in a bunch of city dwellers. Outside a summer night in Tasmania is falling, in large driving droplets, and even the devils and possums presenting themselves at the door of the hut seem to prefer to be inside tonight. Each time I wake I hear it bucketing down.

Light from a sallow sun makes our waterproof pack covers glow as we turn our backs on Waldheim's cosy comfort. Crater Lake is darkly ruffled, like my breath as I coerce protesting legs upward. From the blessed relief of Marion's Lookout, Lake Dove is just as uninviting, and little Honeymoon Island looks decidedly frigid. Bending into an enthusiastic wind I perambulate like a turps drinker lurching from puddle to puddle. Ahead, the ground dissolves into grey cloud, though I'm assured that behind the amorphous

mass hides the scraggy dolerite fingers of Cradle Mountain.

Kitchen Hut at midday becomes an impromptu lunch site, but a cheer from the hardy souls outside announces the emergence of Cradle Mountain. It's still too windy for an ascent today, but skirting around the scarp and through wild mountain scree we are rewarded with brief glimpses of battlements on high, seeming to punch through the clouds. Rain, a burst of sunlight, more rain, cloud, mist and back to sunlight. This is weather in the fast lane — though the fast lane is a slushy bog-like track where I relearn "downhill" — that's where the gushing water rushing along the track is travelling with me and not against me; against is "uphill".

I also redefine "joy" — it is now to be found in Waterfall Valley in the guise of a clearing sky, an

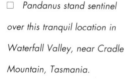

Pandanus stand sentinel over this tranquil location in Waterfall Valley, near Cradle Mountain, Tasmania.

☐ On a frosty summer's dawn a wallaby breakfasts oblivious of Barn Bluff in the background.

already erected tent and a billy on the boil. Trekking can really be a delight. A little caffeine and no pack is a reviver par excellence. It entices me to troop off with Rob, one of the guides, and a small group of trekkers, for a spot of waterfall appreciation. Pressing through the undergrowth we come to a scene of tumbling water. The fall is frozen at a setting of 1/500th of a second on my camera, and smooth at eight seconds of slow shutter opening.

A clear night in midsummer Tasmania equals frost in the morning. It makes the air seem cracklingly fresh and encourages a new day of trekking. A little cluster of pretty faced wallabies are breakfasting as we leave camp. Single file, we traverse open country under the morning gold pinnacle of Barn Bluff. This 1,559 metre dimple on the landscape was first mentioned by the Van Diemen's Land Company explorer Joseph Fossey in an 1826 trip account and named for a suggested likeness to a barn. Seen backdropped by an azure alpine sky,

it is less a barn and more an impressive sentinel mountain in a wild landscape.

Amid the hush of a perfect morning comes "squelch", "squish", "squash" or "oh no!". Slightly boggy, boggy, very boggy and bottomless are the multiple choices for this morning's section of Overland Track. A wrong choice is an unfortunate one.

A rest stop is punctuated by barley sugar and jelly beans. It's a time to share the morning's highs and lows with each other. We all tramp the same track yet spread out in micro clusters the route provides widely varied experiences. For some, birds have a special affinity, others enjoy (or are dismayed at) meeting snakes and lizards, while the rest are captured by flora and landscape — dappled light on dying leaves, and wind rippling branches.

Echoes of an exploitative past crunch underfoot as we move through the stark miniature moonscape of an old mine, cache the packs, and meander on a side track toward Lake Will. The lake was named by a coal prospector Joseph Will in 1839, but for us this beautiful white sandy-shored lake and fringing pencil pines are a perfect site for a beach picnic. Where the lake shallows, its tannin-stained waters take on a soft gold hue. Where the lake ends, calm waters free-fall and create a powerful waterfall which covers the nearby pandanus plants with a fine continuous spray.

Even under the unwelcome weight of my pack, the afternoon is uplifting — vistas of mountains and plains shown in the clearest, purest air possible. Alpine pools dot the landscape, but to eyes trying to

☐ FOLLOWING PAGE On the second day of an Overland Track journey, Lake Windermere backdropped by Mt Oakleigh comes into view.

pierce the afternoon sun they appear a cluster of precious flat plate jewels. On a last ridge I pause to enjoy a panorama of peaks set behind a lake named Windermere. This diminutive untamed Tasmanian lake appears far more beautiful than its namesake in England's Lakes District. Indeed by the time I eventually struggle into camp, the nearly set sun is laying a hushed mask over the lake's reflections of wilderness. As if the scene is being painted by an old master, fringing trees and rocks meld into the lake.

A freshly dug hole 300 metres away from camp serves as the loo. Using it early morning is a livening experience thanks to an ice breeze caressing my white cheeks as I squat and contemplate life. Despite this, I am loath to leave Lake Windermere, the place just cries out for a day or two of mooching about, but organised treks have schedules to keep and this one is no exception.

Cloud and poor visibility are my companions but through it wafts a bird of prey somewhat perplexed by what must seem like slow moving, brightly coloured hunchbacks. The bird effortlessly lifts up and is swallowed again by low sliding cloud leaving me to concentrate on the track. Flatter country leading into Pine Forest Moor (a stand of king william pines) should make for faster walking, but since it is dotted with enchanting alpine pools, some only a few metres across, my progress is a stop, photograph, and go, affair. It stops completely when I sidetrack to take advantage of a wonderful lookout where the clouds lift enough for me to see down into the rugged country of Forth Gorge.

As we nibble a jelly bean or three

one of the guides announces, "For our lunch spot today, turn right just after the wooden bridge over Pelion Creek, there'll be a big red pack marking the spot." Beside the turn off sign sure enough the pack is there. We all see it, bar one who must have tunnel vision and carries on regardless; perhaps Weindorfer's description of Cradle Mountain as a place "where time is not and nothing matters" has been taken to heart. Much wasted energy is expended on the part of the guides before this lost sheep is reunited with the flock.

After lunch, and a cool feet rinse, the track skirts around the east flank of Mt Pelion West, first climbing through a beech forest, then descending into Frog Flats. The flats were supposedly named because of the large numbers of frogs living here, but I believe they were actually named after the antics of trekkers trying to hop across ominous mud pools. Everyone has their own way of dealing with mud. Some quadruple their walked distance by inventing circuitous "dry" routes — making mighty lunges from one dry clump of button grass to another. Others simply ignore everything and walk through anything — which is fine if you don't mind the odd sink-to-the-waist-through-the-mire experience.

My walking style is looking a tad rough and ragged by the time I sight Pelion Plains. Finding my tent amid a stand of peppermint trees I slip off my twelve kilogram pack and find that its departure is like a whiff of oxygen to an altitude victim. Heading towards the stream for a zinging rinse I feel a little light-headed, probably the effect Pat McManus was referring to in his

□ OPPOSITE *In the golden hush of dusk, the surface of Lake Windermere appears like polished glass.*

book *A Fine and Pleasant Misery* when he wrote, "After carrying the pack all day you had to remember to tie one leg to a tree before you dropped it. Otherwise you would just float off into space."

Back in my tent I am a little tardy in zipping up the mesh screen and this oversight is taken by little black leeches as an invitation to come in out of the cold. Moving as if their next meal depended on it a score of them loop across the floor. Like bantam-sized heat-seeking missiles they home in on the only warm blooded thing in the tent, me. They are ejected even faster.

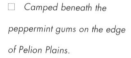

☐ *Camped beneath the peppermint gums on the edge of Pelion Plains.*

Such is the fickle nature of Tasmanian four-seasons-a-day weather that it is fine by sunset. While Pelion Plains campsite lacks the tranquil beauty of Lake Windermere it is a perfect natural amphitheatre — the plains fanning out to bump into towering mountains. To the north Mt Oakleigh's lofty spires catch the last rays of sun and are transformed into spindly blood red fingers. And into the sun Pelion West loses its bulk and becomes just an inky black jumbo cutout in a tangerine sky.

Easy hours pass in campfire-philosophising about the future of this marvellous region with Eric

Sargent, the present day doyen of Cradle Mountain. Eric has been trekking mountain trails here for more years than he cares to admit and has an inherent love of the wilderness. To my eyes the stars above us are a marvellous omen for a fine day tomorrow, but Eric has reservations, feeling they are too bright. He is about to elaborate when all conversation ceases as we witness a rare showing of Aurora Australis.

The scientific explanation for the Southern Lights revolves around the "boiling off" of atomic particles from the sun and the formation of a solar wind which reacts to our upper atmosphere, lighting up in much the same way as a neon tube. Standing in the darkness deep in a wilderness, there's a Japanese lyric poem by an unknown author which seems to mean a great deal more:

> *"The earth speaks softly*
> *To the mountain*
> *Which trembles*
> *And lights the sky."*

I discover the truth in Eric's "too bright stars" when at 3.50 am a storm of wind and water sweeps down from the mountains lashing at the tents. Guides are up and out in the cold checking on ropes and pegs, but I, for once, can just snuggle deeper into the down bag and go back to sleep.

Dawn is an effort. Today is a rest day — cards and chat and nibbling scroggin, we are cosy while the rain pelts down. But our boots can't really get wetter and the chance to do a little packless exploration in a nearby beech forest deep in Forth Gorge is too tempting. The route takes us past an abandoned copper mine and an old miner's hut before skirting under Mt Oakleigh's turrets, and plunging into a world of opulent greens. At the feet of dripping rainforest trees, trickles amalgamate into rivulets to spin and dance their way between the trunks. It's a noisy wonderful place of constantly changing images, but on film I can only attempt to capture an extract of the light reflected beauty. This is yet another sensual day which ends all too quickly.

Morning — well perhaps. It is the grey of light struggling to find a gap in cloud and rain and it is wonderful how it gives life to the beech forest. I've plenty of time to appreciate this as I follow the trekker in front up between the forested flanks of Pelion East and Mt Ossa. At 1,617 metres, Ossa is the highest of all the high Tasmanian mountains and its name is fitting as in Greek mythology giants

piled Ossa on the adjacent Mt Pelion in their war against the gods. Pelion was the home of the centaurs and as I struggle to crest Pelion Gap it seems like a great day for centaurs. In those brief moments when I dare to look up and out all I can see is the belly of a cloud being driven through me at a furious pace. Packweight and momentum are nothing to this wind. It can stop me dead in my tracks or spin me off course in an instant. That I successfully land on the button grass clump I aim for is pure chance.

Mud, glorious mud. Forget about the hard patches, just plunge in and enjoy it. This seems to be a general consensus of correct approach on the squelchy descent to Du Cane Hut. Du Cane, built by hunter and trapper Paddy Hartnett, is also known as Windsor Castle as much for its size as its site under the majestic Castle Crag. For me, it's the place to meet

☐ *The deep greens of the beech forest come to light after days of mist and rain.*

sunshine again. Sunlight is a wonderful spirit lifter. Through the crowns of trees pin points of light dance from a million leaves and where they strike the beech forest floor soft layers of fragrant steam rise as I silently glide by.

I plunge pack-free downhill and this madness has me fully alive for waterfall delights. From precarious vantage points it's a heady experience to be within spray and roar distance of Boulder, Cathedral, D'Alton and Fergusson falls. Clambering back up to the packs I find it is only a short lope to camp, amid the lushness of a beech forest just beside a fast-flowing Mersey River. Any romantic notions I held on camping in rainforests are rooted out in a sleepless night of clinging to the high side of a tent floor shaped not unlike a golfer sand-trap and lined with craggy logs jammed into the ground at crazy angles.

Are the gods smiling, or just laughing? Whatever their game, I'm grateful since Tasmanian mountain trekking under blue skies is phenomenal. Ascending Du Cane Gap is a fun skirmish through a gaggle of thrown together boulders. Stripped of what's been almost continual cladding in wet weather gear, the feeling of sun warmed skin is most agreeable. The blue sky is clear and the air seems washed and every gruff indentation of surrounding peaks stands out in stark relief. With the Traveller Range standing tall in the east, and the impressive peaks of Mt Massif, Mt Geryon, The Acropolis, The Parthenon and Mt Gould seeming so close to the west, the Overland Track passes through a valley of the gods.

Perhaps these ancient stockpiles of rock inspire us, or perhaps, like horses, we can sense "home". Whatever the reason, after a subdued lunch amid a stringy-bark forest, the "trek" to Narcissus Bay is more like a contest between speedwalkers. Fit, finally, after many kilometres of hard travel, walking is pure joy and fast striding is a heady elixir to be savoured. Having to stop at Lake St Clair is bittersweet, but after a boat ride to Cynthia Bay my first hot shower in eight days is luxurious.

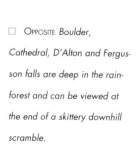

☐ A burst of sunshine, near the southern end of the Overland Track.

☐ OPPOSITE *Boulder, Cathedral, D'Alton and Fergusson falls are deep in the rainforest and can be viewed at the end of a skittery downhill scramble.*

LOCATION GUIDE

Located in the centre of Western Tasmania, Cradle Mountain-Lake St Clair National Park is still known to older Tasmanians simply as "The Reserve". Reserve status for 63,943 hectares of the area came in 1922, national park standing in 1947 and today it covers 131,920 hectares and is included in the World Heritage List. Appreciation of the area's great beauty began in 1835, when the surveyor-general initiated the tradition of bestowing classical names to its majesty, and other cartographers carried on in the same style. Even the post office had high regard for "The Reserve" — to the extent that in 1900 a pictorial series of Tasmanian stamps had a halfpenny portraying Lake Marion and the Guardians, and a fivepenny of Lake St Clair and Mt Gould. This didn't stop a dam being built on the Derwent River in 1937 raising the lake level by three metres and killing thousands of trees around the foreshores.

Within the park is the birthplace of five major rivers, the Forth, Mersey, Derwent, Murchison and Mackintosh. The oldest rocks are schists from the Precambrian era, then comes Permian and Triassic marine and terrestrial sediments and Jurassic dolerite. The numerous shallow highland pools and lakes were produced by glacial action during the Pleistocene period — there were major glaciers above Frog Flats, Narcissus Valley and Mersey Valley. Tasmanian Aborigines are known to have used the area. Artifact sites have been recorded at Mt Rufus and Cradle Mountain and early references to native huts were recorded by S.W. Sharland, a government surveyor, in 1832.

Through the park, running north-south, is the Overland Track. Blazed and marked by Bert Nichols and completed in 1935, the modern version was first regarded as safe for self guided walks in 1937. The Overland's eighty-five kilometres grew from an amalgam of tracks originally blazed through greed and hunger. In the 1920s the Van Diemen's Land Company was locally headquartered in Stanley in the north west of Tasmania. They sent out parties seeking land to exploit and one of them, a Dane, Jorgen Jorgensen, is believed to be the first European to have seen Lake St Clair. In 1826, Joseph Fossey visited the Cradle Mountain area, but the mountain was first climbed in March 1831 by a surveyor, Henry Hellyer. A pressing need to find a way across to the west coast prompted government-sponsored expeditionaries like E.G. Innes, who constructed the section of track between the Old Pelion Hut and Lake Will in 1897. The glittering prospect of mineral wealth drove on the privateers and for fifty years there were prospectors sifting the region for coal, silver-lead, tungsten, tin, molybdenum and wolfram. None had much long term success, though the leftovers from their exploits can be seen at sites along the track.

Tree fellers and hunters trapping wallaby and possum continued the tradition of exploitation. It is Weindorfer who is regarded as the prime force behind the preservation of the national park. He first climbed Cradle Mountain in December 1909 and then spent the remainder of his life working towards a dream which he first expressed on the summit of the mountain: "This must be a national park for the people for all time. It is magnificent, and people must know about it and enjoy it." He is buried near Waldheim ("Forest home").

It was probably raining at the time since, with 3,000 millimetres annual rainfall, fine days are at a premium.

This extravagant precipitation and the park's diverse terrain help to produce widely varying flora (119 different plant communities), from tall stands of eucalypt and dense beech forests in the gorges through to button grass on the plains. The beech is *Nothofagus cunninghami* and grows to thirty metres. *Nothofagus gunnii*, commonly called fagus is

☐ *Mountain flora, including the spiky endemic Pandanus, near Cradle Mountain. This area can be buried by snow during blizzards, which can occur at any time of the year!*

Tasmania's only deciduous beech. Numerous pines such as celery top, king william and pencil are also a feature of the area. Summer's superlative wildflowers include Christmas bells, lemon-scented boronia, and flaming headed mountain rockets.

More than twenty species of mammals can be sighted along the track, including echidna, platypus, quoll, Tasmanian devil, numerous possum, wombat, bettong, wallaby, native rats and, for those born lucky, a marsupial mouse. Mountain shrimp and fresh water crayfish inhabit the streams, tiger, copperhead and whip snakes are seen, leeches are often encountered. In the air are wedge-tailed eagle, sea eagle, peregrine falcon and closer to the ground are currawong, rosella, black cockatoo, honeyeater, wren, finch, thornbill, thrush and the rarely seen ground parrot.

FUTURE PROBLEMS

As the draft management plan for Cradle Mountain-Lake St Clair park stated, "Assuming that the park managed to avoid hydro-electric dams, logging, mining and tourist roads, the major management needs . . . relate to firing and trampling". Although most of the largest fires affecting the park have come from outside the park boundaries, there have been many fires caused by such stupid acts as bushwalkers burning used toilet paper. As more people walk the tracks, maintenance needs grow — as does the pressure to boardwalk difficult sections rather than keep the original style of track which blends with the environment.

THE BASICS

Preparation

Sore muscles are almost unavoidable, unless you are trekking-fit. Minimise the pain by exercising regularly for at least a month before the trip: visit the gym, take stairs instead of lifts, cycle (specially getting off the seat and pumping uphill) and if possible, do some half and full day walks carrying a light pack and walking in the boots you are planning to use on the trek. Trim your toenails. Once on the trek take it as easy as possible for the first couple of days.

Backpack

When stuffing everything into the pack make sure items likely to be needed in a hurry, such as wet weather gear, maps, camera, water bottle and mug, are easily accessible. Using zip lock plastic bags inside the pack liner helps to keep clothing dry, but protect the plastic bags from piercing. Load heavy items higher in the backpack so that they will be close to your back and keep fuel bottles away from everything else.

Once the pack is loaded make sure the straps are free and with the pack facing you lift it onto your right knee using both shoulder straps. Balance it there, hold one strap with your left hand, slip your right arm through the right shoulder strap (left as you face it) then hoist it onto your back. Slip your left arm through the left shoulder strap, bend forward slightly then adjust the waist strap. Standing upright you should feel weight on your hips, then tighten the shoulder straps until they are firm (not tight) and clip the chest strap across. The weight will now be shared by hips and shoulders.

Wet Weather Gear

The relative cost of wet weather gear diminishes as the amount of wetness encountered increases. Standing dry and warm in a shop the price tag might take your breath away. Viewing the inside of a rainstorm on top of a mountain in Tasmania is more likely to make that expensive wet weather jacket seem a bargain. Essentials for a life-long wet weather jacket are fully-sealed triple layer Gore-Tex, roomy and long enough to cover your bum, a bombproof two way zipper covered by an extra wide weather flap, a carefully designed adjustable hood, a waist cord to trap warm air, large flapped external pockets and an internal map pocket.

Feet

Each morning apply a hand moisturiser to your feet, paying special attention to the heel and Achilles tendon. This, along with well fitting shoes and two pairs of clean socks (thin and thick) will reduce the chance of hot spots, which become blisters. Placing hot, tired feet in an icy stream is sheer bliss, but don't soak them. Reapply moisturiser before putting socks and boots back on. Wash and powder feet at night to reduce moisture and stop tinea, and take a good look at them to see if there are problems developing.

Trekking

Once on the track start slowly and try to walk as upright as possible leaning slightly forward to create a momentum of forward movement. Where possible walk gently and rhythmically and at rest stops try to relax totally, pack off, eyes closed, with extra clothing on if it is cold. Airing your feet if they are hot is also a great lift. If your legs are aching, find a flat piece of ground then lie on your Karrimat with your legs up on a laid down pack.

Walking Staff

Those who use them, swear by them. They are helpful in maintaining an easy rhythm, act as a balancing aid when crossing streams and can even become a camera steady.

Dangers

Trekking dangers are usually self-induced. Stepped-on snakes tend understandably to panic and bite at the nearest object, smooth rocks are extra slippery when covered in wet slime, and the teetering edge of a cliff is best viewed without the backpack attached. Travelling too close to the person in front is not only a pain for that person but makes for an excellent chance of a pushed aside branch springing back and smacking you in the face. In dense forest when it's raining don't just put your head down and walk — large tree limbs can grow horizontally and are very unforgiving (as I can testify).

☐ Trekking in wet weather can be either a joy or a curse. With good wet-weather gear and a forgiving attitude, rain can be fun.

☐ FOLLOWING PAGE A wet-footed walk on a track in a beech forest deep in Forth Gorge takes in an abandoned copper mine, a miner's hut, and the striking turrets of Mt Oakleigh.

Trekking the Overland Track — Luxury Check List

Body Protection

Long sleeved woollen shirt
Lifa underwear
Peaked woollen cap, sun hat & bandana
Strong cotton shorts (for the rare days of sunshine)
Long woollen pants
Gloves, balaclava
Strong waterproof boots & gaiters
Change of woollen socks (two each of thin inner
 & thick outer)
Bathers (optional)
Woollen sweater
Down jacket
Gore-Tex waterproof full length jacket with
 hood & overpants (e.g. J & H "Cats & Dogs")
100 per cent UV protection sunglasses
Sunscreen
Rid insect repellent (especially for leeches)

Accommodation

Four season tent, built in floor & insect netting
 (e.g. Macpac Olympus)
4-season Karrimat & Thermarest
Candle/reading torch (spare long life batteries)
Sleeping bag rated as 4-season (e.g. J & H
 Winterlite or Winterwarm)
Gore-Tex bivvy bag (e.g. J & H Hollow Log)
Silk inner sheet

Getting There

Access to the park: the northern end at Cradle
Mountain is eighty-five kilometres from
Devonport and the southern end at Lake St Clair
is 173 kilometres from Hobart via the Lyell
Highway. Both roads can be temporarily blocked
by winter snow. Trekking season runs from
November to March (though it can snow early or
late).

Craclair Tours has been guiding people
through Cradle Mountain–Lake St Clair National
Park for many years. Their "Through the Park"
tour is an eight day, seven night trip and includes
transport, meals, all trekking equipment,
backpacks, sleeping bags with liners, waterproof
parkas and overtrousers. Cradle Huts Pty Ltd
have constructed four private huts along the
Overland Track and run trips using them.
Adventure travel companies also run trekking
trips along the track.

Transport

Bus transport: Devonport to Cradle Valley —
Maxwell's Bus Service; Hobart to Lake St Clair
— Bushwalker's Transport.

Silva type compass
Plastic pealess whistle
Cradle Mountain-Lake St Clair National Park
 1:100,000 map
Nylon cord (>30 m)
Internal framed 65–85 litre backpack (e.g.
 Karrimor Condor series)
Waterproof self-sealing inner bag
Extra waterproof pack liners
Smaller waterproof stuff sacks for clothing

Camping

Matches (in self-sealing plastic bags)
Candle lantern and spare candles
Swiss army knife
Cup, bowl, eating utensils
Trangia stove (with kettle)
Methylated spirits (in more than one container)
Food (worked out for each day & placed in self-
 sealing bags)
Toiletries, toilet paper & trowel
Two 1 litre waterbottles & 5 litre water bag or
 wine cask bladder

Recreation

Slater, Slater & Slater, *Field Guide to Australian
 Birds*, Lansdowne-Rigby, Willoughby, NSW,
 1986
Forest Resources, *Forest Trees of Tasmania*
Flora & Fauna Checklists from Tasmania National
 Parks & Wildlife Service
Siseman & Chapman, *Cradle Mountain National
 Park*, Algona Press, Montrose, Vic., 1979
Camera bodies
Lenses, 24 mm & 35 mm for landscapes, 105 mm
 or 200 mm for other trekkers
Strong torch & flash unit for nocturnal visitors
Shower cover for camera
Light but stable tripod
Slow speed film
Notebook & pen

Further Reading

Donaldson, G., *The Walking Book*, Holt, Rinehart
 & Winston, New York, 1979
Huxley, L. (ed.), *The Journals of Captain Robert
 Scott*, Dodd, New York, 1913
Kuntzleman, C., *The Complete Book of Walking*,
 Simon & Schuster, New York, 1979
McManus, P., *A Fine and Pleasant Misery*, Holt,
 Rinehart & Winston, New York, 1978
Thompson, P., (ed.), *Myles Dunphy — Selected
 Writings*, Ballagrin, Sydney, 1986

ROCKCLIMBING

The ability to climb stayed with human beings even after we moved down from the trees and began to walk about on two legs. The love of climbing mountains however is a more recent development. Mountains were seen at best as derelict and sterile, covered in either bothersome snow or useless vegetation — places of poverty and hopelessness. At worst, mountains harboured deadly spirits, dragons and monsters and were certainly no place for people.

However, curiosity overcomes fear, just as knowledge conquers imaginary ogres. In 350 BC Phillip of Macedon is reported to have climbed Mt Haemus in the Balkans simply to get a view of the Adriatic and Aegean seas. The desire of Peter III of Aragon to see what was on the top motivated his climb of Pic Canigou in the Pyrenees. Both climbers survived their mountain experience. Gradually a love of mountains' inherent beauty grew. In Japan, the mountain they reverently call Fujisan was first ascended in 700 AD by En-no-Shokaku and his footsteps have been followed by countless thousands, and recorded in prose, poetry, film, paint, and a hundred other means. Hokusai's "Thirty-six Views of Mt Fuji" took ten years in preparation of the woodblocks.

Mountain climbing as we would recognise it began, according to Ronald W. Clarke, when: "On Tuesday, June 26, 1492, a few weeks before Columbus set sail a group of men gathered below the precipitous walls of Mont Aiguille, the 6,880 foot rock bastion . . . in Southern France." Antoine de Ville led the successful ascent of what had previously been called "Mont Inaccessible". But it wasn't until the eighteenth

☐ OPPOSITE *The Grose Valley, in the Blue Mountains in New South Wales.*

A climber ascends a natural formation called a chimney.

OPPOSITE Learning to rockclimb can be an intense experience and one in which the rock becomes both friend and foe.

century, with the ascent of Mont Blanc by Jacques Balmat and Michel Paccard, that the first Golden Age of climbing was ushered in.

In Australia, high summits in the Victorian Alps, Snowy Mountains, Blue Mountains and Great Dividing Range were climbed by various explorers, surveyors and pleasure-seekers, following in the footsteps of the Aborigines who feasted high on the slopes of many of the mountains during summer. Though they lacked any formal climbing equipment, the Aborigines were adept tree climbers and also utilised numerous rock

shelters. In the upper Blue Mountains of New South Wales, David Liddle found: "... the Aborigines settled in a snug, east-facing rock shelter on Kings' Table, Wentworth Falls, about 14,500 years ago ... the spacious, river-cut Walls Cave ... provided a temporary home 12,200 years ago."

H.C. Goss is remembered as the first European to climb Ayers Rock in 1873. In the years between 1910 and the 1930s Dr Eric Dark and friends put up numerous climbs in the sandstone cliffs around Katoomba as well as climbing in the Warrumbungles. Formation of the Melbourne University Mountain-eering Club in 1947 was followed four years later by the formation of the Sydney Rockclimbing Club. From this club came Bryden Allen who produced the first guide book *The Rockclimbs of New South Wales* and John Ewbank, who in about 1967 created "Australia's own grading system, a simple cardinal scheme ... it rates the subjective 'value' of the climb from 1 ... with an open-ended limit ...". The highest standard of Australian climbers is currently thirty-one, achieved by Malcolm Matheson and Geoff Weigand. One route, a thirty-second named "Punks in the Gym" was put up by a German, Wolfgang Gullich in the late 1980s.

The reason why people climb has often been dismissed as purely selfish foolhardiness: "because it is there" is an oft-quoted and misquoted reply made by the famous British mountaineer George Mallory in 1923 just before he died on Mt Everest. "Because it is not there" might be a more realistic reason — "it" being a better understanding of ourselves.

Climbing rock is, above all, a mind game. Putting mind in touch with body, spirit in touch with soul, fear in touch with rapture. The reality of climbing borders on the metaphysical. It's an altering of our normal environment; taking the stable horizontal life platform and turning it on its ear: feeling gravity as a foreign force and a friend all at once.

Alas, like other mind-altering experiences climbing has been the target of wild rumour and senseless posturing. Perhaps this is a carry-over from the belief that mountains were ugly, frightening homes of dragons. It is true that climbing can be, and is, often frightening, but the only dragons to be overcome are the internal ones that melt your confidence with their fiery flames.

Climbing's timeless attraction is that it matters not what has gone before in your life. As you stand before a rock face your focus is on a tiny space of time to the total exclusion of past and future. Into the climb the sensation of failing takes hold. The force shakes you, and it won't voluntarily let go. It has to be persuaded into submission by mental aggression, by mind over muscle, body over gravity. As Chris Bonnington writes in *A Quest for Adventure*: "This is not an elitist ethic, but rather the deeper sensuous involvement that the climber has with the mountains around him, a feeling heightened by the stimulus of risk."

Not everyone is suited to rock climbing, but in the category of the unsuited I would not include women and unmacho men. Great bodily strength is less important than strength of mind in a climber.

Modern climbing requires grace and style, and is more akin to a slow, graceful ballet than a rigorous survival exercise. As Royal Robbins says in his book *Basic Rockcraft*: "A climb is a work of art, a creation of the person who made the first ascent."

Unfortunately most mountain rock can't defend itself against being ravaged by human beings. An early siege mentality in climbing led to many routes being permanently disfigured. The attacks on Yosemite, for example, prompted John Muir to help in the formation of the Sierra Club. A healthy change in attitude and the development of more suitable technology allowing the use of less damaging jamming, camming and chocking devices have changed climbing into a more passive sport. These devices are known as "protection" and their existence makes climbing much safer than it first appears. Basically, protection is put in by the lead climber as a safety net in the event of a fall. The type of protection applied depends on the rock. A very small crack can be utilised with the assistance of artificial chockstones (nuts or hexs) which are from about the size of a small fingernail right up to a fist. Friends are camming devices, which are compressed, entered into the appropriate space and released. The cams expand to fit the crack, and provide excellent protection — in climber jargon "bombproof".

Climbers follow a quaint tradition of "naming" each new route, choosing names as weird and wonderful as the climbers themselves. Route names sometimes give clues to the problems which may be encountered — such as

☐ Australian terrain is often a juxtaposition of sandstone and gum trees.

Sunstroke and Echo Crack. Sometimes they are too esoteric to understand — the logic behind names such as Purple Haze and Dogface Wall is as wild as your imagination. Sometimes names are regrettably far too descriptive — Puke and Horrendous Episode leave little to the imagination and engender horror before your first foot is placed on the mountain.

Aside from the enjoyment of having a long term goal of actually putting up a route and thus naming it, having routes named means you can use each area's guide book. They set out the directions to follow each named route, enabling you to choose routes which are within your capabilities. Without a word-based mud map, you could begin a grade 8 climb and, without realising it, meander off into a grade 20 finish.

It is daunting to stand at the base of your first real climb. On paper there is a lot of skill involved between grades 8 and 18, but to a beginner standing at the foot of a hundred metres of soaring rock, they both seem equally impossible. To untrained, nervous eyes the rock surface seems featureless. In reality, close up there are many divots, cracks, scoops, finger, toe and hand holds, to turn the impossible into the attainable.

An angled slab is a gentle introduction easing the novice into new skills. The instructor will demonstrate, often just in sandshoes, how to "walk" up the slope. Then, when it's the students' turn, they discover how deceptive ascending rock can be. Within the first few steps, feet begin to send a slight tingling sensation to the brain; unmistakably it means "this body is about to slip". By the next tentative step, reality has overtaken theory and back down the slope you go. On the next attempt, under the instructor's guidance, the beginner usually finds enough adhesion to achieve a safe, confidence-building ascent.

Moving from climbing angled slabs to vertical walls is the point at which chaff is separated from wheat.

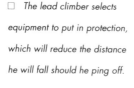

☐ *The lead climber selects equipment to put in protection, which will reduce the distance he will fall should he ping off.*

Now before I go any further, every, and I mean every, rock climber is frightened at some time. Royal Robbins describes his feelings as: "Halfway up a pitch, frozen into immobility by fear of continuing...". It is overcoming that fright which makes climbing such a worthwhile experience.

Naturally, on any competent course raw beginners are not just suspended out in space one false move from annihilation, it just feels that way. There are a number of important steps that are taken to ensure the beginners progress in complete safety. Initially, entering

the "world of rock" is like taking on a new language, but the basics of protecting fragile, breakable bodies are pretty straightforward. First, a climbing harness to which is tied a safety rope is worn. The basic knots, figure of eight and bowline, are learnt thoroughly so that they can be tied with eyes closed. These knots are double checked before each climber begins.

Beginners follow the leader. It's the leader's task to set out the most efficient route and to place protection for himself or herself and the following climbers. To protect the lead climber, the next person to climb is the belayer, who is attached to some solid object. As the leader climbs, the belayer feeds out rope through a friction device. The lead climber puts in protection and then puts the safety rope through a karabiner (a metal snap link device) hung from the protection by a sling. In the unlikely event that the leader falls, downward progress will be stopped by the protection and by the belayer clamping off the rope in the friction device; provided of course the protection has been put in correctly and the belayer hasn't nodded off to sleep.

The leader climbs until the first "pitch" or section of the climb has been completed. This is usually at a point on the climb, like a ledge, where all the climbing party can fit. After being securely anchored to an immovable object, the leader becomes belayer and instructor for the next climber.

As the leader has been climbing, each member of the group watches, taking a keen interest in the leader's technique of overcoming problems. It's usually impossible to remember

☐ *At times climbing can be frightening, but it's the sort of fright that can become highly addictive.*

much after the first few moves; besides, watching and doing are worlds apart.

Your turn to climb is like stepping up to a thirty metre tower with a complex dive to accomplish and hoping desperately you can remember the right sequence. The only difference between diving and climbing is that instead of submitting to gravity you are trying to defy it.

Above you is a patient instructor and below other people in all likelihood equally as nervous as you are. Between the two you negotiate a seemingly impossible morass of obstacles; just getting off the ground in many cases proves difficult. It can be damn embarrassing to "ping off" from the cliff only a metre or so from the ground. Sometimes instructors, knowing that you will try to duplicate their first few moves, will start a climb in a particularly difficult manner. Aside from setting a tough task, it

encourages new climbers to think for themselves, rather than acting like sheep.

Climbing has been likened to walking up stairs, it's just that the treads are exceedingly narrow and the rises quite large.

To climb is to strive for survival. From a sane, rational urban civilised human, you can quickly degenerate into a frantic, whimpering primitive, desperately clinging to existence. Those huge, obvious holds you could remember soon give way to bland, featureless rock offering no assistance. The more you look in desperation the less you see. The harder you try, the narrower your vision becomes. Very swiftly you are stymied — mentally and physically exhausted.

Help is at hand in the form of your instructor, who can usually see at least ten different ways of overcoming the slight obstacle which is threatening to turn you into a gibbering idiot. The instructor's job

☐ FOLLOWING PAGE *Rock climbing has become a graceful ballet where the dancers are dramatically poised between earth and sky.*

is to cut through the waves of confusion which are taking control of your mind, quell the rising panic and make you see — see the finger hold fifteen centimetres above your nose, see the toe hold just above your right foot, in short force you to think your own way out of the dilemma.

If the instructor is competent and you have an aptitude for climbing, you will quickly sort out the obstacles on what is an easy route, then continue climbing and make it to hallowed ground. The hallowed ground can be a seemingly tiny space of rock ledge beside the lead climber. From this heady vantage point you can, once securely fastened to the rock, peer over the edge at the following climbers who get past problem areas you invented for yourself, only to be stopped by new problem areas they find for themselves. Eventually all will be on the ledge of the first pitch in various stages of elation, or panic, depending on their head for heights and their power of imagination.

After achieving the first few not-too-difficult ascents and with a few hundred metres under your climbing shoes, you begin to realise there's more to climbing than first meets the eye. Learning to climb rock is more about attaining grace and style than fighting the mountain. In attaining grace and style first comes the necessary acquisition of technique. As kids, most of us could climb all sorts of vertical objects (usually faster and more skilfully if doing so without permission), but usually in a wriggly-worm fashion, taking bits of skin and clothing off as a natural part of the fun and adventure of it all. Learning the techniques of true rockclimbing you quickly find it's a

definite no-no to leave anything behind you, and that includes skin and pieces of clothing. It seems that for beginners trying hard to stay attached, there's a natural tendency to cling close to the rock face. This unfortunately is the simplest way to fall off. As you lean into the face you lessen the downward force of gravity on your boots, which in turn lessens the adhesion and ping, you're off. Another early problem is to over-reach, ignoring the smaller hold and trying to reach a more substantial one. The end result is the same, off you come.

Climbing is really a set of small moves, carried out with lumbering oafishness or sprightly grace. Once you can keep off from the rock face and work within your natural body, arm and leg reach, climbing becomes less of the one step up two steps back routine. It is also less exhausting if you are not forever on the knife edge of your wits and strength, just hanging on grimly. When you can grasp the idea of actually transferring weight in each of the moves, along with it comes the birth of smoothness and fluidity, the first glimmer of grace and style. It is a beautiful feeling.

Much of the pleasure in climbing comes from achievement: not giving way to fear, overcoming a problem, feeling like you are beginning to use your body well, and putting together a series of clean efficient moves and thus creating a fine climb. It's a personal achievement rather than a "conquest". Climbing rock is only dangerous in its sensual nature. It is as if something powerfully addictive has slipped inside you, sneaked beneath the outer layer of skin, and nestled comfortably up alongside your bones. Feeling the enticement of climbing makes you realise why many mountains are religiously revered and aesthetically appreciated by so-called primitive peoples.

My climbing experience is set in the Blue Mountains National Park.

An Attempt On Mt Banks

At Perry's Lookdown we pause to gaze across the Grose Valley and soak up a long distance view of Mt Banks. Even from far away it's big — the highest total cliff line in the

Blue Mountains. This morning the tiers of the huge walls look sombre and are set deep in shadow. Even the clouds hovering over it look dark with foreboding. What is that traditional Japanese saying? "May our five senses be pure and may the weather on the honourable mountain be fine." Strange how it seems to have picked up a faint trace of humour in the translation.

Descending into the abyss, each tenth step down my pack seems to weigh a few more grams, pressing itself down my spine and into my knees. "This is a bit tedious," says Andrew, in typical understatement, as we go on and on down what are becoming tortuous drops. I call a halt when the sound of my knees crying "murder most foul" becomes unbearable. No one objects. Dropping my pack may dent the path, but I can't raise the energy to worry.

A drink and cool water enters my system to be immediately evaporated off the back of my neck. There's a crackling warmth to the forest on this, the sunlit side of the valley. I get up and swing the pack aboard, but getting the old legs to move is like hand cranking a supercharged V12. Eventually they fire, but I'm missing a cylinder or six.

Blue Gum Forest heralds the valley floor, and staunch, softly grey-blue trunks are studded through the bush like a motionless guerrilla army. This is still a precious place of tranquillity. It is interesting to speculate what would have been here if the original idea of ringbarking the lot had been carried out — too horrible to contemplate. I mosey under the big gums and give silent thanks to conservationists who purchased this parcel of land for 130 pounds at the end of the Depression, and then had to run innumerable fund raising events to scrape up the money. I take a five minute break and stretch out looking up at the canopy of blue gums — it is gently restorative.

We trudge onward towards the Grose River. Doddering along the track I have an inkling of being

The first few steps can be the most daunting.

☐ *At the end of the Depression a group of conservationists purchased the area known as the Blue Gum Forest and gave it to the State for all to enjoy.*

ninety-five years old — it's not a nice experience. Following the stream's path we go upstream taking in the little dips and hillocks with an ever slowing pace.

Andrew spots the crossing point and he also manages to negotiate a leaping rock-to-rock path across the stream. We find a great spot for lunch: I exaggerate, this spot is nice, but anywhere would be fantastic for lunch. Lunch means less to carry, and a pack-free half an hour.

After sating my appetite, I find a new definition for bad news. There may be no water on the mountain so we have to carry it all. My share is a four litre drum, but there must be some mistake. The Grose River is surely radioactive. One muscle-bursting feel of my newly weighty pack and I'm certain that it's "heavy" water I'm carrying. It is 1,000 feet to the base of Mt Banks' cliff line — not 300-odd metres — a thousand painful vertical footsteps

conveys the pain much better. Half way up I'm having no trouble identifying with Balmat as he trudged up Mont Blanc in 1786: "I no longer had any strength to go higher; the muscles of my legs seemed only held together by my trousers." My only problem is that I am wearing shorts!

The sun has arced across to four o'clock by the time I catch up with Andrew and Mick at the crest of this dusty sliding scree. At times my climbing pace is down to one step for each breath so when I rejoin my companions I'm worn, weary and very ragged. There's a hint of joy there too, but we haven't yet begun to climb. And we won't either if the bush has anything to do with it. At the end of a slight track is a grey-green wall worn by the feet of successful abseilers coming down the mountain. Impenetrable is a term usually associated with jungles, and this comes damn close to it. At one stage the only way we can make forward progress is by using our overloaded backpack-carrying bodies as a crude form of battering ram and falling into the wall. The vegetation varies from open, sun-baked scree to dank, slippery rainforest, with some mad-matted jumbles of scrub in between.

In nearly two hours of struggle we have achieved 600 metres through the scrub and stand with some pride at the base of the climb. The idea of actually climbing has never been so appealing. We scramble up and unpack the climbing ropes and equipment atop what the guide book calls a "distinctive large rock about fifteen feet high". History in the form of twenty-four metres of rock face swirls above us. This route was first attempted by climbers from the then just formed Sydney Rockclimbing Club in 1951, without success. The "Rockies" came together with the aim, expressed in their first meeting records, "to pioneer in surrounding mountains" and "to help others to obtain aesthetic pleasure in mountaineering". As befitting the last years of the British Empire, Mt Banks was then called King George. In the summer of 1953, Russ Kippax, Dave Roots, Enn Truupold and Owen Llewellyn, managed to make it to the top — in sand shoes.

As we lay out the gear — climbing boots, climbing harnesses, a wide range of protection, ultra-strong Kernmantle ropes and friction devices — I think about what it must have been like to climb in the '50s. The leader used a 7.5 metre waistline of thirteen millimetre nylon rope looped six or seven times around the waist and tied at the ends with a fisherman's knot. Unfortunately this type of rope could be cut by the extremely abrasive effect of sandstone on nylon — it occurred at least three times in the Rockies' history, with one fatality (Barry Willis on the Three Sisters).

With Mick comfortably belaying through a Sticht plate, Andrew begins to climb, working slowly upwards. In the '50s the second climber (who belays the first) was advised to "wear gloves for belaying. [Gardening gloves were recommended.] The burning of one's hands may be so severe that it might leave the second incapable of further action in case of a fall. There are cases where the second's rope burns are worse than the leader's injuries."

I lay back on our rock platform to watch Andrew climb. It should be simple, but life is never simple. Six hours of struggling through the bush carrying overlarge packs combines with friable rock to create the ingredients of an epic. Initially, Andrew puts in protection about four metres up, but it's really just a token. In the quest for something better he moves up slowly, carefully. As he climbs further above his protection the sandstone seems to tire of staying as stone and is keen on becoming sand. Every hold becomes suspect.

An air of quiet expectation plummets to icy tension when Andrew's distance from his protection begins to exceed the distance from the protection to the ground. A twelve metre fall is far enough to make a large dent in

☐ *Bathed in afternoon light, Mt Banks takes on an air of benevolence.*

☐ The lead climber, Andrew, begins to scan available sites to place further protection.

Andrew and he knows it. Upward progress ceases as his experienced eyes scan the available sites to place protection, and find none. He faces the three choices leaders have faced since organised climbing began: go on and possibly risk his life in a major fall, climb back down or put in artificial protection — a bolt. In the 1960s when expansion bolts called Terriers first made an appearance on the Australian climbing scene they caused the same conflict as they had caused all over the world. Virtually anything can be climbed if you are prepared, as some were, to lay siege to it and cart portable generators for power impact drills to lay a track of permanently fixed bolts. But is it climbing or in the true language of the British, does it go "beyond the pale"?

I loathe the idea of putting a bolt in the sandstone, but it's not me leading, my life is not at risk. I dig out the bolt kit and hammer, tie it to the rope Andrew is towing and he pulls it up. Once the decision is made, Andrew's problem is that he must balance with both hands free and risk all to two tenuous foot holds. It takes a dreadfully slow ten minutes before we all breathe a little more easily. At least he isn't going to spear to earth, though above the bolt things don't improve. Often his is an uneasy choice between climbing on moss covered rock and lightly attached flakes. With agonising care Andrew inches up towards what, to me, seems like a cave. At least I hope it is. Daylight is rapidly retreating.

Once Andrew is secure he belays me as I climb. Seconding reduces the climb's difficulty and I'm about five metres up and feeling confident when a large chunk of apparently solid rock comes off in my hand.

Confidence evaporates and I'm gratified to finally make it to the top. My perceived "cave" is really an airy rock platform less than a metre wide with a no less than thirty metre drop straight off the edge. But at least it's a big enough ledge, just, from which to haul up the gear. Even with a Yosemite ascenders-style set up, this proves a struggle, particularly since the packs seem to have a magnetic attraction to every niche, crack, bush and overhang on the slope. By the time all our equipment is sharing space with us on the ledge and Mick is able to climb, we are joking about testing out his night vision.

The climbing ropes keep us firmly attached to the rock face. After a balancing act dinner, by torchlight we find enough lengthwise space for three bodies. Andrew and Mick sleep in an upper level which is wide but short, I get a lower narrow slot which resembles a grave. At least it's a grave with an awesome view.

I'm only half awake when a surprised rock warbler lands beside my head. I'd swear it does a double take at seeing me cocooned in my rock grave before leaping off into space. I envy its freedom. A few moments gliding and it could land on the little patch of sand I can see far below and dabble in cool river water. From our perch we breakfast as the mantle of green cloaking the Grose Valley catches its first rays.

As a belay point we set up a

☐ *The bivvy ledge on which we perched for a night on the mountain.*

☐ *Nestled precariously in a cleft of rock, we get breakfast underway.*

vibrant pink sling around a half-tonne rock. Andrew steps out of the semi-darkness of his cocoon-like ledge, and disappears upwards into the sky. I belay him, reading his progress in the stop and go movements of the rope. "Safe" comes his faint call — he's at the top. I follow and find I'm climbing a scrabbly set of miniature terraces, interspersed with clumps of tussocky grass. This is shades of the 1950s when climbing was a natural extension of bushwalking. The feeling is reinforced as we again haul the gear. It comes with sticky, begrudging slowness.

A cleanish twenty-three metre following pitch encourages Mick to change from last climber to first. His moves are smooth and positive, but it's like watching a black swan gracefully moving across the surface of a lake. Above, all is calm and serene, but underneath, like the swan's quickly paddling feet, Mick's mind is running at full speed. Two metres below is his last piece of protection. He asks Andrew for advice on what to place. A mistake here means a four metre fall before splattering against a sandpaper-coarse surface. As his toes nestle into holds, fingers touch down on niches,

a suitable location presents itself and a Friends cam bites home. Renewed confidence transforms itself into fluid weight transference and he's soon to the top.

Andrew follows, belayed by Mick taking out the protection as he goes. After an age of struggles, the gear has been lofted and Mick calls down "climb when ready". It is my cue. Foreplay is tightening the laces of my foot-hugging climbing shoes. I feel the formed leather become almost one with my feet, but like a ballet dancer's pumps they feel awkward on the ground. One step into the vertical world and they feel completely natural. I hate beginnings — just a metre off the ground and I'm seemingly stymied. Solving the problem, I try for that elusive delicate touch, but it becomes more than a little frantic as my adhesion to the rock changes from positive to

tentative. Trying not to hug in closely, I pause on a tiny ledge and make a definite attempt at relaxation. Legs extended, I consciously relax both arms, retake my hold, lean out a tad to increase my scanning angle and keep climbing to the top. We take morning tea on an overhung ledge. Below is a dazzling view of valley, to the side are golden coloured cliffs, and above is a ceiling which resembles a peeling parchment more than rock.

Unfortunately the next pitch is almost vertical bushwalking rather than climbing. Andrew leads, gardening on his way up and as I follow I leave a trail of falling mulch. Again pack hauling soaks up time like a parched sponge. A half scramble takes us to the start of the next pitch, a soaring sun-scorched crack, but as we contemplate this marvellous looking section the

reality of our situation is sinking in. It is now approaching three o'clock and we have only attained the first major ledge. With two of the party needing to be back at work tomorrow morning, we aren't going to make it.

It's always hard to accept defeat and we all seem depressed while recoiling ropes and restuffing packs. Escape from this ledge is theoretically possible and we begin another session of scrub wrestling. But the mountain hasn't finished with us yet and lays a series of obstacles in our path. After three hours of struggle, sweat and bush-pushing we emerge just under the summit, scraped, bleeding and feeling castigated by the barbs of the mountain's dominance. Just as in 1951, Mt Banks has proved harder than anticipated, but it will be here next time.

☐ *A panoramic view of the Grose Valley from our resting place, part of the way up Mt Banks.*

LOCATION GUIDE

The Grose Valley and Mt Banks are within the Blue Mountains of New South Wales. When Australia was just a part of the huge continent Gondwana, the Blue Mountains formed the western edge of the Sydney basin. "Marine silts . . . in the . . . Grose and Jamieson Valleys, were covered . . . Quartz-rich sands flooded into the area . . . cemented to form the Narrabeen Sandstones, those wondrous vertical cliffs of the upper Blue Mountains." Vegetation covers a wide range: stunted mallee on ridge tops, sheltered pockets of rainforests, hanging swamps, heaths and outstanding tall eucalypt forests. Diverse wildlife includes such wonderful creatures as crimson rosellas, gang gang cockatoos, tiny thornbills, melodious golden whistlers and grey shrike-thrushes, numerous honeyeaters, bossy currawongs and cheeky rock warblers.

Aboriginal cave artwork is evidence of long term habitation. The Daruk tribe is believed to have inhabited the Blue Mountains, with many caves being occupied in excess of 20,000 years ago. After the white invasion, the Blue Mountains remained a tough, rugged, apparently impenetrable wilderness and a source of frustration for the early colonial powers as attempt after attempt to cross them was beaten back: 1789 Dawes, Johnston and Lowes, 1793 Banks and Paterson, then Hacking and Bass, 1802 Barrallier got to within thirty kilometres of the Jenolan Caves, before finally a route was found by Blaxland, Lawson and Wentworth, and on 28 May 1813 they stood on the edge of the western escarpment.

A road was constructed, then a railway and a second major road to service towns and tourist resorts and the wilderness values of the Blue Mountains were well on the way to extinction.

But many hundreds of conservationists and one in particular, Myles J. Dunphy, turned the tide. Describing the region Dunphy wrote in the *Katoomba Daily*: "grand scenery of stupendous canyons and gorges, mountain peaks and plateaux up to 4,400 feet altitude, uncounted thousands of ferny forest dells and gauzy waterfalls, diversified forest and river beauty, much aloof wilderness . . .". But he also foresaw "Over expansion of mountain towns at the expense of equally valuable wilderness . . . pollution of more, or all streams, interference with swamphead sources of rivers . . .". Sadly this has come about, despite the formation of the Blue Mountains National Park. Dunphy had first vocalised the idea of a Blue Mountains National Park in 1922, and in 1931 formed the National Parks and Primitive Areas Council — the same year that bushwalkers discovered that the Blue Gum Forest was to be ringbarked. The Blue Mountains National Park was finally declared during the 1950s and presently covers more than 200,000 hectares from Newnes in the north to the Wombeyan Caves in the south.

THE BASICS

Fitness

Leg muscles and power to weight ratio are important. Age is no particular barrier, but being

□ OPPOSITE *A soft misty dawn brings the Grose Valley out of its slumbers, just as it has for many hundreds of thousands of years. Tragically, urban developments on the escarpments threaten the purity of the once pristine Grose River water.*

overweight at any age just means there's extra weight to lug up the cliff. In preparation for climbing, ignore lifts, instead take stairs two at a time to build up the leg muscles and develop stretching ability. Arms tend to tire once raised above heart level and chinups are a worthwhile exercise.

Pain and pleasure are twins in climbing. The pain sometimes begins as soon as you put on climbing boots. These specially designed friction boots are meant to be natural extensions of your feet. As such they need to be very tight, not crippling, but too tight to stroll comfortably more than a few hundred metres. Climbing in them is superb, with only the occasional prickle of pain — usually in hot weather. In one way it's possibly an advantage to have hurting feet at the beginning, at least that way your mind is taken off the additional pain associated with toes, finger and hand jams.

Jamming is a technique which allows you to achieve what may have seemed the impossible. Literally it means placing a fragile part of your anatomy into an appropriate crack in the rock, then expanding it so it jams firmly in the niche. To get your foot into a vertical crack you move your knee out sideways, place your then near-vertically aligned toes into the crack and bring your knee back. This twists and jams the foot enough to climb on it. Although it is temporarily painful, at least your feet are covered. When your hand and finger jam it's a case of gentle skin against unforgiving granite crystals. Do it right and there's minimal pain and blood. Get it wrong and at the critical stage when you most need it, the hand or finger slips out of the crack leaving copious quantities of skin attached to the rock. Rock climbers are not usually chosen to demonstrate the benefits of elegant jewellery displayed on fingers and wrists.

Pain in climbing is also associated with failure. Situations can quickly develop where you are using apparently all your physical strength and mental endeavour just to stay on that rock face. It's not often that you are actually at that point, rather you have just stopped thinking. In Royal Robbins' words: ". . . don't give up . . . . Most people fall on a practice climb only after they have given up, and they never approach their real limits."

☐ A selection of climbing gear, including a helmet, a kernmantle rope, slings, carabiners, nuts, hexs, chocks and Friends.

☐ OPPOSITE In the Blue Mountains a climber is easily dwarfed by the vertical cliffs of softly glowing sandstone, known as the Narrabeen Sandstones.

ROCKCLIMBING, MT BANKS — LUXURY CHECK LIST

Body Protection

Long sleeved cotton shirt
Bandana
Broad brimmed hat (with chinstrap)
Strong, long cotton pants
Dunlop Volley sandshoes for walking
Socks
Woollen sweater
Gore-Tex waterproof full length jacket (e.g. J & H "Cats & Dogs")
100 per cent UV protection sunglasses
Sunscreen

Accommodation

Bivvy bag
3-season Karrimat or Thermarest
Candle
Sleeping bag rated to 0 degrees C (e.g. J & H Bushlite)
Silk inner sheet
Torch (spare long life batteries)

Getting There

Air to Sydney, train to Blackheath, taxi to Perry's Lookdown

Climbing

Blue Mountains Climbing School: P.O. Box 42, Katoomba, NSW 2780

Walking Grose Valley

Out & About Bush Ventures
49 Jersey Ave Leura NSW 2780

Transport

Silva type compass
Plastic pealess whistle
Blue Mountains map
Internal framed backpack (e.g. Karrimor Hot Rock series)

Camping (in Bivvy Cave)

Matches (in self-sealing plastic bags)
Swiss army knife
Cup, bowl, eating utensils
Trangia stove (with kettle)
Methylated spirits (in more than one container)
Food (worked out for each day & placed in self-sealing bags)
Toilet paper & trowel
1 litre waterbottle & 5 litre wine cask bladder for each person

Climbing Gear

Two 50 m, 11 mm Kernmantle (dynamic) ropes
One 50 m, 9 mm hauling rope
A rack of Friends
A rack of wires
A selection of hexcentrics
General karabiners
Quick draws
Tape slings
Climbing harness
Sticht plates
Figure of 8 descenders
Climbing boots
SRT ascenders
Bolt bracket
Bolt kit & light hammer
Chalk bag
Helmet

Recreation

Hungerford & Donald, *Exploring the Blue Mountains*, Kangaroo Press, Kenthurst 1982
Craig D., *Native Stones*, Fontana Paperbacks, London, 1988
Camera bodies
Lenses, wide (18 to 35 mm) short telephoto (105 mm)
Slow & fast speed film
Notebook & pen

Further Reading

Bonnington, C., *Quest for Adventure*, Hodder & Stoughton, Great Britain, 1981
Clark, R.W., *Men, Myths and Mountains*, Weidenfeld & Nicolson Ltd, Great Britain, 1976
Colley, A., "The Greater Blue Mountains National Park", *National Parks Journal*, Vol. 28, No. 5
Friend, J., *Classic Climbs of Australia*, Second Back Row Press, Katoomba, 1983
Liddle, D., *Blue Mountains Wilderness*, Second Back Row Press, Katoomba, 1987
Robbins, R., *Basic Rockcraft*, La Siesta Press, California, 1982

PHOTOGRAPHY

Although the developer of the daguerreotype, Daguerre, said, "I have seized light, I have arrested its flight" back in 1837, and a few calotypes were made in 1850, wilderness photography in Australia began in earnest as a wet affair — not really conducive to rugged outdoor travel. For the next thirty years, to create a lasting image the photographer had to first place a collodion-coated plate in sensitising solution, then insert the plate into a holder, take it to the camera, expose it on the subject for a number of seconds, return to the darkroom and develop it immediately.

Despite the limitations of requiring a multi-second exposure and the completion of the whole process while the plate was still wet, early photographers did produce wilderness images. In America in the 1860s Carleton Watkins used a specially made 18 x 22 inch camera to capture the rugged beauty of Yosemite and at the same time, Richard Daintree, working in north Queensland achieved marvellous results transporting all his photographic equipment, including a tent darkroom, overland by pack-horse. To negate the need for carrying trays and chemicals, Daintree "... made a 'dry' preservative solution of his own from the resin of the eucalyptus tree". In other parts of the country photographers moved like gipsies in horse drawn caravans. Some, like Charles Walter, travelled alone in the bush, hauling camera, tent and paraphernalia on their backs.

The big boost in technology for wilderness photography came with dry plates. In Tasmania, John Beattie set off in 1879 with a group using horse and cart. They headed for beautiful Lake St Clair and, according to Margaret Tassell and David

☐ OPPOSITE *Exploding upwards a flock of water fowl attempt to eclipse the sunset with sheer weight of numbers.*

Wood, "Their use of gelatin dry plates for the first time at this location was possibly also its first use in Australia." At last the beauty of the Australian bush could be shown in reality (albeit in black and white or hand coloured), rather than interpreted by the eyes and brush strokes of European painters.

Just as the American landscape photographer William Henry Jackson helped to create the world's first national park, Yellowstone, in 1872, so too were early photographers of Australian wilderness drawn to conservation. As he trudged into rugged, remote regions of Tasmania, John Beattie recorded in his notebooks "... nothing gives me greater delight than to stand on the top of some high land and look out on a wild array of our grand mountains. I am struck dumb, but oh! my soul sings... I must confess, however, to a feeling of sadness at this speculation [west coast mining], for what lover of nature can stand unmoved and contemplate her glories swept away by the tide of humanitarianism, — the axe and the horrid sulphur fumes...".

In the 1890s William Saville-Kent photographed submerged corals for his book *The Great Barrier Reef* and Charles Kerry slung a huge camera and tripod over his shoulder and headed up into the Australian Alps by horseback and snowshoe to record snowfields. And, while leading the 1904 Transcontinental Expedition, Richard T. Maurice produced haunting images of a vast landscape with a panorama camera.

Frank Hurley was another photographer to embrace wilderness conservation, being instrumental in the declaration of Macquarie Island as a sanctuary and thus engineering an end to the killing of its sea lions and penguins. On his way to the Antarctic with Mawson, Hurley filmed the slaughter of whales in the hope of stopping this ruthless trade. He passionately described in his notes "... men hurrying with flensing knives, and power saws, to dismember bloody carcasses, of cranes lifting red, steaming masses of flesh and bone, of figures, Lilliputian, moving to and fro among a scene of gory carnage, too horrible and loathsome to describe, and too nauseating to regard."

One of Hurley's greatest photographs crafted deep in the Antarctic shows two small figures struggling to collect ice as a blizzard rages around them. Another series shot during the ill-fated Shackleton expedition in 1914 displays the *Endurance* captured by pack ice yet seeming to rest comfortably. However, the ship is being crushed into a pile of splintered wood and fallen rigging.

Hand colouring was always popular, but amazingly, Australians had access to natural colour prints on paper after a Swiss photographer, James Aebi, made the first colour print in Australia in 1905. On the way to modern colour materials were an array of methods including Autochrome using dyed granules, Paget and Finlay two plate additive systems and Dufaycolour, before Kodachrome offically arrived in Australia during 1937.

Just as John Beattie in the previous century had struggled against what he called "the devastating influence of the 'guns and snares' of our ardent colonial fowlers" so too did one of Australia's greatest wilderness photographers, Olegas Truchanas, use colour images against a pro-development Tasmanian Hydro Electricity Commission. Olegas did this through arduous journeys on foot and by kayak into areas that few, if any, human beings had glimpsed. The public showings of his photographs alerted many thousands of people to the fragile beauty of Tasmania's south west and thus helped to build a tremendous groundswell of support for conservation, resulting in the declaration of a valuable huon pine reserve. Tragically, nearly all of his photographs were destroyed in a fire in 1967, and the place he fought so hard to preserve, Lake Pedder, was drowned in an act considered by many as official vandalism. Olegas lost his life during a journey down his beloved Gordon River. Yet out of all of this grew a strong conviction in the worth of wilderness.

Carrying on that wilderness tradition is Tasmanian landscape specialist and protege of Truchanas, Peter Dombrovskis. Writing in his magnificent book *Wild Rivers*, he touches on why many photographers in Australia have surged to the forefront of conservation: "... the rivers ... disappeared; their forests drowned, their rushing waters trapped behind grey concrete walls.... The [Franklin] river... was grander, wilder, more remote and touched me more deeply than any other place I had known."

Each of us has our own perception of the world. Wilderness photography provides a means of sharing these perceptions with others. For some photographers their work is a chance to make a statement about our fragile planet. Others use images to provoke discussion,

encourage preservation, or simply to record what priceless beauty has been lost.

Whether photography is, or is not, art, is unimportant. It can be delicately artistic or the crudely basic produce of a heavy-handed artisan. As the great American landscape photographer Ansell Adams said, photography's purpose is to capture the "extract, not the abstract". Adams likened a negative image to a musical score, where the

print is the performance; so in essence a photographer composes and performs to produce photography.

A wilderness photographer seeks to observe the whole and represent it through key elements. In the same way that "simplify, simplify" was the creed of philosopher Henry David Thoreau, so too is it the guiding principle for wilderness photography. Through a wonderful interaction of eyes, brain and photographic equipment riveting impressions of life and death have ensued.

Photography is one of the least damaging human activities in terms of its effect on wilderness. No matter how glowingly presented, hunting to kill is a violent base act — not a challenging sport but a carry-over from Neanderthal days. It is an activity whose time has past.

☐ *Soft light on ancient images in Arnhem Land.*

Hunting by camera however, is still consistent with the primitive skills of knowing a wilderness, tracking with stealth, blending into the environment, patiently waiting for the right moment and smoothly squeezing the trigger. The distinction is that by creating its photographic image, a wild animal remains free, instead of being reduced to a stuffed trophy.

The physical challenges for a wilderness photographer are also abundant. Hills and mountains are just as large as they were a hundred years ago and although photographic equipment has become far lighter since the time of gigantic cameras, modern glass and metal still combine to be a demanding load. The perverse nature of wild light, zestful insects and the impatience of companions are added distractions. Few great images are ever accomplished by pure luck. They usually emerge from intuition: "seeing" the right combination of light quality and suitable subject, seeking out the best vantage point — habitually the coldest or hottest, windiest or most exposed — then battling with unco-operative weather in order to capture a brief magical slice of life.

Three bushwalkers cresting a peak together, dropping their packs and looking at the same scene will see different images: one will see sun rays splayed on far-ranging peaks, another will see soft gold light caressing leaf patterns on the ground, and the photographer will see problems. Good wilderness photographs are worried out of life. And learning how to worry your way to good pictures is not easy — some might say it is impossible.

Everyone can improve their photographic skills, raise their confidence in handling equipment and build a memory bank of experience, but a good photographer also needs the gift of seeing, of isolating photographs from life's images. As American photographer Alfred Stiglitz puts it, "The ability to make a truly artistic photograph is not acquired off-hand, but is the result of an artistic instinct coupled with years of labor."

Even though this is an age of autofocus zoom lenses, bayonet-fitted to autoexposure, and autowind cameras with built in flash, many of the best wilderness photographers choose to use only the manual setting of their 35 mm single lens reflex cameras or use primitive large format cameras designed last century. It may seem that these photographers are nostalgic romantics preferring past to present, but in reality it is a reflection of the fact that you make, rather than take, memorable photographs.

Unfortunately much hot air is wafted in foolish debates about "purity". For every advance in photographic technology there have been people who have decried loss of control; from magnesium powder to through-the-lens metered electronic flash, from hand operated exposures to stepless electronic shutters, from exposure by guesswork to onboard computers. All of these things combined have only produced a greater number of correctly exposed, in-focus colour pictures. They have not and cannot make good photographs. Quantity is not quality. Essentially wilderness photography is a search for just that, quality. Quality is tough to define, but easy

to recognise. For a photographer, amateur or professional, it is finding that moment when a scene is blessed by what Ansell Adams called "soft rich light". Other photographers describe seeing smooth grey light, feminine light, or clean, pure light. We are all seeking light. As the great photojournalist Galen Rowell writes of most amateur photographers, "They tend to forget that they are never photographing an object, but rather light itself... no light... no picture... remarkable light, they may have a remarkable picture."

Being aware of light quality is only the beginning. Making good photographs is seeing how the elements of a scene may be composed into a fluid, captivating image, assessing how the highlights and shadows will respond on film, choosing the right shutter speed and aperture combination (see page 82) and then, before it all disappears, tripping the shutter. And tripping it again, half a stop less, and again half

a stop more, then changing lenses and reshooting, a practice known as bracketing (see page 82).

Ansell Adams considered bracketing for protection a sign of insecurity. This is quite true — I acknowledge feeling insecure when confronted by what I recognise as the makings of an excellent image. But I'd also add that since processing labs are prone to dropping, scratching and losing your best photographs, the time to make a duplicate is the time when the original is captured. I also agree with the old adage that film is cheap, relative that is to the amount of effort you have expended to get body and equipment to a particular place at a special moment. To scrimp on the number of photographs at that point is foolish.

It's also foolish to get hung up on film. It's not only beauty which lodges in the eyes and brain of the beholder, it is also the perception of colour. Green is green and red is red,

except when reproduced on film, then it might seem a yellowish green or an orangey red in comparison with your memory of the "real" colour. Which transparency film you use is a matter of personal choice but you should be more concerned with your own response to whether it reproduces "true" colours for the type of photography that you enjoy. One film will be excellent when exposed in intense sunlight with action-stopping shutter speeds and another will give wonderful results at eight seconds of slow shutter opening.

Sharpness or fineness, however you define it, is a strong aspiration among wilderness photographers intent on obtaining the greatest detail possible in the final image. In the past, the format used, whether miniature half frame or 10 x 8 inch

sheet film, had a dramatic effect on the final image quality, particularly when reproduced in magazines or newspapers — a larger original was always better. Today, with improvements in film and computer printing technology, the perceived differences are much less, and it is the portability and speed of the equipment and final purpose of the photographs which dictate the format.

Peter Dombrovskis doesn't carry his leadlike Linhof Master Technika 5 x 4 into the wilderness because he likes the solid weight of it crushing his spine. Using a 5 x 4 inch piece of film for each image can produce excellent results, as Dombrovskis' marvellous posters attest. However, the view camera's bulk, slowness and limited film stock are a great disadvantage when photographing a bells-and-whistles audiovisual, or when you are locked into an adventure tour with limited time to actually take photographs.

Great poster-sized images are also possible by loading a 35 mm camera with top quality slow speed film and using the camera in a similar manner to a view camera, i.e. on a tripod and setting off the shutter by a cable release.

Whether using a large format camera or a 35 mm compact, taking an age to make one exposure is not a judge of photographic excellence. Nor is working quickly a precursor to making poor images, it just means you don't waste quality light or try the patience of your subjects. A cheaper camera body is also not necessarily a justification for bad photographs. What is of vital importance is that piece of glass through which the image flows onto the film. Again, quality is paramount. With a limited budget it is always better to choose a smaller number of quality lenses over a bag full of cheap ones. Usually this means buying top brand names at top prices. Secondhand is a cheaper alternative but beware of worn out optics (see page 82 for simple testing).

What lenses to own should be dictated by need, not desire. Start with a 35 mm as your standard lens and let agonising frustration dictate which direction you must follow. If the 35 mm just won't allow everything you want in the frame then buy a wider lens or if it is just too broad then go larger. All photographs in this book were taken with fixed focal length Nikon AI lenses including 18 mm, 24 mm, 28 mm PC, 35 mm, 105 mm, 200 mm and (rarely) 300 mm and 500 mm.

However, the great bulk of wilderness photography can be handled very well by a light outfit comprising only 24 mm, 35 mm, and 105 mm lenses. It is far better to carry an extra camera body (or two) in preference to extra lenses.

Since the ideal place for a camera is in an airconditioned, dust free studio, thrusting delicate tidbits of technology into a wild environment racked with heat and dust or cold and wet is asking for trouble. Cameras can be protected from anything, but you must temper protection with accessibility. Storing the camera inside two plastic bags and one rubber bag and wrapping it inside your sleeping bag should ensure it makes the distance. How many photographs you can take with it on the trip will be another thing entirely. At the other extreme, leaving the camera dangling freely

☐ An egret, captured with a 300 millimetre lens and motordrive set on continuous.

from your neck as you ford swollen rivers ensures you capture every bit of action, including the camera's drowning. Somewhere between those extremes is an ideal compromise. I haven't found it — yet. Camera bags are mostly designed for wedding photographers, and for the benefit of chiropractors since all the weight is swung off one shoulder. Karrimor and Lowe do make a range of outdoor camera bags that have both shoulder and waist straps to share the load. They work very well, except when you carry a large backpack at the same time, then the two waist straps competing for one waist become a problem. Specially-made chest bags using an interconnecting web of clips and photographers' pocket-mad vests always make me feel like a human bomb going into armed combat. Leaving cameras and lenses in the main backpack demands the energy sapping ritual of unloading for every photo opportunity.

I try to work on a kind of minimum protection plan which varies according to the level of danger to the camera. Trekking or bushwalking means wearing a camera body and lens (or two, one set long and one short in the photojournalist tradition) and using a single elastic chest strap to stop it swaying about too much. In light rain I add a home-made vinyl weather cover; in heavy rain I retreat from constant access, storing my camera in the pack and using a tripod and umbrella (the latter only if the load isn't too horrendous). Basically, as the odds shorten for me (and cameras) being smashed into rocks or trees, overturned in canoes, swamped in rapids or buried in snow,

I increase the level of protection. As a result I only lose the occasional camera.

Just as personal risks versus obtaining the shot have to be weighed, for a wilderness photographer not only is there the challenge of propelling self and camera to the right place at the right time and in functioning mode, but there are the not insignificant dilemmas arising out of wilderness ethics — cameras don't lie, their handlers just bend the truth a tad.

For some photographers, waiting for the right light or climbing to the best vantage point still isn't enough, they have to add a bit of creative "zest" to life. This can be nothing more than spraying water on ferns to make them sparkle, distorting distance relationships with ultra wide or super long telephoto lenses, engaging in a little "gardening" to clear away unwanted bits and pieces, trampling young plants that intrude into the frame or breaking off branches that disturb compositions.

Moving up the ethical consider-ation scale, is the construction of composites. Compared to the drama of storm clouds nothing is as boring as bald sky. To overcome this some photographers keep a library of sky "effects" to build stunning composite pictures. Gustav Le Gray began this technique in the 1850s by making prints from separate negatives of sky and water. Today, it is possible to add split screen filtration for instant sunrise oranges, or to use computer enhancement in the lab and darkroom to achieve an almost guaranteed show-stopping image.

Then there's the photography of wild, wild animals. This can range from providing freshly killed fish to sharks so they can be seen "attacking", to chasing, capturing and corralling animals so they can be photographed in a "natural" setting, and annoying snakes and lizards enough to make them adopt an aggressive stance. Also popular are the methods of making nocturnal animals temporarily blind by using high powered flash units tripped by infrared beams and of putting insects in an icebox so they are chilled enough to pose.

Most people would not equate these actions with the rape and pillage engendered by uncontrolled forest clear-felling, yet on a miniature scale they reflect the same callous disregard for flora and fauna. Given a thousandfold increase in the numbers of wilderness photographers such unethical behaviour can start to impinge on the "wild" in wilderness.

My chosen wilderness photography experience is in Kakadu National Park and Arnhem Land in the Northern Territory.

Spirit Of The Land

In choosing Kakadu and Arnhem Land I'm attempting the impossible, to photograph the spirit of the land. And yet, as the remaining wilderness is in essence an untrammelled link with ancient time, by softly infiltrating a pristine environment we can begin to become closer to it. The challenge of managing a wilderness today is therefore evident in how much of the original spirit of the place remains. On the way down from Darwin it's evident that perishingly little spirit remains outside the boundaries of Kakadu National Park. Much of the

With almost regal stature a jabiru strolls on the edge of Yellow Water Lagoon.

landscape evokes a feeling of sadness — it's been ripped and torn and burnt and developed into temporary submission. Artificial crocodiles and soulless accommodation centres add little to the landscape. Once within the park boundaries I'm hoping a little of the spirit still survives, but this seems improbable as I join a dozen photographers jovially jostling for position on the edges of Yellow Water Lagoon.

Oblivious to our manoeuvrings, a big tropical sun dips into a last sliver of clear sky. A few disheartened clicks register audible contempt at the lack of a classic cloud-induced sunset. The disappearance of the sun's image in viewfinders persuades cameras to vanish. The click of camera shutters is replaced by the ubiquitous crack/hiss of stubbies giving the Northern Territory kiss of life.

The dust settles from retreating four wheel drive vehicles — my fellow snappers have left me to the company of ravenous mosquitoes intent on quenching their blood lust. At least they don't chatter. I am enjoying the feeling that a modicum of peace has returned to the lagoon when, in the half-light, black shapes gently part the waters, then move across it with infinite slowness. Crocodiles exist in their own primeval time-frame. I stay beside the camera and tripod waiting for the brief period of the day when, under some mystical command of "bring up the light!", fading light revives to ochre in a tropical afterglow similar to the alpenglow so cherished by mountain photographers. It comes, briefly, and through my 105 mm lens a pair of trees make a perfect, if lonely, joint silhouette against a yellow brown sky whose softly graduated tones are akin to the most delicate watercolour.

My wristwatch alarm jangles me awake to pitch black. Starlight is the only natural illumination on the sixteen kilometre track to Jim Jim Falls. I'm heading down this sandy avenue before morning, before black is washed into grey, before grey turns to gold; and hopefully before the bloody wind gets up. What I'm seeking is a breathless hush personified in the surface of a still pool, and I want to see it when it's dressed in a cloak of soft light. By torchlight I track through scrub to the dampened edge of a long pool. Showing black against a now soft-grey sky, the gorge walls seem to tower. Focussing on the pool, I frame time-bleached fallen trees that mirror the venerable age of surrounding rocks. Their relative eras stretch apart again as undiluted sunlight edges over a cliff-line horizon. Its arrival heralds a radical

☐ *An aerial photograph of Twin Falls, taken with my feet jammed hard against the empty aircraft door frame in a futile attempt to counteract air turbulence.*

change. Just as my ears record clinking voices of the morning's first day-trippers, an invisible hand of moving air slips through the trees to give the water surface a damned good shake, shattering the mirror. What I have glimpsed, and hopefully recorded, is gone.

A couple of hours later I'm using lung power to fill a borrowed air mattress. Camera bodies and lenses are wrapped in towel padding and placed into a waterproof river bag. Balancing this precious cargo on the lilo, I push off into a deep long pool. The sun is high enough to light the surrounding steep gorge walls but it is a harsh cold light and does little to bring out the rock's true oranges and reds. Rock hopping takes me to the next pool and finally, I paddle up to be bathed by spray at the very edge of the twin waterfalls.

Twin Falls is now actually a joke. Typical of the wet season excess and dry season poverty of this landscape there's hardly enough of a trickle to keep the rocks glistening. What a far cry from the frequently promoted image of this place as two roaring storming bodies of water competitively lunging over a massive drop. Even with an almost waterless waterfall I can enjoy the challenge of photographing pale skin against ebony rock. Ignoring a dark-induced exposure reading from the rock, I meter off the back of my hand, then use a 24 mm lens to show a diminutive human figure pitted against a Goliath-sized wall.

After a night in the bush I'm back on Yellow Water Lagoon and photographing scenes of life and death. My guide cuts the motor and we glide silently by. Through a tripod-mounted 300 mm lens I view a

With a 300 millimetre lens I captured this frighteningly powerful crocodile.

motionless crocodile — an armour plated monster with uncleaned fangs. Many wildlife photographers try to gain extra stillness by shooting in between their heartbeats, but, as the image of the crocodile grows in the viewfinder, it's getting harder to find a gap between my heartbeats. The crocodile is motionless, its mouth is open but it shows no other signs of life; until, that is, I take my eye from the viewfinder to find a different angle of approach. Then it moves with explosive energy and disappears into the murky waters of the lagoon.

We move on past a flock of ducks jostling for foot holds on the bank and are soon captivated by a tall egret acting out the part of an ivory statue. The act is perfect, but for a couple of feathers vibrating in the breeze. As I photograph it while it stands motionless, my feelings are of wonder and enjoyment of its loveliness and perfection, but then again I'm not the frog that it knifes down on like white lightning. The egret moves off to munch in private.

Back on land I head off to Nourlangie Rock, the site of some of Kakadu's spiritual strength and its most famous rock art. When I first saw this place many years ago, it was a daunting experience. For me this feeling has now been neutered by guide rails, signs, boardwalks and silicon water prevention lines — all no doubt necessary to keep moronic fingers away, but depressing none-the-less. It is as if Kakadu rock art is now simply a saleable product used to inject money into government coffers — merely a five minute pit stop on a tick-the-features coach tour.

As I head out of the park and towards Arnhem Land, thunderstorm clouds appear clamped on top of the ancient grey-brown cliffs. I emphasise the scene's majesty by using a 200 mm lens and exposing more for clouds than cliffs.

A few hours later, at sunset, and only a few kilometres down the track, smooth-barked gums footing the cliffs are bathed in soft pink light allowing them to become almost effeminate. To keep the entire scene in focus I select an aperture of f22, but need a tripod-mounted 105 mm lens to cope with the ultra-slow shutter speed.

I'm back next morning before dawn, but the scene merely goes from slate to bright.

With an access permit organised, I can confidently pass a sign warning of dire consequences for illegal entry, and cross the East Alligator River. After hours of sand track, four wheel driving I arrive at a bush camp to meet a guide who looks like he has stepped straight out of a hunter's annual — "In a past life" he assures me as we move through dense dry rainforest and out onto dry floodplains. On the edge of the plain is a very tall and very dead tree holding off the inevitable in an off-

☐ Gathering clouds create a silhouette of rock on the edge of the Arnhem Land escarpment.

vertical last ditch stand of stubbornness.

Moving around it, I manage to find the right angle to the sun where my polarising filter cuts out light scatter from the bark. A 24 mm and narrow aperture lens allows me to place the tree in its environment and capture a passing cloud at the same time.

☐ *With an 18 millimetre lens, this immense Northern Territory sky can almost be contained.*

We bounce from rut to rut across a track which will be at the bottom of a gigantic river flood plain in a few months time. Then we board a flat bottomed punt which is ideal for moving through shallow reed-fringed water and also makes good "ground" for my tripod. We quiet the noisy motor and drift to the sound of magpie geese. I begin to feel this place has retained its wilderness spirit when the sound of the geese is swamped in thundering wingbeats as they rise. Trying to frame images is a nightmare of overabundance — front lit it's a mass of moving colour; back lit, silhouettes melt together forming strange masses of black. It is exciting, frantic stuff where focussing is a hit and miss affair, but the light is fading fast. I'm using wider and wider lens openings, then slower and slower shutter speeds and finally my eyes are protesting at trying to see into a viewfinder in the semi-darkness.

After a night's sleep we head out to a recently rediscovered group of caves.

The trek is hot and thirsty work: along with the harsh crackling of breaking leaves arising from beneath my feet there is a light layer of dust. It catches on sweat globules on my legs and gathers to give me not a bad looking instant Arnhem Land tan.

My guide stops to point out edible plants, and to sample a few which can be eaten raw. Rock replaces forest and in some ways the rock seems more gnarled than the trees. But it goes unphotographed because the light is harsh and uncompromising, creating intense highlights and deep shadows. Certainly there is a maze-like quality here as we slip 'twixt sun-heated giant tors and through little connecting passages of chilled shade. There are so many twists and turns that but for occasional glimpses of sun my internal compass would be completely spun.

Our maze-walking only ends when we slip under a boulder overhang and lie down on smooth cool rock. With my head cradled on a convenient slab, my eyes are free to absorb thousands of years of life pictured above me, its spirits, fellow creatures and prey, all laid and overlaid on the dry ceiling and walls. This is life and death lived, recorded and communicated by countless artists in an unbroken link from the Dreamtime.

As we move from gallery to gallery I speak only in whispers or not at all. For me this sacred site has become sacred.

Moving through a series of caverns

and rock arches that have been made smooth by a thousand wet seasons, we arrive at the entrance to a cave where the floor is grey dust. My eyes take a little time to adjust, but eventually I can absorb the fringing rock art and begin to analyse it in terms of a photographic problem. What stops me is the sight of my country's ancestors lying silently and untroubled. Lovingly wrapped in the soft folds of paperbark are the bleached bones of other human beings. People who had loved and were loved are now laid to rest in this place of peace.

A trembling rises in me and I can hear in my mind the wails and chants of grief long past. As the tears well, run down my cheeks and fall into the dust, I shake with grief, sharing an overwhelming sense of loss of my ancestors. Wearing white skin has no significance, the people here are part of my country. And for the first time I can share a sense of unity with ancient times. My cameras remain unused.

LOCATION GUIDE

The Arnhem Land Plateau is an immense weathered sandstone complex. Its oldest rocks are Lower Proterozoic sediments from 2,000 million years ago. The region's western margins, along with the flood plains and the estuarine coast, contain Kakadu National Park. The park, 200 kilometres east of Darwin, is the traditional land of the Bunitj clan of the Gagudju language group. Kakadu was first proposed as a park in 1965, but following the introduction of the *Aboriginal Land Rights (Northern Territory) Act* it was successfully claimed, leased in 1978

☐ *In this area of natural water worn passages, light seems to struggle in, almost be-grudgingly.*

to the Australian National Parks and Wildlife Service, then proclaimed as a park Stage 1 in 1979 (Stage 2 in 1983, Stage 3 in 1989), and placed on the World Heritage List in 1981. Arnhem Land remains Aboriginal land and an access permit is required prior to entry by non-Aboriginal persons.

The continual presence of Aborigines in the region, since they crossed land bridges to Australia more than 40,000 years ago, has meant an outstanding array of rock art has survived today. Explorer Leichhardt first recorded rock art in 1845 and now there are more than 1,000 surveyed sites in the region. They fall into three main periods beginning 35,000 to 40,000 years ago: Pre-estuarine — hand prints, hunters, dynamic figures, stone axes, simple spears and boomerangs; Estuarine — many fish including barramundi and X-ray art; and Contact — rifles, steel axes, sailing boats.

Europeans ascribe two seasons to the region, "wet" and "dry", but in Aboriginal language there are six seasons: beginning in January there is Gudjewg (monsoon), Bank-Gereng (knock 'em down storms), Yegge (cooler but still humid), Wurrgeng (cold weather), Gurrung (hot dry weather) and Gunumeleng (pre-monsoon storms). With a terrain that ranges from bare rock to rainforest the region contains more than 1,000 species of plants including Carpentaria palms, wild orchids, and lotus flowers. Half the species of Australian birds can be seen in the region — many in air-filling thousands, particularly at the end of the Gurrung season when waterholes begin to dry up. Long-legged brolga

and jabiru are the tallest birds on the ground, and the sea eagle rules the skies, but the lotus bird would have to be the most charming as it traipses delicately across tethered plate-sized lotus flower leaves on the surface of the water. Beneath the waters, and frequently basking on the banks, are many fresh water and so-called saltwater crocodiles (they also frequent fresh water).

FUTURE PROBLEMS

Within Kakadu's geography there is a township, Jabiru, a uranium mine, Ranger, a motel/hotel at Cooinda and another on the South Alligator River, and the park is bisected by a high speed bitumen highway. An ever-increasing number of tourists continue to apply pressure for upgraded "facilities" which slowly eats away the possibilities of wilderness experience. At present an environmental impact study is being conducted in relation to a proposal by BHP to mine for gold at Coronation Hill within the "conservation" zone. Since Australia has a miserably small percentage of land protected for permanent conservation, there is no place for mining within national parks.

THE BASICS

Formats include tiny pieces of film, half frame, Instamatic, through to chunks of 6 cm by 7 cm and even 10 x 8 inch sheets. My preferred format is 35 mm using a single lens reflex (SLR) camera. With an SLR, light enters through the lens, is bounced upwards into a pentaprism and to the eye of the photographer. At the

☐ OPPOSITE *In the afternoon, the harsh tropical sun of Kakadu and Arnhem Land is transformed into soft, rich light.*

instant the shutter is released, the mirror flips up and the same light strikes the film. What you see is almost what you get, keeping in mind that most viewfinders do not show the entire image.

Automatic cameras will handle many lighting situations but are commonly fooled by dark images on light backgrounds, light images on dark backgrounds and when shooting into the sun, contre jour. The essential ingredient is to decide which is the most important then to set your exposure for that, and bracket. Bracketing is taking exposures either side of the suggested one.

Correct exposure involves a balance of shutter speed and aperture. The faster the shutter speed, e.g. 1/500th of a second, the less time the light has to penetrate through to the film. Fast shutter speeds will stop fast action. A slow shutter speed, e.g. 1/30th of a second, gives more time for light to pass, but will allow some moving objects to blur.

Aperture is expressed as "f stops"; a low number is a large lens opening, a high number is a small lens opening. Going up from one f stop to the next, e.g. f5.6 to f8, light is halved. Going down each f stop, e.g. f11 to f8, light is doubled. A small aperture, e.g. f16, lets a small amount of light reach the film, but will keep more of the image sharp (in focus). A large aperture, e.g. f2.8, allows in a large quantity of light, but only a small section of the picture will be in sharp focus.

Depth of field (the area of sharp focus) also increases as the lense gets wider. A 50 mm lens at f8 gives a smaller depth of field than a 24 mm

lens at the same aperture. Gaining even more apparent depth of field is achieved by using hyperfocal distance. In essence this is initially focussing on the object close to the camera, then refocussing a fraction beyond the foreground image. What will actually be in focus is a portion one third in front of the subject and two thirds beyond it. Guiding distances are shown on some lenses and are most effective at very small apertures.

Composition has more rules than a game of chess. The rules are okay as a beginning point but eventually you are seeking to achieve a simplification of life's clutter into a focal point within a photograph. The viewer's eyes should move smoothly to somewhere in the frame, rather than bouncing around the image like a pinball.

Filters are many and varied but most of them are designed to create fiction. Filtration should still keep the lighting as real as possible. To do that I use three: a UV often — to keep scratches off the lens; a polariser frequently — to purify tones and cut surface reflections; and a neutral density occasionally — to reduce the overall amount of light.

Purchasing a secondhand lens is fraught with dangers, but a simple lens sharpness testing method can be achieved using a tripod and ensuring the camera is square to the subject; e.g. photograph the classified section of a tabloid newspaper. Use all apertures at two different subject-to-camera distances (take notes). For short decision times use print film (one hour processing), or an E6 process slide film (three hours processing) then review the sharpness with a magnifier.

☐ OPPOSITE *Wilderness photographer Rob Jung — a study of concentration.*

PHOTOGRAPHY, KAKADU AND ARNHEM LAND REGION — DRY SEASON LUXURY CHECK LIST

Body Protection

Long sleeved cotton shirt
Bandana
Broad brimmed hat (with chinstrap)
Strong cotton shorts
Long light cotton pants
Dunlop Volley sandshoes
Socks
Bathers (optional)
Woollen sweater (for night)
Spray jacket
100 per cent UV protection sunglasses
Sunscreen
Rid insect repellent

Accommodation

Roomy tent, built in floor and insect netting
3-season Karrimat, Thermarest or Lilo mattress
Candle/reading torch (spare long life batteries)
Sleeping bag rated to 0 degrees C (e.g. J & H Bushlite)
Silk inner sheet

Getting There

Air to Darwin, 4 wheel drive to Kakadu/Arnhem Land
Anyone undertaking commercial photography in Kakadu requires a permit in advance from ANPWS Canberra
Entry to Arnhem Land requires a permit from the Northern Land Council

Transport

Silva type compass
Plastic pealess whistle
Cahill & Jim Jim 1:100,000 topographical maps
Nylon cord (>30m)
Internal framed 65–85 litre backpack (e.g. Karrimor Jaguar series)
Waterproof self-sealing inner bag
Extra waterproof pack liners
Smaller waterproof stuff sacks for clothing

Camping

Matches (in self-sealing plastic bags)
Swiss army knife
Cup, bowl, eating utensils
Trangia stove (with kettle)
Methylated spirits (in more than one container)
Aluminium billy (for fire)
Toasting fork
Food (worked out for each day & placed in self-sealing bags)
Toiletries, toilet paper & trowel (if bushcamping)
Two 1 litre waterbottles & 5 litre water bag or wine cask bladder

Photography

Slater, Slater & Slater, *Field Guide to Australian Birds,* Lansdowne-Rigby Willoughby, NSW, 1986
National Parks & Wildlife Service brochures & flora & fauna check lists on Kakadu
Moldray, *National Geographic Photographer's Field Guide,* National Geographic Society, Washington D.C.
Two or three camera bodies with at least one motordrive
Karrimor or Lowe camera bag — with waist strap
Waterproof river bag
Lenses: 24 mm, 35 mm, 55 mm micro, 105 mm, 200 mm, 300 mm (with matched 2Xs multiplier or a 500 mm mirror)
Sturdy tripod & cable release
UV, polariser & neutral density filters
Matched metal lens hoods
Slow & medium speed film
Notebook and pen

Further Reading

Bickel, L., *In Search of Frank Hurley,* Macmillan, South Melbourne, 1980
Dombrovskis, P., *Wild Rivers,* P. Dombrovskis, Sandy Bay, 1983
Newton, G., *Shades of Light,* William Collins, Sydney, 1981
Rowell, G., *Mountain Light,* Century, London, 1986
Tassell, M. & Wood, D., *Tasmanian Photographer,* Macmillan, South Melbourne, 1980
Techniques of the World's Great Photographers, QED, London 1981

UNDERWATER DIVING

Insects are the most efficient sub-aqua explorers. The whirligig beetle has a divided eye, one half to see above the surface and the other to see underwater. Mosquito larvae breathe through a short snorkel at the end of their abdomen, while very long snorkels are utilised by voracious water scorpions. Even scuba diving is easily managed by insects; backswimmers simply take a bubble of air down with them.

Many thousands of years before Sophocles wrote of "Plunging beneath the waves, Which cover the keel" Australian Aborigines were accomplished divers. Early European anthropologists noted Tasmanian women carrying plaited grass baskets diving for abalone and scraping the tenacious animals off the sea floor with wooden chisels. Not only could these divers cope with the extreme cold, they could also stay beneath the surface for long periods. In Western Australia, Daisy Bates recorded similar experiences: "mussels are caught by diving; the women performing this work... they carry a spinifex net with them and, holding this in their mouths, dive to the bottom of the water, catch the mussels... and in a short time fill their bags."

Extending one-breath diving limitations has been a problem which has plagued humans since ancient times. Solutions have ranged from the practical to the bizarre, and have prolonged time below the surface from a few minutes to forever. Aristotle (384 to 322 BC) wrote of specially equipped divers sucking air from the surface. Paintings from the sixteenth century depict divers walking on the sea floor using an inflated skin bag as an extra lung. Papagrigorakis gives an Englishman, James, credit for designing the first self-

☐ OPPOSITE *Protected by the fronds of its host, an anemone fish peers out in safety.*

contained apparatus using compressed air in 1825. But as he points out, no one had as yet discovered a way of regulating the air supply.

Hard hat diving enabled longer periods on the bottom, but the diver was weighed down and attached by an airhose to a surface compressor. The quantum leap in recreational diving came when Jacques Yves Cousteau and Emile Gagnan developed an Aqualung. For the first time human beings could experience freedom of movement, and breathe regulated air below the surface. Cousteau wrote of his enchantment in the classic text *The Silent World*, and the same underwater world awaits for today's self-contained underwater breathing apparatus (scuba) diver.

The early days of scuba in Australia were pretty basic. As Neville Coleman relates in his excellent dive guide, "In the 1950s scuba sets were being sold in some sport store shops, together with a phonograph record that explained the few known rules of staying alive while scuba diving." Since then great developments have taken place in both scuba equipment and methods of teaching underwater skills (see pages 90 and 101).

For a diver, the sea is an entry point to an underwater wilderness. By taking the plunge you will discover what a fraction of the total world you previously inhabited. An underwater wilderness is a stunning world within a world. On the surface the ocean can be storm-tossed, sparkling with dazzling pins of sunlight, or threatening deadly-grey, but below the surface, life goes on oblivious to these changing moods. The natural world's use of colour, texture and design seems unleashed with heady exuberance. Everywhere the brilliance of one creature seeks to outdo the brilliance of another. It's a bewildering, enchanting macrocosm, and one in which we enter on trust.

Unlike a landscape where the pressure of feet on ground leaves an ever increasing scar, it is possible for thousands of people to dive an underwater wilderness and leave absolutely no trace of their passing. However, just one diver can wreak death and destruction in this fragile waterscape through nothing more than being clumsy. Even the most slightly built, land-balanced person can become exceedingly clumsy underwater.

On land, balance, weight, height and body shape have a great bearing on how easily we move about. Underwater, the rules change: large awkward people achieve grace and poise hitherto undreamt of. Lumbering turtles, awkward sea

☐ *An almost weightless diver fins towards the surface.*

lions and seemingly foolish bopping penguins once beneath the sea move with poetic beauty, and blend with their environment. Underwater, few humans can even begin to approach this level of harmony, yet the chance to develop new moving skills in a fresh environment is just one reason to become a diver.

A skin diver is literally a naked human with a taste for adventure. A smooth body moves underwater powered by kicking legs, and by lungs that will carry enough air for a short period. From that most basic level you simply add more clothing and equipment to make the diving experience clearer, easier, longer and safer — even colour co-ordinated!

An outer skin of form hugging neoprene wetsuit allows movement through the water but insulates against quick heat loss and gives positive buoyancy. A snug fitting silicone face mask provides an airspace between eyes and water, allowing clear, though magnified and narrowed, vision. A self draining, large volume snorkel tube allows ease of breathing while you're head is down and you move across the surface. Fins simply make feet more efficient.

Once flotation, clarity and efficient movement are taken care of, the only people who can't go surface snorkelling are those who can't breathe. Snorkel diving is more strenuous, so being swim fit is a great advantage. But only a person with zilch imagination could stay paddling on the surface forever and look at everything from a distance. To easily snorkel dive wearing a wetsuit you also need to wear a weight belt. The belt shouldn't have so many lead weights

that you sink like a brick immediately after you stop swimming, but just enough so that at the surface you still have a slight positive buoyancy (flotation) and at the bottom a slightly negative buoyancy. Take a deep breath, bend at the waist, push your legs straight up and their weight aloft will push you down. For a splashless descent don't start to kick until your fins are below the water. Otherwise every fish in your diving area will be spooked.

In some places, the fish might unfortunately be spooked anyway. A sad common thread runs through snorkel diving in Australia and it is recorded in photographic images of dead fish. Most people's introduction to snorkel diving (mine included) revolves around adrenalin-pumping hunting exploits — getting into the water, killing something and getting out again. Even sadder today, despite the development of simple to use underwater cameras and the incredible growth in conservation

☐ Snorkelling requires only basic equipment and the ability to swim.

☐ FOLLOWING PAGE A school of reef fish move slowly aside to let me pass.

87

□ *A pupil sticks close to the diving instructor. The structured approach of professional diving schools eases fears and quickly builds underwater confidence.*

awareness, some people still snorkel dive simply to kill fish and crustaceans (spearing while using scuba equipment is illegal in all States).

However, for most divers learning to scuba is the zenith of diving. Its physical demands are much more extensive, not so much in your level of fitness but more in your physical makeup so a thorough medical is essential (see page 101). After the medical, it matters little whether the dive course is run by PADI (Professional Association of Diving Instructors), SSI (Scuba Schools International), FAUI (Federation of Australian Underwater Instructors), or NAUI (National Association of Underwater Instructors), each organisation covers similar ground and passing the course allows you to

hire scuba gear and dive world-wide.

Many courses begin in a pool so that learning takes place in clean, clear water at a pleasant temperature with no turbulence or currents. Above water learning concerns diving physics and equipment, the two stage reduction of pressure from the air tank to the regulator in your mouth, the buoyancy control vest, weight belt, wet suit, pressure and depth gauges, fins and mask. Water-bound learning involves a range of necessary manoeuvres mainly involving taking off and putting on the gear underwater, and safely descending and ascending.

At the end of a scuba course your first open sea dive is sure to be mindblowing. Descending beside your diving "buddy" (with the instructor nearby), the sea floor seems to come up to meet you in delicious slow motion. It only takes a little compressed air in the buoyancy vest to create weightlessness. Hover motionless, do a handstand on one finger, lie upside down gazing at the surface — this is a world of perfect and effortless gymnastics.

Everything is fascinating: the way your exhaled bubbles flatten like mushroom caps on their way to the surface, how well sound carries, what a lovely silvery sight the surface makes, how fish are curious, how touching distance is so hard to judge and how there's a complete, new world down there waiting for you to discover it.

My featured diving experience is on Lady Musgrave Island, a coral cay on the Great Barrier Reef.

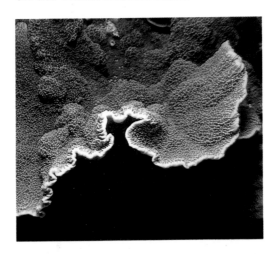

CORAL ISLAND

Out to sea, looking like the jagged teeth of a crosscut saw, an angry horizon eats into the sky. Leaving behind the smoothness of the Burnett River, we find powering rounded walls of water which pick up and drop the *Lady Musgrave*, like a bathtime rubber duck, even though she's a well founded sea-going twin engined catamaran. Successive days of strong wind warnings have kept us holed up on shore. Finally the winds have abated to twenty knots.

As the boat muscles its way through rolling swells, I seek fresh air on the aft deck. Wind whipped spray sparkles in the sun as gannets, boobies, shearwaters and terns revel in their preferred environment. Some of these sea birds seem to strafe the waves, some fearlessly plummet, some mirror the craggy sea surface and others wheel, turn and grab at an awesome pace. All make life a long-odds gamble for schools of small fish.

The probability that I will donate breakfast to the fish is quickly increasing, but I'm saved by a stretched blimp stuck on the horizon. The image of Lady Musgrave Island grows larger by the minute until it can be seen clearly as a strip of yellow below a gangly bunch of green. Not that this little coral cay shows much above the ocean's surface. It is, if you like, the very pinnacle of a gigantic mountain range poking out of a layer of cloud — the cloud being crystal water covering a formidable mass of coral. A dramatic lightening in water colour signals that we are nearing the island's outer fringes, though even from just off the edge of the reef it seems a tiny "mountain"

☐ Hard corals form the backbone of the Great Barrier Reef.

91

☐ *The coral cay Lady
Musgrave Island is surrounded
by a closed ring reef and offers
superb diving.*

On the outer edge of the reef huge waves arrive and die on the jagged coral in a last gasp of angry white foam. In 1768, the navigator Louis de Bougainville arriving outside the outer barrier reef saw a similar sight and turned his lumbering square rigger away from danger. But we are inside the reef. We can enter a natural channel through the fringing coral to enter a lagoon where the water has undergone reef wizardry — all is sleekly serene. Dotted across the lagoon's pale green floor are large black shapes, which, as they slip harmlessly past the boat's hull, turn out to be bulbous coral clusters alive with fish.

We are keen to set foot on land, but day visitors have priority. They are off-loaded to float about in glass bottomed boats and scoot ashore for a short peek at a coral cay. Finally it is our time to go ashore. Weighed down with dive equipment, food and camping gear, our backpacks are large and heavy and we stagger a little on the way to the boat. This attracts the interest of a garishly

dressed day tripper. He asks how long we are staying and echoes our reply of "A week!", though his rendition is filled with incredulity. "What are we going to do staying on a deserted coral cay for a week?" I suppose it is a fair question. E.J. Banfield, who wrote *The Confessions of a Beachcomber*, chose his island for its beauty and productiveness. He wouldn't have chosen Lady Musgrave Island.

Barely above high tide and open to every breeze, the place doesn't even have water to drink. Given reasonable weather, the first two are no real problem. It is the lack of fresh water which is the biggest bugbear. We are just lugging the last of our rented twenty litre water barrels along the beach as the *Lady Musgrave* heads back towards Bundaberg. Its departure alters our perspective and reinforces the solitude of this little coral cay on the Great Barrier Reef.

To dive next morning we cross-island trek into a dark, white spattered forest which smells like an unkept bird aviary. All the night inhabitants are out earning an honest living catching fish, leaving an eerie, hushed, smooth barked forest of old giant pisonia trees. We occasionally emerge into sunlight amid the tangled wreckage of trees decimated by the last cyclone.

Pisonias give way to pandanus and then an open sky and a lagoon is at our feet. Donning wetsuit, weight belt, fins and mask, and carrying underwater photographic gear, we take snorkels into our mouths and push off from shore. What on land had seemed to be blue green water surrounded by brown masses, is transformed underwater; the blue green is sand, but the brown is living corals and home to a myriad of fish. So complexly colourful are they that each one is a piece of mobile excitement.

As I swim unhurriedly across the surface, a slowly changing panorama slides by only a metre or two below my face mask. Here a cobalt blue starfish, there a curious wrasse of rippled red and green. Motionless, I take a deep breath, tilt down and bring my legs up behind in the air. Dip diving brings a general scene into close focus — softly swaying anenome and hard antlers of coral. To the surface again and breathing once more, then again becoming a part of the wonder of it all. I fin along further until a brighter than bright colour or a little movement captures my interest and has me sliding down for a closer look.

This is the garden with Kenneth Slessor's "flowers turned to stone", where reef fish are graceful lively birds moving effortlessly through forests of corals. A moorish idol, its

long snout sampling delicate morsels of food, reminds me of a flycatcher's perfect hovering to pluck spiders from their webs. A small group of parrot fish rip and tear at the coral, like a bunch of galahs getting stuck into banksia blossom. And a cloud of miniature fish emerge from the fine filament branches of coral, only to disappear again when startled, like a flock of silvereyes flitting through heath.

Like their land-based counterparts these underwater "birds" are always watchful, always slightly wary, for a coral reef is where, as E.J. Banfield put it, "no creature is safe unless it is agile and alert, endowed with giant strength or encased in armour". He left out cunning and camouflage, both factors that are exhibited by a large octopus which first tries to slip past unnoticed, then makes a quick dive for the sea floor where it melts, into the background.

☐ With bark not unlike the boab, pisonia trees are the dominant forest species on Lady Musgrave Island.

My Nikonos displays a disappointing resistance to winding on, which signals thirty-six exposures is not enough for a coral island dive. It is probably just as well since I am learning that a three millimetre thick long john wetsuit over a full body lycra suit is not quite enough to keep the cold at bay. It takes two hot drinks for me to stop shaking.

As warmth is returning to my body, the last of low tide water escapes from Lady Musgrave Island, leaving it surrounded by a vast mantle of coral stretching off into the far, far distance. In this first dive we have explored maybe two hundred square metres. There's only 1,000 hectares to go — so much for what to do for a week!

Days later and we are still only scratching the surface of possible dive sites in the lagoon when a strong wind-shift turns our semi-sheltered campsite into a raging blast zone. But on an island circled by reef, finding sheltered diving is always possible. We batten down the tent then move around to the south eastern beach for the day to take a closer look at a turtle trap — a large deep pool surrounded by shallow water in an extensive area of coral.

Finning slowly out over the shallows we come across a manta ray busily interested in something on the bottom. It allows us to approach quite closely before making a few silky strokes with its wings to fly off. Effortless poetry in motion. Seeing it move so wonderfully it seems to me that if many reef fish are like small birds, then the manta ray with its easy, almost lazy flying style, placid gregarious nature and ability to filter feed, is very akin to a pelican.

Cruising along behind a smaller ray leads us right into the turtle pool we are seeking. The slowest fin beat is too fast for diving here. I begin to realise the true complexity of a coral reef when there's too much for me to see even if I hover and simply allow the slight joggle of surface water to move me along. The outer perimeter is a cliff-like coral jungle which at first glance is solid to the sandy bottom. By taking a deep breath and holding upside down I can look underneath the coral and discover that what I presumed to be solid is really a honeycomb maze. Little beams of light dance through from the surface and allow just enough illumination for me to see solid clusters of immobile fish, which begrudgingly move away from my gaze, backing further into their secret hideholes.

Searing lungs remind me to surface. Half a dozen more dives and a bump from my companion directs my attention out rather than down. During my inverted exploring we have been joined by a school of barracuda who are in no hurry to

leave. They glide about the place looking like true lords of the realm.

In slow motion we complete a circumnavigation of the pool. No turtles today, but a score of sand rays all flopped over each other as if the little coral caves are doss houses. Lack of water on the receding tide eventually forces us back to shore.

As sunset approaches the breeze subsides. Carting cameras and a tripod to the northern end of the island, we get good seats for the evening performance of the arrival of the black capped noddy terns. The overture to the performance is a golden ball in a pale blue sky on a shimmering sea. The sun goes, leaving in its wake a rich sky of luscious reds and yellows. It would have been enough just to enjoy the sunset, but this is not our sole reason for being here.

As regular as the tide and the moon they come. In the furthest distance the scale makes them seem like insects. Insects which grow in size and numbers until they are recognisable as sea birds. The black capped noddy terns are coming together to create living sky sculptures. Imagine a gigantic flying Chinese dragon stretching half a kilometre and made up of thousands of birds. As the leading hundred lift and turn, their movement is echoed like the travelling kink of a flicked rope. Their movement so fast it is hard to see — the birds form an awesome slow motion aerial display. Against a deepening sky they wheel, creating fluid images, only to destroy them and recreate new ones. For twenty minutes this performance goes on. But then a large group turn and head for the island with single minded purpose. Only a few metres above the water surface a thousand birds are heading straight for our dress circle seats. For long seconds our world is a vision of incredibly agile birds avoiding each other at high speed, whistling past us with a soft thunderclap of wings, and making a last gasp dash for their roosting sites. We sit in silence and in awe as wave after wave hurtle past, returning to their little coral island amid the wilderness that is the Great Barrier Reef.

☐ The deep blue of the ocean fades to softer hues when it encounters the shallow ring reef of Lady Musgrave Island.

LOCATION GUIDE

There are seventy coral cays and 2,500 reefs which make up 2,000 kilometres of Great Barrier Reef, the largest animal created structure in the world (including human created structures). Lady Musgrave Island (23° 54'S; 152° 25'E) is the second southernmost island on the Great Barrier Reef and about fifty kilometres off shore, north east of Bundaberg. The cay covers between nineteen and twenty-seven hectares (depending on tides and seasons) with the long axis running north east–south west. The surrounding reef is ten square kilometres and completely encloses the cay to form a huge lagoon — access to it is via a narrow natural channel in the northern corner.

Lady Musgrave is one of the Capricorn-Bunker group of islands discovered in 1803 by Captain Bunker in his ship *Albion*. Could they write, green turtles would have marked the date ten years later under the heading catastrophe. These marvellous creatures were initially killed on an opportunistic basis by passing outrigger canoeing Aborigines and European sailors, but then the first commercial factory was set up. Right up until 1950, when they were finally protected, green turtles were killed for soup and meat. It wasn't until 1968 that all species of sea turtle were protected. Guano mining (bird droppings for use as fertilizer) and bêche de mer harvesting also took place on various islands of the Capricorn-Bunker group, including Lady Musgrave.

As with many other islands off the Queensland coast, at one time goats were introduced, supposedly to provide meat for stranded sailors. While waiting to be put on the menu the goats passed their time by eating everything that would stand still. Elliot Napier in 1935 reported, "All the undergrowth has long since gone . . . and even the bark upon the trees has been gnawed away to a height of several feet." The last of the goats was removed in 1974 and the island has been slowly recovering since.

Today, Lady Musgrave Island is a marine national park (declared in 1967) and part of the Capricorn Section of the Great Barrier Reef Marine Park (declared in 1979). It comes under the authority of both the Queensland National Parks and Wildlife Service (QNPWS) and the Great Barrier Reef Marine Park Authority (GBRMPA). Except for a miserably small portion within the northern side of the lagoon which is classed as a conservation zone, all the remaining reef surrounding the land above high water is zoned as General Use B — no commercial fishing and no live coral or shells may be taken.

While this zoning sounds fine, in practice it means killing in a national park is condoned. On land the QNPWS would prosecute anyone caught shooting fauna, yet it is quite okay for a snorkeller to take a speargun into the Zone B area and hammer hell out of the fish population. Perhaps GBRMPA should erect signs underwater directing fish to the safe conservation zone. It would be far better to take on board the idea of preserving all fauna in a national park and declare the whole reef surrounding Lady Musgrave as a conservation zone, instead of kowtowing to the Queensland frontier attitude.

☐ OPPOSITE *A mass of black-capped noddy terns creates dynamic formations in the sky.*

We should be amazed that GBRMPA exists at all. Were it not for the long running national campaign run by conservationists including John Busst, poet Judith Wright, the Littoral Society, and belatedly the Australian Conservation Foundation, the priceless Great Barrier Reef would have been a platform for oil drilling as well as the raw material for limestone mining. This conservation battle began in 1963 with the first applications to mine Ellison Reef and is detailed by Judith Wright in her excellent book *The Coral Battleground*. In essence, by 1967, eighty per cent of the Great Barrier Reef had been leased by the Queensland Government for oil and mineral exploration.

As usual, conservationists were accused of emotional over-reaction. In the event of an oil rig blowout, to protect the incredible diversity of life forms found on the reef the Queensland Mines Department were planning to spray dispersal detergents on the slick within twenty-four hours. Around that time there was a blowout off shore from Santa Barbara in California and experts later testified that the oil slicks had spread 160 kilometres, and more than six months after the first leakage it could not be stopped. Little wonder Sir John Barry said "Australia would soon be a quarry surrounded by an oil slick"

"Save the Barrier Reef" stickers blossomed and what followed was a long drawn out struggle requiring great personal dedication by conservation volunteers. The campaign then culminated in a protracted states rights battle, eventually won by the Commonwealth (and the people of Australia). Lady Musgrave was within the first section declared under the GBRMPA Act.

Now it seems almost inconceivable that such a conservation struggle was needed at all. Even before seeing the Great Barrier Reef its life force statistics are awesome. Just in species numbers there are 400 corals, 4,000 molluscs, six turtles, 1,500 fish and 240 birds. The number of individual creatures is uncountable; in sea birds alone species can have from 250 to more than 1,000,000 breeding pairs.

To some species of sea birds Lady Musgrave is a permanent home, and to others it is a migratory breeding site. Brown booby, wedge-tailed shearwater, sooty tern, bridled tern, black noddy (white-capped), crested tern, lesser crested tern, roseate tern and black-naped tern all nest within the Capricorn-Bunker group. The Royal Australasian Ornithologists Union (RAOU) regard fairy terns as a rare species and the little tern as endangered; both are under considerable threat from human impact on nesting sites. The RAOU have a creative "adopt a tern" programme through which it is hoped to raise money for research into the management and conservation of these species.

Peak time for seeing immense numbers of breeding birds is October to November. Lady Musgrave Island has a permanent colony of white capped noddies which leave with the first rays of dawn and return after sunset. There are also groups of reef herons, sooty and pied oystercatchers and silver gulls around the reef edges. Inland are scores of tiny silvereyes and strutting around your tent will come buffbreasted rails.

Lady Musgrave Island is a vegetated sand cay surrounded by a closed ring reef. The reef comprises an inner and outer reef flat and a reef rock rim — all exposed at low tide. This structure is formed from the skeletons of coral and is built by coral polyps (animals). Most polyps extend their tentacles at night to catch some food but have a symbiotic relationship with algae which, through photosynthesis, provides most of their food. This is one reason why living coral reefs can be easily killed by siltation.

Growing above high water within the Capricorn-Bunker group are sixty-nine species of flowering plants. Dominant is *Pisonia grandis*, a large smooth barked tree which grows to twenty metres. It is both helper and killer to the immense numbers of white capped noddy which use its branches as nesting sites but are caught up in the sticky substance exuded by ripening fruit. Aside from the delightful coastal

sheoak (*Casuarina equisetifolia*) and sandpaper fig (*Ficus opposita*), my favourite island tree is the screw pine (*Pandanus tectorius*), found thriving close to the edges of Lady Musgrave. Cribb says that pandanus is derived from the Malay word pandan and the trees were called breadfruit because of a superficial resemblance to true breadfruit. I've also heard them called manroot trees — once you see the large root props you'll know why.

Lady Musgrave Island is a nesting site for adult loggerhead (*Caretta caretta*) and green (*Chelonia mydas*) turtles and a nursery ground for juvenile and sub-adult turtles — they can frequently be seen just off the beach at high tide — particularly late in the afternoon. Courtship and mating peaks in late October, with egg laying taking place high up the beach at night weeks later. Hatchlings dig their way out seven to twelve weeks after that and make a dash for the sea. Many don't make it.

FUTURE PROBLEMS

Compared with its planned life as a drilling platform and limestone quarry, cocooning the Great Barrier Reef inside a marine park and listing it as a World Heritage property should ensure a fair chance of long term survival. It doesn't of course as long as huge tankers and freighters continue to make a shipping channel out of waters James Cook called "the Labyrinth". There have been more than 500 ships wrecked on the Great Barrier Reef, and not all in the days before engines and radar. As an example, on 25 March 1985, *TNT Alltrans*, a 35,000 tonne bulk carrier loaded with alumina and bound for New Zealand went aground on the reef surrounding Lady Musgrave Island. Thankfully it caused only localised damage.

"Localised damage" is all relative however, particularly with the crown of thorns starfish (*Acanthaster*

planci). Eminent scientists are still arguing over whether starfish plagues are induced by human beings or are natural cyclical occurrences. Taken as a whole, damage to the reef has been limited, but as noted authority on the reef Professor Endean points out, "140,000 (crown of thorns) would destroy the hard coral cover of an average reef of ten square kilometres in two or three years". Lady Musgrave reef is exactly that size!

Visitors to Lady Musgrave Island are also responsible for causing localised damage by, for example, anchoring over coral, using spearguns to kill fish, taking live crustacea, interrupting and confusing nesting birds, egglaying turtles and escaping hatchlings and bringing domestic animals ashore. These problems could be overcome by changing the zoning, educating visitors and enforcing fauna regulations.

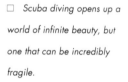

☐ *Scuba diving opens up a world of infinite beauty, but one that can be incredibly fragile.*

THE BASICS

A modern diving outfit consists of a two piece neoprene wetsuit (three millimetres to seven millimetres thick), often worn over a lycra skin suit, a clear mask with provision for simple equalising (self-pressurising of the middle ear air spaces and eustachian tubes so that the pressure outside and inside is equal), a large volume self-draining snorkel, wetsuit booties and well fitting fins, a quick release weightbelt, lead weights and knife (for cutting free of entanglements, not attacking sharks). Scuba gear consists of the diving outfit plus a diver's flag, buoy and mooring weight, a high pressure tank, regulator, pressure and depth gauges and buoyancy vest.

To complete an internationally recognised scuba course you need to be water fit and to pass a medical which should include a chest X-ray, respiratory function test and audiometry test. For your own safety, the more strict the check, the better. If, after the check up, all your medico can determine is that you have one heart, two lungs and blood pressure, find another doctor. Underwater you will be existing in a very different environment and breathing air under pressure. Sudden unconsciousness is usually fatal. Those people not safe candidates for scuba diving are anyone pregnant, asthmatic, with lung cysts, epilepsy, or any diabetic on insulin.

Once you decide scuba is for you, successful completion of the course is likely, though everyone has a few hurdles to overcome on the way. When kitting out at the start ensure the wetsuit is a firm fit with no big gaps — keeping warm is essential.

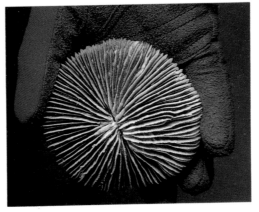

☐ *An azure starfish and a mushroom coral.*

Mask clearing is a problem for some people. Take extra time to ensure the mask fits neatly and comfortably — with head down check the fit by breathing in through your nose — the mask will stay on unsupported if it is a snug fit. With a flooded mask everything is blurred and a little frightening, but clearing the water is very easy. Other people have a problem taking the regulator out of their mouths underwater and sharing it with their partner. A few have trouble equalising the pressure in their ears, and others forget to keep breathing underwater — the most important rule in scuba.

Unless you are using a special regulator, breathing dry compressed air makes you dehydrated. Keep up your liquid intake, but not so much that you are desperate to urinate the instant you get into the water. Avoid alcohol and tobacco before a dive.

The theory of diving is a natural adjunct to practical skills in a swimming pool. Each day you will come to understand a little more about what is happening to your fragile body in an alien environment and why it happens. The laws of physics are also particularly relevant and become fascinating to the diver.

The end product of the pool work and the theory is to build your confidence underwater. When it comes time to do a sea dive you'll feel calm, and be assured of what to do when everything is going well, and you'll also know how to cope in the unlikely event of something going wrong.

Dangers

Dangers are perceived to abound underwater. It's amazing that there's enough water to fit the number of sharks waiting to eat you, let alone the plethora of other wild creatures just aching to bite, sting, or poison you.

Or at least that's what non-divers think. The truth is much calmer. With rare exceptions — you have more likelihood of being struck by lightning than eaten by a shark — most wild underwater creatures will greet your quiet presence with shy curiosity. Should you (as a large creature) attempt to touch or catch a smaller creature you may frighten it and it will try to protect itself. Many reef animals are very good at self-protection; that's why they are still living. If you regard diving on a reef in the same way as being in a room filled with priceless fragile glassware — you move carefully, look with awe but don't touch — then there is almost no chance of coming to grief on a reef.

Boring things like getting severe sunburn from snorkelling all day and acquiring nicks and scratches are the most common dangers. Coral cuts are easy to get if you blunder around, but very hard to clean and cure. Wear a full length body suit and be aware of where you are and where the coral is.

Hyperventilation (pumping in super large gulps of air then holding the last and diving) was first used by Pacific Island divers. Through this they could manage depths of thirty to sixty metres, spending up to four minutes looking for sponges and pearls. Aside from the fact that it greatly enhances your chance of blacking out, on a shallow reef there is no reason to use this technique. Likewise scuba diving in shallow water (less than ten metres) negates the chance of decompression sickness (bends).

☐ *With the correct equipment, a dive flag and a competent buddy, underwater diving is much safer than it is often perceived to be.*

UNDERWATER DIVING, LADY MUSGRAVE ISLAND – LUXURY CHECK LIST

Body Protection

Long sleeved cotton shirt
Broad brimmed hat (with chinstrap)
Cotton shorts, long light cotton pants
Dunlop Volley sandshoes
Socks, bandana, bathers
Woollen sweater
Gore-Tex waterproof full length jacket (e.g.
  J & H Cats & Dogs)
100 per cent UV protection sunglasses
Sunscreen
Rid insect repellent

Accommodation

Roomy tent, built in floor & insect netting able to
  stand strong winds (e.g. Macpac Olympus) &
  sand pegs
3-season Karrimat, Thermarest or Lilo matress
Reading torch (spare long life batteries)
Sleeping bag rated to 0 degrees C (e.g. J & H
  Bushlite), silk inner sheet
Tent torch & spare long life batteries

Getting There

Air to Bundaberg
Lady Musgrave Cruises to island
Coral Cay Camping Permit (can be arranged
  through Lady Musgrave Cruises) or Queensland
  National Parks & Wildlife Service, Bundaberg

Transport

Internal framed 65 – 85 litre backpack (e.g.
  Karrimor Jaguar series)
Waterproof self-sealing inner bag
Smaller waterproof stuff sacks for clothing

Camping

Portable radio — for weather forecasts
Matches (in self-sealing plastic bags)
Candle lantern & spare candles
Swiss army knife
Cup, bowl, eating utensils
Trangia stove (with kettle)
Methylated spirits (in more than one container)
Food (worked out for each day plus at least three
  extra days & placed in self-sealing bags)
Fresh water in barrels (can be hired from Lady
  Musgrave Cruises)
Lots of fresh vegetables (can
  be ordered from Lady Musgrave Cruises)
Toiletries, toilet paper

Recreation

Skin suit, wet suit, weight belt, fins, mask,
  snorkel, gloves
Light day pack for beach picnics
Slater, Slater & Slater, *Field Guide to Australian
  Birds*, Lansdowne-Rigby, Willoughby, NSW, 1986
Saenger, P., *The Great Barrier Reef — A Diver's
  Guide — Australian Underwater Federation*,
  Scientific Committee, Australian Underwater
  Federation, Brisbane, 1977
Edmunds, Dr C., *Dangerous Marine Animals of the
  Indo-Pacific Region*, Wedneil Publications,
  Newport, NSW, 1978
Flora & Fauna Checklists from Queensland
  National Park & Wildlife Service
Nikonos amphibious camera, close up kit, Aqua
  Sea 140 strobe, camera bodies in waterproof
  container
Lenses, wide (18 or 24 mm) for low tide reef &
  telephoto (300 to 600 mm) for birds
Strong torch & flash unit for nocturnal visitors
Shower cover for camera, sturdy tripod
Slow & fast speed film, underwater notebook,
  pencil and fish recognition charts

Information

Australian Underwater Federation:
  P.O. Box 1006, Civic Sq., ACT 2608
Great Barrier Reef Marine Park Authority:
  P.O. Box 1379, Townsville, Qld 4810
Queensland National Parks & Wildlife Service:
  138 Albert St, Brisbane, Qld 4000

Further Reading

Banfield, E.J., *Confessions of a Beachcomber*, Angus
  & Robertson, Sydney, 1968
Bates, D., *The Native Tribes of Western Australia*
  (edited by I. White), National Library of
  Australia, Canberra, 1985
Coleman, N., *The Underwater Australia Dive Guide*,
  Nelson, Melbourne, 1987
Cousteau, J., *The Silent World*, ISIS, London, 1989
Cribb, A.B. & J.W., *The Plant Life of the Great
  Barrier Reef and Adjacent Shores*, University of
  Queensland Press, St Lucia, 1985
Napier, E., *On the Barrier Reef*, Angus &
  Robertson, Sydney
Papagrigorakis, E.E., *The Underwater Man*
  (translated by P. Ramp), Dymocks, Sydney, 1981
Slessor, K., *Selected Poems*, Angus & Robertson,
  Sydney, 1977
Wright, J., *The Coral Battleground*, Nelson, West
  Melbourne, 1977

CAVE EXPLORATION

Caves were our primordial homes. They offered security from wind and rain, were less extreme in temperature and were defendable against attack. Yet it seems for all human beings that once we moved out into the light and air, caves began to be at once both frightening and fascinating. Leonardo da Vinci experienced this when he wrote: "... I came to the mouth of a huge cave, before which I stopped for a moment, stupefied by such an unknown thing.... After a time there arose in me both fear and desire — fear of the dark and menacing cave; desire to see whether it contained some marvellous thing."

To the Australian Aborigines, caves contain many marvellous, mystical and terrifying things. In the Nullarbor, the vast region Aborigines called Kattaoondiri, the intricate network of caves was the home of Jeedarra, devil serpent of the plain. In the creation of these caves scientists talk of drifting continents, changing ocean temperatures, uplifting, and the cutting power of fresh water on limestone, but Aboriginal legend tells a different tale. According to Douglas Kemsley in a 1 November 1957 edition of *Walkabout* magazine, "Yugarilya (the Pleiades) chased Jeedarra with their digging sticks. In his flight Jeedarra pushed up the cliffs of the Great Australian Bight and slid into hiding holes in Kattaoondiri."

It was believed that when Jeedarra became angry it lashed itself about so fiercely that terrible dust storms swept across the plain. Despite the presence of such creatures, some caves were worked as flint mines as far back as 20,000 years ago, some were used as storage areas for sacred artifacts (often to keep them from the eyes of women), and others were sacred

□ OPPOSITE *A speleologist peers into the depths of Koonalda Cave.*

sites in themselves where elders would give life and colour to the walls with intricate paintings.

Archaeologists have found much evidence of frequent Stone Age usage in such diverse places as Kutikina Cave (Tasmania), Kenniff Cave (Queensland), Koonalda Cave (South Australia) and Malangangerr (Northern Territory). Cave exploration in Australia by Europeans began almost with the First Fleet because of the colony's need for building lime. Limestone and marble are used in a crushed form as the base material in cement and concrete mixes, and in the iron and steel industry. Describing Bungonia Cave in New South Wales, explorer and botanist Allan Cunningham recorded in his journal for 27 April 1824: "We found the land exceedingly cavernous, orifices four feet in diameter connected with capacious subterranean excavations... of whom some presented yawning fissures of apparently great depth...." Unfortunately with too few exceptions the discovery of a limestone cave meant its ultimate demise.

☐ *Ready to go underground, the caver is equipped with overalls, strong boots, a miner's light and a hard hat.*

Wild cave conservation, as opposed to the Victorian age's attitude of creating a fairyland like the Jenolan Caves, really only started to take shape with cave explorers such as Captain J. Maitland Thompson and his expeditions into the Nullarbor in the 1930s. Australia's first caving club, the Tasmanian Caverneering Club was founded in 1946, while the Sydney University Speleological Society began in 1948. In those early days there was virtually no specialist equipment for cavers: ropes were hemp or manila, lights were household torches or carbide lamps and miner's helmets were made of compressed cardboard. Wire ladders came later as did the miner's light and what was at first very hairy cave-diving using a gas mask, a length of hose and a pair of foot bellows. Ian Lewis of the Cave Exploration Group of South Australia (CEGSA) is credited with pioneering new techniques for safe underwater cave exploration.

Caving expeditions of the past were major logistical events. Take one of J. Maitland Thompson's epics where he set up a petrol dump, and needed two cars and a truck loaded — till the springs flattened — with 600 litres of water, an extra seven drums of petrol, surveying instruments, camping equipment, a twenty-five metre Jacob's ladder, a winch and a derrick, photographic equipment, powerful petrol lamps and a three metre metal canoe — a total load of about four tonnes. Today, thanks to modern four wheel drive technology, frequent fuel stations and lightweight camping gear, getting to wild caves is considerably simpler.

While it has become generally easier to go caving, the quality of the experience remains as unchanged as the caves. A wild cave is still exactly the same as it was fifty years ago, or in some cases, five thousand years ago.

Descending into the tranquil, awesome world of a natural cave is physically taxing, exciting and addictive. To plunge into the depths of a cave is to tap into the primitive nature of the earth. It's tampering with the sensory framework that is the basis of our existence by removing key parts of the perceived world. Bruce Bedford viewed the essence of caving as "The silence. The blackness. Both are absolute, both slipping back to the borders of

☐ A caver descends into a cave using a wire ladder attached to the bull bar of a four-wheel-drive vehicle. Additional security is provided by a safety rope belayed from above.

nothing." And he posed the interesting question "Are you listening to the silence and watching the blackness, or watching the silence and listening intently to the blackness?"

Blackness underground is absolute; not the greyness of a starlit night. It is when you bring your hand close to your face yet cannot see it.

Not many people would enjoy the challenge of being a kilometre underground with a dead light and no way out. Escaping to the surface could be impossible. Aside from those caves where there is a wind blowing, in a moment of inattention it is impossible to tell whether you are going away from or towards the entrance. The realisation of this has, in the past, sent people insane. However, today there is little likelihood of a total blackout. It is standard caving safety routine that three independent light sources are carried. They usually consist of a

miner's light clamped on a safety hat and powered by wet-cell batteries, a dry-cell powered hand torch, and a further safety net is provided by one of the earliest forms of light — a candle and waterproof matches.

Caves can be wetter than wet and dustier than imaginable and it is for this reason that tough protective overalls and strong boots are de rigueur for speleologists. Steep entrances can call for wire ladders or abseiling/jumar rope.

Aside from the excitement of discovering the skeleton of an extinct species, some of the most extraordinary experiences come when your headlamp plays across a stunning example of nature's cave art. The most prolific cave minerals are carbonates, with calcite the most common, producing classic stalactites, stalagmites, columns, curtains, straws and rimstone pools. Calcites also produce more exotic creations like cave pearls, twisting

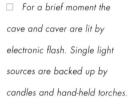

☐ For a brief moment the cave and caver are lit by electronic flash. Single light sources are backed up by candles and hand-held torches.

helictites, pendulites and cave corals. Porous limestones can create gypsum flowers and salt can produce haltite flowers.

Many caves have some creatures anchored permanently underground. Some wander in, become disoriented and die, others simply trip over an edge and fall to their deaths. Naturally some unfortunate creatures enter the caves protesting at being a predator's takeaway meal, only to then become prey to owls roosting in the caves. But not everything is frighteningly deathlike. Beyond the edge of light penetration, lives a wide range of intriguing creatures, though most plants are beaten by their inability to photosynthesise in total darkness. Some creatures such as bats, birds, crickets, snakes, lizards and centipedes come and go as they please, but others like eyeless shrimps and beetles stay in caves for their whole lives. On the surface, winter rains may freeze and summer sun scorch, but below ground, conditions are very stable with life lived at an almost constant mild temperature. Bats make use of this by roosting in the dark zone and utilising the high domes of caves as nurseries.

The underground environment may be stable in temperature and humidity, but it is not necessarily still. Astonishing as it is to first experience, many caves "breathe", that is they have a wind drafting in or out. Scientific explanations of this revolve around the stratified nature of limestone and how blowholes occur in the upper layer, acting as a break in the impervious surface crust through which the lower layer is able to breathe. The result is winds of up to sixty kilometres per hour ripping out of the caves, and howling in. At different times of the day blowhole wind acts as a giant vacuum, sucking in passing small birds and animals. In other types of caves air motion is theorised to have multiple causes, for example, changes in atmospheric conditions, two entrances separated by large distances, resonance (much the same as the sound created by blowing over the mouth of a bottle), or breathing associated with thermal convection.

The natural landscape within caves can also differ greatly from the surface. While no water collects on ultra-flat desert plains, caves underneath them may contain rivers or lakes. The sumps (lakes) can range from tiny sluices of water just big enough for a hot tired body, right up to immense sumps six kilometres long. In such lakes lots of fun can be had with an inflatable boat and snorkel gear, but they are fully explorable only by experienced specialist cave scuba divers, preferably with glaciated nerves, good wetsuits and strings of compressed air tanks.

Even if you stay out of the water

☐ A "wind" rips out of a breathing cave on the Nullarbor Plain.

there are plenty of challenges: squeezes are those body-hugging narrow bits where two immense pieces of earth are parted just enough to wiggle through — if you breathe out and don't panic; and it doesn't pay to start to think about earthquakes with solid rock pressing hard on your ribs and backbone. Aside from squeezes, wild caves present other little tests: monster boulders seemingly thrown together, steep slippery drops, suspect stale air and all-pervading dirt which seems attracted to eyes.

Despite a comforting light from the strongest of torches it pays to focus your attention to each twist and turn and to make a mental (or jotted) note of each major ground feature. Many caves resemble a major city's underground train system, having maze-like multi-level intersecting passages. It is breathtakingly easy to let a few moments' inattention lead you hard up against a dead end. Dead ends are bad news but are not a time to panic or to shout, since sound is often deflected underground and can appear to be coming from anywhere. Calm reasoning and careful backtracking will soon have you on course to the surface and fresh air. Otherwise you may develop first-hand knowledge of what it's like to be a cave victim.

I was doing my best to control the length of my visit when caving under the Nullarbor Plain.

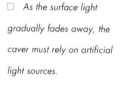

□ *As the surface light gradually fades away, the caver must rely on artificial light sources.*

BENEATH THE NULLARBOR PLAIN

Flames licking into dry timber create prancing shadows on the walls of a cave called Murrawijinie. We sit around the campfire and are drawn into contemplation by its mesmerising powers. But for our modern clothing and light skin, this scene could have been set in any period over the last forty millenniums, since that is how long caves under the Nullarbor have been visited. Dousing the fire we turn in, but I'm gripped by a restless excitement. Looking up I view the stars through rock-fringed windows.

Swallows greet the new day with a burst of spry flight. I emerge from the comparative warmth of the cave to icy, pre-dawn light. As the sun lifts, it casts rays across a landscape so devoid of variation that I could swear that it is possible to glimpse the curvature of the earth and to grab hold of the concept of being on an immense spinning orb.

Out across this plain of 200,000 square kilometres of flatness we search for something in the midst of nothing: a something called a doline, a collapsed cave roof which creates an entrance of a size which may range from a velodrome to a two metre hole in the earth. In his nine extensive explorations of the caves from the 1930s to the 1960s, Captain J. Maitland Thompson used marine navigation techniques with a compass, distance log, chronometer and a sextant.

The good captain navigated in true sea-going tradition perched on the "bridge deck" of a charabanc (the roof). Messages were relayed to the engine room and wheel house (the cab) in simple style; one thump of his

Dolines are collapsed cave roofs that create entrances to their intricate tunnel webs. They range in size from a few metres to this very large one at Koonalda.

hefty boot on the roof translated into "steer to port", two thumps meant "turn to starboard" and three thumps were the comforting "steady as she goes". Our leader, Iain Greenwood of Osprey Wildlife Expeditions is relying on Landsat photographs and aerial surveys, but actually finding a cave entrance still demands precise topographical map and compass work, and sometimes, just a smidgen of luck.

Koonalda Cave's entrance is huge, more than sixty metres in diameter, but it is encircled by sad, degraded landscape eaten bare by sheep. Edging into the cave I leave the broad surface images behind, replacing them with images of a micro world shown all too briefly by a narrow piercing beam of light from my headlamp. For thousands of years this cave was an underground Aboriginal quarry producing valuable flint nodules; now it is a treasure trove for archaeologists. For me it provides the mind-altering challenge of a "squeeze". I wiggle, grovel and slither through a section of cave where the roof and floor become intimately associated, all the time inadequately suppressing my fear of becoming a permanent fixture. Upon returning to the cave entrance the surface air smells sweet.

☐ *The caves under the Nullarbor reveal an assortment of fossils. The shell fossil dates from a time when the Nullarbor was the floor of an ocean, and the skull dates from a time when now extinct animals roamed the forested plains.*

Our next challenge is a fossil cave set in a unique, cragged landscape full of bleached limestone. After camping near it we are all keen to venture past the ancient, lichen-encrusted quandong skeleton which has guarded the entrance for many, many years. (In researching this chapter I uncovered a 1930 photograph showing the same cave entrance with the dead quandong looking equally gnarled and ancient.) As I slide down the tree trunk, its deeply fissured bark feels smooth to my skin. Being inside this cave is like being in a terrarium. Collapsed roof holes around the edges are windows to the sky and little clumps of

greenery take heart where they strike. I move as if there are eggshells underfoot. Animals are everywhere — life, flesh and blood departed, leaving scattered bones, skulls and perfectly preserved dried specimens, like the fox my headlight falls across, with its skin pulled back leaving its face perpetually locked in a silent scream.

The cave may be a death trap for animals, but it is also deep in silt-covered treasure — archaeological treasure. Patient digging reveals a fascinating array of creatures which once roamed the Nullarbor. McNamara and Murray's *Prehistoric Mammals of Western Australia* describes a wombat weighing between 100 and 150 kilograms, one of its relatives the size of a rhinoceros, a marsupial leopard with front teeth six centimetres long and a giant kangaroo standing about two and a half metres high. The likelihood of being confronted by living specimens of these creatures is zilch; all of them disappeared at least 15,000 years ago. However, fossil remains are always an exciting possibility. Gently probing with spatula and paintbrush on behalf of Flinders University we unearth ash from an ancient campfire, pieces of bone (later dated at 1,000 to 6,000 years old) and the skull of a strange carnivore (later identified by Dr Rod Wells of Adelaide as a *Sarcophilus harrisii*, Tasmanian devil). Tassie devils have been extinct on the mainland for thousands of years.

It rains overnight, but by morning there is no trace of the deluge. The Nullarbor is like some huge sponge greedily soaking up any water. Where it goes I discover later in the day when we arrive at the doline to

Weebubbie — a cave entrance which dwarfs us all. Local Aborigines feared and hated Weebubbie Cave, calling it "the place of hidden feet", but later used it as a storehouse for sacred artifacts to keep them from the eyes of women. In the days of the overland telegraph line, Weebubbie was a picnic spot for telegraphists from the Eucla transmitter station.

We descend via a wooden ladder, a metal ladder and then loose scree which ends in a lustrous green lake. My headlight pans across the surface of the underground lake until it fades off into blackness, its power defeated by sheer size.

A wetsuit is barely adequate against the cold waters as I take a waterproof torch, snorkel and mask and push off into the blackness. Weightless and immersed in an invisible liquid, I glide across an unseen surface, a sensation like that which an astronaut must feel being set adrift outside an orbiting space capsule. My torchlight arcs down through water I know is there but which in its purity is invisible. Where the light does finally strike is more than thirty metres down amid pinnacles of fallen grey limestone rocks each the size of a giant's plaything. Between the rocks and the surface is nothing. It is a bizarre sensation.

I quench the light. Weightless and sightless, I'm adrift in an amorphous black envelope, cut off from every normal landed, sighted sensation. It is incredible.

Ascending to the real world again we find it is cold and punctuated by misting rain, but the rain stops by the time we establish a new camp near Cocklebiddy Cave. Dawn is an endless line of old gold which eats into a black sky, then turns it blue. At Cocklebiddy the daylight filtering down from the entrance is just visible from the shores of another subterranean lake. Dinghy inflated, we paddle to an island to set up magnesium flares, sparklers, torches and candles in a briefly successful attempt to view the immensity of the cavern.

Paddling on further I encounter a lowering roof and miniature stalactites. Roof meets water and I stop, but the water doesn't. This is the largest underground lake in Australia and the longest cave dive in the world (Ian Lewis of CEGSA describes it as the world's longest sunken bathtub). It has drawn cave scuba diving expeditions from all

☐ *Simon paddles us to the junction where Cocklebiddy's roof meets its sump lake.*

over the world. First charted as a source of water in 1900, the known length of the sumps has simply grown and grown. During the first dives in 1972, 100 metres were explored; this was pushed out to one kilometre in 1976. By 1979, a large Australian expedition of nine scuba divers set a world underwater cave diving record of three kilometres, later extending it to four kilometres. In 1983 a French team pushed to the end of the third sump — at just less than six kilometres, travelling with submarine scooters. Where the French stopped, believing they could squeeze no further, an Australian

diver, Hugh Morrison, removed his air tank and, by pushing it in front of him, managed to get through for another 240 metres.

Up until now we had been spending a few hours at a time cave exploring then re-emerging to the surface. Our chance to spend a full day underground came at Mullamalang. This cave was discovered during a 1963 to 1964 Sydney University Speleological Society expedition, and was named because of the large amounts of dry sand found in the cave. Getting underground is a bit of a rough rock scramble which eventually pans out as the track follows an ancient stream bed 100 metres below the surface. Just when I think that the day underground will be a doddle, all progress ceases with an amazing sight. Set beneath an impressive high-domed cavern is an intimidating sand dune, called The Dune. The track skirts around this monster so we leave the bats roosting in the high dome at peace.

I'm pondering how natural forces can create a sand dune underground when my quandary is partially answered. I round the next corner and am confronted by a squeeze, through which pipes a good facsimile of the southerly buster. Battling through the flying sand here is like coping with a gale on the beach. With sand dunes and gales behind us I'm not really surprised to be strolling through rolling sands before encountering the next obstacle, a brace of boulder-strewn hills.

Cresting the last hill we combine our torch light which forces its yellowing way for fifty metres then bounces back as pure white. Scrambling downhill proves difficult

☐ *To descend into the tranquil world of a cave today is an adventure.*

as distances seem to increase and decrease under the flickering torchlight. One poorly judged leap would result in an awkward injury, so everyone is moving carefully. Finally we arrive at the base of the hill and the reflected white turns out to be pure gypsum walls, with "flowers" of crystal "growing" on the surrounding rocks. This gypsum also just happens to be fringing the exquisite turquoise waters of White Lake. Hot and tired, we slip out of our clothes and into the cold water.

In one day of walking, Mullama-lang is barely glimpsed, since the cave has at least twelve kilometres of passages. This cave was the site of a major expedition by a team of forty-five speleologists from CEGSA. The group included a core of twenty people who camped underground for fourteen days, plus a support crew of cave "sherpas" who relayed equipment from the surface.

After the immensity of Mullamalang, Nurina Cave is almost too small to contemplate. And it is nearly too small to find. Entering a tight-angled squeeze we struggle, then wriggle through a couple of body-hugging passages, and slide down a vertical drop before standing upright for the first time. Moving torch beams create eerie shapes as they paint in details of the main chamber: a diamond-shaped cavern floored with tranquil calcite surfaced pools and decorated with free-flowing natural limestone sculptures.

An electronic flash reveals the cave in a brief blast of light. For a milli-second total black is defeated and the cave's intricate details are naked. As the image, etched on overexposed retinas, fades, blackness returns.

"Ready to leave?", our assistant guide Andrew's voice drifts into our chamber. Simon, Rod and I have been taking photographs for nearly an hour and Iain's assistant, Andrew, has come down part way to check our progress. "Yes, just packing up, we are right behind you," Simon replies. It takes a few minutes to secure the camera gear into a padded backpack for the rough return journey to the surface — a few minutes too long. We casually troop from a side tunnel into the main chamber, then up the climb and start on the ultra-twisty section. It is slow going. The bag of cameras needs to be pushed and hauled through small gaps, then balanced in place while the lead caver moves to the next secure point. In tight spaces my view is limited to Simon's back and reflected torchlight from Rod. When Simon's head appears in front of me I presume we have a problem. "We've come to a dead end" he says.

I join him squeezed on a confined ledge. Headlamps off, we are confronted by nothing; no welcom-ing shaft of light, not even a calming patch of grey, just black. Somehow we have missed the way out. Headlamps on again and as light plays on blank walls of limestone my imagination flicks into overdrive. In October 1966, a team of scientists came across the carcass of a Thylacine (Tasmanian tiger) with so much of the skin and hair intact that it appeared to have died only months previously. In fact carbon dating later revealed it to be 4,600 years old. The idea of us being perfectly preserved for a similar length of time before discovery is of little comfort. By backtracking and rethinking our passage, the correct route rewards us with a glimmer of surface light. We pop out of Nurina like champagne corks at a plush wedding.

Twelve hours is enough time for our fright to diminish and on the way to Eremophila Cave everyone is keen to be a troglodyte again. Finding the cave is not easy since the entrance is only about a metre across. Ultimately we discover it partially hidden by emu bush. The bush is shimmering and shaking like there's a mad-as-hell emu rattling it, but the cause is wind — hard enough to easily inflate a three person tent held over the entrance to the cave.

Penetrating this cave means dropping twenty metres straight down, so we use a wire ladder securely attached to the bull bar of the four wheel drive, which each caver belayed on a back-up safety rope. I draw the short straw. It is a struggle to get started, but once I'm clear of the ground I can hook my heels behind the ladder and so keep my centre of gravity close to it. Even so, it is all too easy to bang into the surrounding cave walls and set off miniature rock falls.

By half way down, intense surface light is just a soft blue filter and I am relying on the miner's light. As the ladder sways and spins my light pans across receding walls. By the time I hit bottom the cave has become thirty times its entrance size. I call up "down and safe" then unclip the karabiner-ended rope from my harness and watch it snake upwards into the darkness.

I step away from the rock fall zone, moving carefully on a white pebbled surface. The "pebbles" are bones covered in the dust of ages, and debris from fallen stalactites. Clustered near the cave edges are a bunch of stalagmites. Suddenly the hard surface under my feet changes and I tread on something that makes a curious booming sound. Standing stock still I bring the miner's light down and discover I'm not alone. There is a kangaroo, fully grown and large, but perfectly preserved and hollow and well past caring about me. The kangaroo's skin is drum tight over its ribs and pulled back from the teeth leaving the appearance of a permanent cry of pain.

I'm willing the next descending caver to hurry up when a movement catches the edge of my light beam. Not everything that's come into Eremophila Cave is dead. A banded gecko is unconcerned at my presence, staring at me as I stare at it, before it easily begins a vertical ascent on a huge fallen rock: no problem for it to come and go. Seeing this little living creature gives the cave a more friendly atmosphere and I begin to enjoy the quiet calm. Calm? I suddenly realise that standing on the floor of this cave there is no perceptible air movement. A gale is drafting out of the entrance, yet twenty metres down all is hushed and still.

We arrive at our last Nullarbor camp in the dark and after living with desert quietness for so many days, the roaring sea sings a strange bedtime lullaby. As the dead blackness of night is overcome by the living colours of dawn I am perched on the edge of tremendous limestone cliffs marking the current beginning of the Nullarbor Plain. Cumbersome rollers thunder against the Great Australian Bight and the place has so much power I can believe explorer John Forrest portrayed the truth in 1869 when he wrote: "... after looking over the precipice, we all ran back quite terror-stricken." I ignore the opportunity to retreat and instead look through the viewfinder of my camera, then open the shutter and let those faintly lit ocean rollers paint themselves across my film.

☐ *Though it is small and protected by tortuous passages, Nurina Cave is no less fascinating than the bigger caves. It can be even more exciting if, as we did, you take the wrong turn and become temporarily lost.*

LOCATION GUIDE

The Nullarbor Plain is an uncompromising place: freezing in winter; instant dehydration in summer. As the explorer Giles wrote in his diary, it was "a region utterly unknown to man and as utterly forsaken by God". This largely treeless plain covers an area three times the size of Switzerland, but the Nullarbor's mountains and rivers are hidden beneath the surface.

Edward John Eyre was the first European to make an overland crossing (along the coast) in 1841, writing in his notes that the edge of the Nullarbor was "indeed a rich and gorgeous view for a painter". Bushmen Miller and Dutton discovered the plain, and in 1866, surveyor Alfred Delisser saw it as "null arbor" (treeless) and he took poetic licence to coin the word Nullarbor ("nulla" also means none or not any in local Aboriginal language).

For nearly a hundred years this huge, arid plain was a barrier between the east and west colonies. The Overland Telegraph line (completed in 1877) formed a tenuous repeating stations link; the Trans-Australia rail link was completed in 1917. Captain J. Maitland Thompson began the first of his nine cave searching expeditions in 1932. In 1941, 400 workers were employed to clear, grade and gravel a road across the plain.

Early settlers saw not a fragile wilderness, but the chance to exploit. In their desire to make good this chance, many pioneers died of thirst and exposure, but many more brought death with them, treating a great world treasure with contempt. Overgrazing, overburning and the introduction of imported pests damaged a fragile environment and doomed many native plant and animal species. Cave sumps were regarded as reservoirs to be pumped and some are now littered with pipes and pumping equipment. A thoroughly-researched report calling for extensive conservation measures was produced in 1978, but legislative response and active management has been particularly slow. A relatively small area (231,900 hectares) was declared as Nullarbor National Park in 1979 by the South Australian Government and ten years later this was increased to 593,000 hectares. Beside this National Park a 2.28 million hectare regional reserve was created which gives a much lower status than national park as it unfortunately tries to juggle the concept of multiple use.

The Nullarbor would appear to be just another big desert, but it conceals more than it shows. It is one of the world's largest regions of karst, or subterranean drainage. The oldest exposed rock in the area is of the late Eocene age (forty million years ago). Twenty to twenty-five million years ago the Great Australian Bight was inundated by an ocean reaching at times more than 200 kilometres inland. What once was an ocean floor became limestone and in it were left fossilised mollusc shells, corals and other marine creatures. Rainwater sank through the raised surface and carved an intricate maze of caves. Under the "billiard" table that is now the Nullarbor Plain are more than 200 subterranean caverns.

☐ OPPOSITE *A caver descends by a wire ladder into a Nullarbor cave. The preserved body of a kangaroo lies on the floor. Aborigines believed that the labyrinth of caves under the Nallarbor was the home of Jeedarra, devil serpent of the plain.*

This underground network is an international magnet for cavers, even if visiting the caves takes a good deal of effort, perseverance and in some cases special permission from a range of government departments in two states. South Australian and Western Australian caving groups organise expeditions, and one Adelaide-based adventure travel operator, Osprey Wildlife Expeditions, runs twelve-day commercial caving trips in the region. Individual cave exploring is possible at some well known cave locations but for most, finding each cave is a nightmare — thanks to the combined efforts of road making crews, dozer drivers and locals.

There was a continuous, nomadic Aboriginal presence in the Nullarbor. Daisy Bates makes the point that, "this apparently great treeless and waterless plain did not necessarily isolate the peoples living around it from each other". The Aboriginal people had, and still have, a distinct relationship with many caves. Most of the Nullarbor Plain was covered by the tribal territory of the Mirning and Pindini. Madura was lived in, Weebubbie was used as a storage area for sacred items, and Murrawijinie is still marked by the sign of the red hand as an "off limits" cave. The feeling of entering ancient, precious treasures is with you in these subterranean caverns.

Birds of prey such as eagles, goshawks and owls hunt and forage down as far as the dark zone, searching for animals that have strayed or fallen into the caves. Beyond the light, Nullarbor caves are the province of some strange creatures — blind spiders, a species of tenebrionid beetle and an endemic cockroach. The caves are also home

to colonies of the little chocolate bat, the lesser long-eared bat and the long-eared bat. The bats utilise the caves not only for roosting during the day, but they also select domed areas for rearing young. The domes provide warmed air essential for the bats' first few weeks of life. It seems strange that bats can find warm areas for nurseries in a region where the surface temperatures are so extreme — 0 to 50 degrees C. Helping in the bats' survival, most Nullarbor caves are a pleasant 19 degrees C year-round.

Hairy-nosed wombats are common and frequently seen resting on the surface after their work of tunneling new Nullarbor caves. Echidna, native cat, bandicoot, possum, desert rat-kangaroo, wallaby, kangaroo, potoroo and native mouse are also present in the Nullarbor region. Endemic animals include a species of dunnart and a skink lizard. Shrubs

and low trees dominate the vegetation including saltbush, acacias, tea tree, mulga, mallee and casuarina. The Nullarbor frankenia is endemic to the region.

FUTURE PROBLEMS

Caves are easily damaged and polluted by uncaring visitors. Weebubbie was the subject of a volunteer clean up in 1985. Basically it is remoteness and their difficulty in being located which protects the Nullarbor caves — even those within the protection of the National Park and the Reserve.

Another concern is that fossils sell for large sums overseas. The existence of extensive fossils in unprotected sites underscores the need for active management of the Nullarbor caves. Given that the Nullarbor is a region of international significance in terms of geology, anthropology, paleontology, history and scenic beauty, it is hoped to be soon protected under a joint South Australian and Western Australian national park/recreation park amalgamation and eventually included in the World Heritage List.

THE BASICS

Descent into caves is by foot, via steel-runged, wire ladders, on single ropes or in some cases by swimming when either free-diving or carrying full scuba equipment. Strong, comfortable and waterproof boots are essential in all but the latter method of entry. Hanging mid-air on a wire ladder, you can usually get some comfort from the thought that the ladder is backed up by an attached safety line belayed from a firmly anchored position. In single rope descents cavers utilise rockclimbing technology and abseil, wearing a climbing harness and using a friction device. Ascents are achieved by prussiking, using a special ascending device. For novices, cave diving is still the most dangerous form of scuba diving.

Lighter, longer-life batteries, plastic and fibreglass helmets and synthetic ropes have helped to make caving a little less taxing. Even so caving can be extremely strenuous so wear shorts and a light top under strong overalls. After a day of rock scrambling hands become chapped and dry so take some moisturiser or wear light gloves.

☐ *A group of cavers just returned to the surface.*

CAVE EXPLORATION, BENEATH THE NULLARBOR PLAIN – LUXURY CHECK LIST

Body Protection

Long sleeved cotton shirt
Bandana
Broad brimmed hat (for surface)
Cotton shorts
Strong overalls
Strong waterproof boots
Socks
Bathers (optional)
Woollen sweater
Light spray jacket
100 per cent UV protection sunglasses
Sunscreen
Rid insect repellent
Waterproof gloves

Accommodation

Roomy tent, built-in floor and insect netting.
3-Season Karrimat, Thermarest or Lilo mattress
Candle/reading torch (spare long life batteries)
Sleeping bag rated to 0 degrees C (e.g. J & H
  Bushlite)
Silk inner sheet

Getting There

Air to Adelaide, four wheel drive to Nullarbor
Access permits SA & WA Government
  departments.
Tour: Osprey Wildlife Expeditions, 27B
  Strathalbyn Rd, Aldgate, SA 5154.

Transport

11 mm static rope
Karabiners
Descenders & ascenders
Climbing harness
Slings
Figure of eight friction device
Miner's light & wet cell batteries
Candles & waterproof matches
Hand torch
Fibreglass or plastic helmet
Silva type compass
Plastic pealess whistle
Regional topographical maps
Aerial survey & landsat photographs
Internal framed 40–65 litre backpack
  (e.g. Karrimor Hot Rock series)
Waterproof self-sealing inner bag
Extra waterproof pack liners
Smaller waterproof stuff sacks for clothing

Camping

Battery charger
Matches (in self-sealing plastic bags)
Candle lantern & spare candles
Swiss army knife
Cup, bowl, eating utensils
Trangia stove (with kettle)
Methylated spirits (in more than one container)
Aluminium billy (for fire)
Toasting fork
Food (worked out for each day & placed in self-
  sealing bags)
Fresh vegetables
Toiletries, toilet paper & trowel
20 litre water barrels (surface)
1 litre water bottles (when caving)

Recreation

Slater, Slater & Slater, *Field Guide to Australian
  Birds*, Lansdowne-Rigby, Willoughby, NSW,
  1986
Flora & Fauna Checklists from SA National Parks
  & Wildlife Service
Montgomery, N., *Single Rope Techniques*
Camera bodies in well padded, waterproof
  container
Lenses, wide (18 or 24 mm) & 55 mm or 105 mm
  micro for caves & closeups
Sturdy tripod
Numerous flash units, plus charging units
Magnesium flares
Slow, fast & superfast speed film
Notebook & pen

Caving Clubs

Australian Speleological Federation Inc:
  P.O. Box 388, Broadway NSW 2007.

Further Reading

Bates, D., *The Native Tribes of Western Australia*
  (edited by I. White), National Library of
  Australia, Canberra, 1985
Bedford, B.L., *Challenge Underground*, Allen &
  Unwin, London, 1975
McNamara, K., & Murray, P., *Prehistoric Mammals
  of Western Australia*, WA Museum, Perth, 1985
Pavey & Montgomery, *Australian Natural History*,
  Sydney, June 1975

BUSH EXPLORING

Mapmakers of old abhorred blank spaces. They would fill the gaps with such encouraging observations as "thar be dragons here", or let their desk-bound imaginations run riot with sketches of whirlpools, ogres and the worst possible terrors. And still it was always the blank spaces, those untracked wildernesses, which acted as overpowering magnets for adventurous souls.

Unknown locations beckoned, drawing in the fearless and the foolhardy alike, allowing them to chance their lives on a quest for discovery.

Patriotism, egotism and greed all played a part in explorers' attempts to fill the gaps in Terra Australis. Sadly some of the early explorers regarded indigenous people with contempt, choosing not to acknowledge the wisdom accumulated from their 40,000 years of survival in Australia. The Europeans preferred to rely on their own technology and an attitude that wilderness could be fought and beaten. Many explorers, like Burke and Wills in 1861, died needlessly, while others like King were fed by Aborigines and survived.

Of those that did succeed in exploring new regions, many travelled through the country at times of great local abundance, such as the wet season. Based on the sight of temporary vast fields of tall grasses wreathed by strongly flowing rivers, the explorers' glowing reports helped generate a land grab. This ultimately opened up tracts of fragile land to clear-felling and overgrazing, which in turn created serious land degradation.

It was only through the persistence of conservationists such as Myles J. Dunphy in the early 1900s that the desire to

☐ OPPOSITE *A wilderness area deep within the King Leopold Ranges in the Kimberley.*

☐ *Precise map and compass work is required of bush explorers.*

explore and map areas grew out of a pure love of the bush and a strong desire to protect it for the enjoyment of later generations. Paddy Pallin, who was at the forefront of bushwalking, described Dunphy as "that extraordinary man who did more for bushwalking and the cause of conservation than any other individual in Australia".

Instead of heading off into the wilderness with horses, camels, portable whale boats, a small army and a vast array of accoutrements, Dunphy and his frequent compatriots in the Mountain Trails Club (formed in 1914), which included Bert Gallop and Roy Rudder, sought to travel light either overnight bivouacking in the open or sheltering in lightweight hikers' tents first made of calico then later japara. The small tent was a symbol of the exploring walker.

Dunphy and Gallop perfected the "Dungall" version of the swag which was humped by swaggies all over the country. The Dungall had a ground sheet and cape, towel shoulder pad, light belt-axe, nested billy cans and food — a self-contained bush explorer's kit which laid the foundation for bushwalking. The more body-forgiving rucksack (backpack) took over in Australia

around 1927, though it too was a development of a much earlier two shoulder-strapped haversack which was used by armies all over the world. In the late 1920s Paddy Pallin established a small business sewing external framed backpacks and simple "A" frame canvas tents — at first supplying his friends in the Sydney Bushwalkers, then catering for an ever-growing percentage of the Australian public.

From these humble beginnings have grown the traditions of today's bush explorers, who are imbued with a strong desire to experience untouched enclaves and leave nothing but quickly fading footprints. There is no need to strip tree bark for overnight ground padding, to kill native animals or to build stone cairns on high peaks. Rather than seeing rock and mountains as barriers to mineral extraction, the wealth of the landscape is recognised as perennial but fragile, and dependent on remaining undisturbed. The objective is to travel light, carry everything in strong backpacks, pad quietly across the landscape, sleep on the ground or in little tents and cook on small campfires which are then extinguished, dispersed and covered.

The knowledge that following a serious accident, possible rescue or assistance can come only after days of walking, places an enormous responsibility on the bush explorer's shoulders and at the same time it bestows a heady wave of freedom. It also helps to keep small sections of Australia wild and unsubdued.

Walking is simply lifting each foot in turn and placing it in front of the rest of the body. However, with a quarter or more of bodyweight saddled in a backpack and toted over uneven boulder-strewn valleys and up and down mountains, bush exploring is both a trial of will and perseverance, whose stress depends on the state of your joints and cardiovascular system. The price is some pain, discomfort and varying degrees of hardship; the reward is a beautifully functioning body — tougher, leaner and trimmed of excess fat — and a clearer, in-tune mind.

In an age where satellite imagery can clearly photograph any two metre square on the entire planet, you'd think that there would be no bush exploring left. Yet even when these astounding photographs are produced, it only takes a roadless remote leafy canopy to produce an appetite for exploration.

A successful bush exploring expedition has always been a product of shared bush skills and motivation. Between a group of intrepid walkers a diversity of bush skills such as the ability to research, plan, organise, navigate, cook, camp and handle first aid, makes life comfortable. Motivation is both the impetus and life blood for adventure, that is, for getting the trip underway. This often means long periods on the telephone gathering local knowledge and setting up transport, and keeping things on track even if the weather turns bad, possums share the food, the navigator becomes disoriented, the doctor falls in love with his or her sleeping bag and group members develop a pathological hatred of each other.

Research into a trip to a protected wilderness is sometimes assisted by national parks and wildlife services, but often the rangers are so overworked and the parks so poorly funded that wilderness sections of parks are as much a mystery to them as to anyone else. Unprotected wilderness — and there is a lot of it in Australia — is even harder to research, given that virtually nothing stands between it and exploitation.

Mining companies and forestry departments rarely promote the beauty of a wilderness before they commence operations. Dunphy learned this early in his conservation career when, with the intention of creating a public reserve, he told a New South Wales Forestry Commission officer of a newly-discovered wonderfully forested

☐ *Enjoying a bush exploring trip can sometimes be a matter of attitude.*

canyon. They promptly went out and logged it! Conservation groups, museum and university field research staff and bushwalking clubs can be good sources of information, though there is sometimes a reticence to share knowledge before they know why you are seeking it.

Planning a bush exploring trip really gets down to hard detail over topographical maps and a few mugs of coffee. Deciding the route and its timing is a matter of experience. Carrying loads in excess of twenty-seven kilograms, the Roman Imperial Army legionaries endured training marches of thirty-two kilometres at five kilometres per hour. John Hart in the Sierra Club guide, *Walking Softly in the Wilderness*, suggests allowing two hours for every five kilometres plus an extra hour for every 300 metres climbed. Paddy Pallin suggested two hours for every three kilometres in rough country, plus a similar allowance for height gains.

Organising, provisioning and cooking depend very much on the length of trip, the relative strengths of group members, whether or not food caches can be arranged, and whether you share the cooking. For a twelve day trip, in a group of four each person can carry a billy, eating utensils, three group lunches and dinners plus their own breakfasts. This way weight relief is rotated equally and you only have to cook every fourth day.

Navigation is not just map and compass work, which in itself is a vast subject and beyond the scope of this chapter section, it also includes making educated guesses based on the terrain as to the probable location of water, making allowances to cope with extremes of temperature, and keeping within safe limits of the group members' climbing abilities, general level of fitness and current health. Leading such a trip also requires the ability to swallow one's pride, take advice and change your mind.

Camping is using the barest minimum that conditions allow. Mid-summer high altitude trips in Tasmania may mean pitching a snow tent in carefully chosen protected sites, cooking on lightweight stoves and sleeping in winter-rated down sleeping bags. On the other hand, venturing mid-winter into the Kimberley means finding just enough flat space on the earth for a ground sheet, then sleeping in a lightweight down bag and cooking on a small campfire.

Most first aid courses seem designed for city based accidents. Their usefulness for back country trips is minimal, other than to keep the patient alive for a longer period. Not everyone can choose a doctor as one of the trip members, so undertake a course in wilderness survival such as the one run by Wilderness Expeditions in New South Wales (all participants must have a current first aid certificate as a basic requirement).

Regrettably the nature of bush exploring necessitates the carrying of a heavy backpack (see page 145). "Heavy" is a relative term: for some people just a jumper and sleeping bag are beyond the pale, while for masochists (especially the long-legged thin variety) excess is approached when trying to carry more than their entire body weight. Bush explorers become paranoid about weight, and are able to smell a camping store "ultra-light" sign at a five kilometre distance — not personal weight, burning off thousands of kilojoules per day takes care of that, but carried weight. Some notable extremes are a passion for silk underwear, drilling holes in a toothbrush, cutting up a field guide to leave only bird pictures, carrying film without canisters and having bare skin as the only change of clothes.

Without doubt, the lighter the pack the greater the enjoyment. It comes down to what each individual regards as essential. A tripod, a book, clean socks, or a portable compact disc player can all slip from luxury to essential, depending on your outlook. One way of cutting down is to do it progressively. On each trip make a list of the items you took but didn't use — then leave them at home next time. Ultimately you will end up carrying a pack so light that you'll hardly leave footprints in the soil!

In my chosen bush exploring experience in the Kimberley, the lead-like camera gear we were carrying ensured that it was wonderful to take the backpack off at the end of each day.

By Foot In The Western Kimberley

Livistona palms set their dusky green against the ochre walls of an alluring gorge. It is fine, however, only for rock wallabies: it provides no way through for us — except back, around and up. Even the lesser ascent we choose is twenty metres of semi-vertical, casually-fitted rock plates. Each needs testing before chancing weight on it. And each lift is taxing when there's an extra third of body weight riding on hips and shoulders. As we climb higher, each step makes me more wary than the previous one.

Tension eases once astride a

☐ *Part of the way up a saddle in the King Leopold Ranges. Even in mid-winter it is 30 degrees celsius and rock scrambling with a full pack is difficult.*

jutting swag of rock, looking down
on grey-green palm crowns. Out on
the distant black soil plains, our four
sets of just padded footprints are
invisible. It is sad country: once
delicate and bountiful, but now torn
apart by overgrazing, it is a
collection of dry, harshly flattened
dust bowls, and good to leave
behind.

Ahead is more climbing — a full
morning's worth before blue sky-
light through the trees signals the
crux of this lower saddle of the King
Leopold Ranges. In Kosciusko, on the
other side of the island, temperatures
are probably well below freezing.
Here, life is lived on the high side of
30 degrees C — heat enough to suck
the moisture out of overladen bodies
and to encourage naked revelling in
the first large tranquil rock pool we
encounter.

Downstream this swimming,
lunching pool becomes a waterfall,
devoid of water. Skirting around it
the rock is smooth — time- and
water-worn. It snakes down at a
feet-tingling pitch, encouraging flat
footed square-on descent. Then it
lands in a bed of caramel coloured
sand and disappears. Stream boulders
and overhanging forest replace the
gorge walls. We play russian roulette
on the rocks: one in every six, or six
hundred, will roll underfoot. The
trick is to pick which one and not go
down in a cursing heap.

Mid-afternoon, and a map
conference suggests we are beginning
on a large sweeping curve. Perhaps a
short cut is in order. From river
stone flatness we traverse up a steep
sided ridge to a white barked gum.
In the strong northern light it shines
for us like a mariner's friend of a
million candle power. Sharing the

□ Opposite *The harsh but
awesomely beautiful landscape
of the western Kimberley.*

tree's lofty vantage point gives us sweeping 360 degree views of a mountain amphitheatre: peaks and rolling tree-strewn hills. No artificial object or human-created scar mars the natural beauty of this scene. A long day's solid walking has taken us into untouched wilderness.

Heaven is a sandy shore campsite beside a deep swimming hole fringed with flaky-barked melaleucas. Under the brilliance of a nearly full moon we dine, rather than just eat, since even bushwalking food gets a taste lift from our perfect al fresco restaurant. Instead of stripping melaleuca bark for bedding as was the local Aboriginal custom, we let lightweight self-inflating mats take shape before laying on them and snuggling into lightweight sleeping bags.

Like a ray of life, a descending swath of morning sunlight fans down the vertical walls of a surrounding gorge. Where it touches the walls, the rock glows with vitality, the reflections cloning themselves on soothed river water. We drown and bury the fire and then restore our sleeping sites before moving off.

After barely a kilometre I'm stream-crossing when my number in the "pick the wrong rock" stakes comes up and I, along with the camera, splatter across unforgiving granite. There are no broken bones, but a healthy show of blood. Thankfully this is a short distance day and we are soon stopped by another deep, water-fronted campsite, this time backdropped by a convoluted mass of orange rock pumping up a hundred metres into the sky. I have time to lick my wounds, strip the camera and bake it dry on a hot rock.

One of the joys of bush exploring is to be able to drink from cool, pure fresh water streams.

An early start means a no-fire, cold coffee breakfast, but things warm up quickly with an awkward rock scramble. Funny how the prospect of a vertical fall of five metres sharpens the reflexes. Descending back to river level, the water makes a hard right sweep, slap bang into a vertical-walled amphitheatre at least 120 metres high and almost a kilometre around. From

a great height rocks glower down at me. This place is unnamed but it has such majesty and strength it makes me feel as permanent as the blip on a cardiograph.

Led out by our slowly descending river, we leave behind the amphitheatre and our backpacks to more easily explore a miniature side gorge sheltering a swag of palms and a little cluster of remnant rainforest trees.

Cool memories of lunchtime swims are fading as the landscape opens up and we encounter parched river scree of a trillion boulders bedecked with teatrees and wattles bent over in memory of the last wet season floods. There have been a lot of long dry months since the rains fell here. Struggling through the thickets I begin to imagine that tonight's camp will be a dry affair.

Wrong: we are doing a meandering follow the leader through a maze of house-sized tors when David spooks a freshwater crocodile. Its hasty bow-waved exit denotes water and an enchanting campsite. Using the last few minutes of sunshine I try to capture on film some of the place's harsh elegance. It seems to be summed up in a scene of exposed rock which is supporting boulders. The boulders are backdropped by leafless kapok trees strewn with yellow flowers.

A warm afterglow accompanies our dust removing rinse, though in the fading light we are still on the lookout for crocodiles. David is the keenest so he is stripped and soaking while we are still divesting clothing. His dissertation on the eating habits of freshwater crocodiles is rudely interrupted by an impertinent, obviously starved, native fish. In a life-like imitation of a crocodile (so David suggests) it sinks two rows of teeth into David's large toe. He exits at a startling pace, proving the untapped power source to be found in loud yells.

Good intentions of an early start are stymied. We are up and packed while there's still a crackling tinge of crispness in the air, but none of us can resist the sight of a breathless dawn turning melaleuca fringed ponds into highly polished mirrors. Kodak shares notch up another couple of points this morning.

Even after we finally tear ourselves away from the river pools and head through a gap in the ranges it's a terrible day for anyone trying to conserve film. Everywhere I look there's another stunning image. I resolve to photograph only the outstandingly outstanding, but it doesn't work. We ascend what appears to be only a slight rise, but it's high enough to open up a stimulating vista of rugged escarpment and treed valley; an immense untainted environment. Silently I soak it all in.

☐ *Unnamed and probably unseen by many people this amphitheatre of rock is truly awesome in size and colour.*

Using a gold-coloured boulder as a skyline beacon we come to its base, and find a playground of giant's tors. Packless, we each head into the labyrinth to explore: up onto sun warm rock faces, on through squeezy passages and corridors and into cool, grey lit caves. Although there are no traces of usage by today's Aborigines, the clear, beautifully preserved paintings of long, long past remain. Lying on my back I follow a recent snake track and wriggle to within arm's reach of paintings created by another human being many generations before mine. Only my eyes brush across the ancient ochres of the paintings and in silent reverence I watch these images from a dreamtime artist.

I rejoin the others, but we are one down. Calling, whistle-blowing, retracing steps and climbing to vantage points elicit no sightings or a response. Mick, who was bouldering when we discarded our packs for easier exploring, has slipped past without noticing us. Suddenly the landscape becomes a little more intimidating and I feel dwarfed by it. In any direction it is many days walking to outside assistance. This is out of the question so we press on, following the river, calling, whistling and cooeeing as we go, believing that Mick would have stayed close to the river. He has, and reunion is a natural high. Even being waylaid by devilish clumps of spinifex doesn't matter much after we are a group again. Well, perhaps that's an exaggeration, the stuff is mongrel in the extreme. With honed-tipped points it can drive through all but the toughest of gaiters, entering bare flesh then breaking off to fester and eventually

fall out. Following donkey tracks across river flats the sticky spinifex resin french-polishes our gaiters and sandshoes, giving them a rough smell synonymous with the Kimberley.

Surprise is another Kimberley feature. Doing a dance on ankle-sapping river stones leads us to a heat-baked gorge where colossal granite tors are made almost dainty by the towering rock walls. This place looks like it was made yesterday — a yesterday which took 300 million years to pass. Yet, amid the arid desolation there are pools of cool water and immature waterfalls. In its peculiar loping flight an egret wends its way up the gorge. Its calmness is visibly shaken by the sight of four strange creatures with

large humps on their backs awkwardly trying not to fall into rock layered crevasses. The crocodiles are also a bit surprised to be caught sunbaking.

Beyond the crevasses and the toe tingling slopes of rock, just where the river is forced to make a gigantic right hand sweeper, is an elevated platform of accumulated sand.

Not one human footprint marks this sand, just a myriad of prints from the local fauna: wallaby, dingo, snake, and the results of a crocodile's hasty exit. How many humans have been here? Who can say, certainly none since before the last wet season, perhaps ten months ago.

Amid our "private" wilderness,

dropping a pack never felt better. Stripping off and easing into deep fresh water brings down my soaring body temperature and massages away my aches and pains.

The water is cold enough to enjoy the sensation of cooled flesh on the sleek sun-warm rock.

Next morning starts the longest day of the century. It begins typically; me stopped in my tracks to photograph the reflection of gorge walls on unruffled pools. Then comes a knee crunching ascent from the river level to a high saddle. Once reached, we revel in the sight of the wild beautiful country which surrounds us. The saddle turns out to be spinifex-guarded gorges chock full of loose rock. This gives way to

□　It is not hard to feel insignificant in this vast landscape.

seven kilometres of savanna plains running at the foot of a steep edged escarpment. While the map promises "waterfalls" every kilometre, the track serves up black stained rock and dusty creek beds.

Thirty degrees Celsius is just a memory as we push through rough scrubby wattle and teatree, up and down gutters of rocks then finally into a shaded gorge. Skimmed with a milky slime, the pool feels cold and uninviting — not unlike the gorge, which turns out to be impassable. The way around leads up vertically stacked layers of crumbling rock. Ascent is slow and hairy; traversing around the next peak is even more so.

Far below a live waterfall trickles. Carrying only our lunch and waterbottles we light-footedly descend and soak up a little rest and recreation while Rob creates johnnycakes. Laden with lunch and

still in the heat of the day the climb back up negates any benefits of the brief rest. What is supposed to be a twenty metre gain on the map turns out to be a frustrating two hours of walking up either on rocks resembling badly formed ballbearings hidden in long grass, or for light relief, evil, slippery, fallen palm fronds. A waterfall climb with our full packs twists the knife just before a marvellous last saddle appears.

Our appearance startles a bunch of kangaroos, but they needn't be frightened of us. I'm certainly not a threat — lying down seems hard yakka. Lured on by talk of deep water swimming pools, I crank up my rapidly aging body and use up the last of my knees on a vertical descent into a dry creek bed. In my wavering state it seems this creek stays dry for the next fifty kilometres, but it's really only a couple. Fading light is a good excuse to camp on flattish

☐ *Snake, kangaroo and crocodile tracks are the only evidence of inhabitance in this truly wild landscape.*

☐ *The red-flowering kurrajong* (Brachychiton populneum).

rocks just upstream from a poor excuse for a trickling brook. We have walked for nearly nine hours in the heat with a vertical gain of more than 300 metres and I am beyond stuffed.

Over breakfast we contemplate a short day. A couple of kilometres down, the map shows the meeting point of two creeks. There's some running water there, so that's where we leave the packs in preparation for the night's camp. Day-packing, we are following a creek just as bland as the map suggests, nice but nothing special.

However, about three kilometres downstream of the junction what shows as a twenty metre drop on the map turns out to be a series of wavering waterfalls and graceful pools. Surrounding this oasis are clusters of ferns and magnificent palms, with masses of lichens clinging to the rock faces. The rock is so deeply coloured we decide to name the gorge "Orange Slice". A thousand millenniums of water has polished the rock smooth — almost like it has been melted. And this magnificent place is not even marked on the map!

Our last night in the King Leopolds is to be on the top of one of the tallest peaks in the Kimberley. As food is consumed and the packs are made lighter they are reloaded with extra water. Out of the deep reaches of little gorges we slowly emerge. With each metre gained, more of the surrounding wilderness emerges. Ahead and above, the mountain peak beckons and cajoles as the air temperature turns each hard-won metre into a sauna-like activity. Lying prone on a ridge top rest point I'm so tired that I rest comfortably

☐ *The red-flowering kurrajong* (Brachychiton populneum).

on a spinifex bush with aching feet propped up on an opportunely placed rock. By not looking at how far there is to go, but by just taking in the valley below, the dark slashes of gorges that we have clambered through and the rolling far distant hills that we've climbed, it seems we've travelled a long way.

Threatening skies, spitting rain and visibility drowned in a soup of humid air encourage us to erect a rain fly for the first time on the trip. Like four cocooned insects on a tree branch we are temporarily attached to this wild mountain top on a black, moonless night.

As needle-sharp points of spinifex scythe the cool air, I stare out at dawn from my snug abode. A short winged bird of prey drifts past, probably trying to make out what we are. Photographic desire forces me out and with chattering teeth, I wander down to an overhanging rocky perch to sit. From here I witness the sky gradually clearing and beams of sun setting near and far peaks alight. It bestows on this wild Kimberley landscape a rare benevolence and beauty.

☐ Following page *Poised on top of the King Leopold Ranges.*

LOCATION GUIDE

The specific location of the Experience section was deliberately vague, because, sadly, at time of writing, the area walked was unprotected from exploitation and destruction. With a total land mass of around 320,000 square kilometres, the Kimberley is an immense rugged region in the far north of Western Australia. Running from the Indian Ocean to the Northern Territory border its vastness unfortunately encourages the myth that wilderness qualities are protected by size, remoteness, and difficulty of terrain. In an age of aerial surveys and an explosion in the number of four wheel drive vehicles, nothing could be further from the truth. The reality of the Kimberley is that only a miserable few per cent are actually protected in national parks and reserves, and even that token portion may be open to mining.

The King Leopold Ranges are located in the north western section of the Kimberley. They extend for roughly 300 kilometres from Walcott Inlet on the coast to Margaret River, west of Halls Creek. The range was named by explorer Alexander Forrest in 1879 after Leopold of Belgium. In his glowing testimonial for the Kimberley, he estimated there were ten million hectares of fertile land and encouraged squatters to start on overlanding cattle drives across thousands of kilometres from Queensland and New South Wales.

This brought the settlers into open conflict with the Aborigines — conflicts which were settled by deception, violence and the mounted police. The journal of one such officer, Sergeant Pilmer, describes the local King Leopold Ranges Aborigines as "... magnificent... intelligent and not lacking in bravery. They would attack and fight at the least provocation." Mounted Constable Hemmings reported that the Aborigines "had sworn to cut the kidney fat out of every tracker they could catch". And even as late as the 1940s, author Ion I. Idriess described this region as "the last wild area of the Kimberley".

Idriess wrote of mounted police hunts through precipitous gorges and razorback spurs, chasing "naked men, with bodies as slippery as the gleaming bamboos". And of bringing captured Aborigines back in chains (neck chains were still in use in 1948). Except for a period when an ex-tracker, Pigeon, led a briefly successful uprising against squatters and police, the pastoral industry and later the mining industry have had free rein in the Kimberley.

The so-called "kings in grass castles" took control of a rich landscape abundant in food, both vegetable and game, and turned a proportion of it into eroded dust bowls. In a submission to the Pastoral Land Tenure Review (1985), the Conservation Council of Western Australia described the Western Australian pastoral industry as having "a record of degradation of natural resources probably unequalled by any other industry... caused by hard-hooved herbivores... largely uncontrolled by generations of understaffed, underfinanced, uncaring and or uncommitted Government agencies". Leigh, Hoden and Briggs of the CSIRO Division of Plant Industries stated "81.6 per cent of Kimberley pastoral

areas are of low or very low pastoral value... with as much as 130,000 hectares urgently requiring treatment. Fifty-four species of native plants have become extinct and a further sixty-nine species are under threat as a result of pastoral activities." Take, as an example, the uprooting for later sale in Perth of livistona palms on Doongan Station in August 1988 — cut down on a leasehold property.

With such an extended history of exploitation it is not surprising that

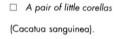

□ *A pair of little corellas*
(Cacatua sanguinea).

even the most recent proposals to upgrade reserves and national parks are lacking in vision. As David Poland of the Wilderness Society group Friends of the Kimberley points out, "abandoned cattle leases, left over lands, disused stock routes and old mining leases have all been proposed as inclusion for park. On the other hand prime wilderness areas which are not vacant Crown land have been excluded from the proposals. In any land use conflicts, conservation is considered the lowest priority." As an example of this, the King Leopold Ranges National Park (a minuscule 10,500 hectare

proposal), would only be declared, according to the report *Nature Conservation Reserves in the Western Australia Kimberley* (Burbidge, McKenzie and Kenneally) if it was not needed for pastoral pursuits.

The Kimberley has an unrivalled magnificence and grandeur, with few areas more beautiful than the King Leopold Ranges. Precipitous quartz sandstones run from white to pale pink, buff to purple and pale brown and are backdropped by wonderful granites. In a broad larger-than-life landscape, ranges reaching to almost 1,000 metres dominate everything. And once feet and balance have been tested in jagged and boulder strewn ascents, the scarps provide magnificent panoramic views over an ancient landscape. The oldest rocks are the Halls Creek group which are between 1,800 and 2,750 million years old.

Back in 1882, E.T. Hardman, a government geologist, reported the occurrence of huge Diprotodon bones in the Lennard River. Today there are thriving numbers of freshwater crocodiles. Not so intimidating and weighing in at an astounding four grams fully grown, the smallest known marsupial is the rare Kimberley planigale or marsupial mouse (*Planigale subtilissima*). Other mammals to be found in the King Leopolds include the water rat (*Hydromys chrysogaster*), euro (*Macropus robustus*), northern quolls (*Dasyurus hallucatus*), rock ringtail (*Pseudocheirus dahli*), sugar glider (*Petaurus brevbiceps*), brindled bandicoot (*Isoodon macrourus*) and a rock wallaby (*Petrogale* sp.).

Birds commonly seen while bush exploring are the red collared lorikeet, red backed wren, red tailed

black cockatoo, black faced cuckoo shrike, wattle bird, little wattle bird, lyre bird, great bowerbird, azure kingfisher, blue winged kookaburra, nankeen night heron, cormorants, koel bird, barking owl, jabiroo, crane and numerous birds of prey including the wedge-tailed eagle and black shouldered kite.

At times the air above the Kimberley is full of white and yellow noise machines. Corellas would have to be the most raucous, playful, fun loving creatures you'd find anywhere. To be walking in one of the gorges when a big flock comes wheeling through is a joyful part of a Kimberley experience. Not so joyful comes the news from the Royal Australasian Ornithologists' Union that at least seven species may be on the endangered/rare list including the partridge pigeon, purple-crowned fairy wren, red goshawk, Asian dowitcher, fairy tern, gouldian finch and the yellow rumped mannikin.

On the ground that most hated of plants, the spinifex, lies in wait, ready to either smear walkers in resin or stab them through anything but the toughest of boots and gaiters. Once seen, never forgotten, the boab (*Adansonia gregorii*) is probably the ugliest tree on the planet. Aboriginal legend has it that the boab was actually planted upside down as a punishment for wrongdoing and what we presume are the limbs are really its roots. However it came to be, the boab has a kind of classically grotesque ugliness which is first barely tolerated, then begrudgingly appreciated and finally whole-heartedly loved.

Other trees include woollybutt, *Eucalyptus tectifica*, hakea, grevillea, turkey bush, kapok tree, kurrajong, pandanus, livistona palms, cycads, a few rare examples of cypress pine and the prolific cajuput (melaleuca). This latter tree was of prime importance to Aboriginal tribes living in the region. William R. Easton wrote in 1901 of the cajuput's use by the Aborigines, "During the wet season they cut strips of bark... which are then bent in a semi circle with the ends stuck in the ground forming a tunnel-like structure... with long lengths of bark which they use as ground sheets and blankets. Some natives also make a bucket from the bark which is fastened together with string (from wattle bark) and cemented with gum.''

Future Problems

Given that park and nature reserves are so limited, threats to the preservation of the remaining wilderness values of the Kimberley are almost limitless: long term land degradation resulting from cattle in the area, a smorgasbord of past, present and future mining projects, bulldozed transects, open cut mines, granite mines, exploration trenches, dumps and haulroads. And lastly, though not the least, four wheel drive based degradation including litter, the need for campfires large enough to barbecue a bullock and an apparent desire to decorate the entire bush with toilet paper. Without greater political foresight the future for wilderness in the Kimberley looks bleak.

The Basics

Clothing

Functionality is above all else in bush exploring clothing. Climates dictate quantity but essentially the objective is to shield easily torn skin from the aggressive attention of spiky scrub. Regions of low temperature and high rainfall demand a top quality outer

☐ These people-like figures, the Wandjinas or rain bringers, dominate rock art in the King Leopold region.

waterproof breathable parka of Gore-Tex or Japara, layers of fibrepile or wool and thermal underwear. High temperatures call for pure cotton long sleeved shirts, double stretch shorts and a hat. One constant, cold or hot, is gaiters: strong, knee high, velcro fastened and well fitted around the ankles, though not tight enough to restrict circulation.

Footwear

Where once boots thundered through the bush, today they gently pad. Softest on the environment (and hardest on the feet) are bare feet, but that takes a long time to cope with. On a very long trip (of over thirty days) barefoot walking may eliminate the common complaint of tinea. Nearly as gentle on the landscape as bare feet are Dunlop Volley sandshoes. Ultra keen bush explorers such as Rob Jung swear by them — he smears Spread-Sole over the stitching — though he makes sure that the food cache a two weeks walk away contains a back-up pair. Between joggers and the thunderers are strong soled boots such as the Asolo KSB which uses a combination of leather, Gore-Tex and proofed materials to achieve strength and light weight. Full leather heavy bushwalking boots are just that, heavy. They do provide excellent waterproofing and superb foot protection, though at a high cost to the environment and to your stamina, since a kilogram on your feet is the same as five kilograms on your back.

Backpack

Choose an internal frame, smoothly-contoured anatomic pack, e.g. Karrimor's Condor, sixty to eighty litre capacity. You are looking for strong puncture resistant material, well stitched with reinforced stress points, padded shoulder straps, laterally adjustable, with a padded hip belt, quick release buckle, external side straps and a generous top pocket.

☐ Two experienced bush explorers, David Poland (left) and Rob Jung, model "tried and tested" bush exploring equipment.

Dangers

Since most bush explorers lack a knowledge of the extensive network of Aboriginal Dreaming or Songlines, becoming geographically embarrassed — lost in other words — can happen to anyone. In his excellent book *Exploration*, Harry Frauca describes an incident when he became lost while collecting insects. It was particularly amusing to him since he had just published a book *Bushwalking* where he described most people who got lost as fools. Paddy Pallin titled his autobiography *Never Truly Lost*, but the title was really tongue in cheek, since he admits at times to being "somewhat bewildered" at his position. Map, compass, skill and experience lessen, but don't fully negate, the chances of becoming lost.

□ *Padding softly through an*

unspoiled wilderness.

FOOD
(*List supplied by Rob Jung*)

□ OPPOSITE *Waiting for our*

pickup vehicle after ten days in

the King Leopold Ranges.

		WEIGHT IN GRAMMES	
		Person	*Group (4)*
BREAKFAST (*catered for individually*)	Muesli	200	
	Powered milk	20	
LUNCH	Johnnycakes etc.		500
	Cheese		160
	Salami		160
	Spreads & butter (*tinned*)		150
DINNER	Packet soup		70
	Carbohydrate (*pasta, rice, cracked wheat etc.*)		500
	Protein (*lentils, dried peas, nuts, cheese, sprouts, bean mix, TVP, sauces*)		500
DESSERT	Dumplings, preserved fruit, custard, pancakes etc.		400
TRAIL SNACKS	Nuts & sweets		300
DRINKS	Tea, coffee, powdered milk, hot chocolate etc.		200
AVERAGE TOTAL PER PERSON			3,160

BUSH EXPLORING, THE WESTERN KIMBERLEY — DRY SEASON LUXURY CHECK LIST

Body Protection

Long sleeve cotton shirt
Bandana
Broad brimmed hat (with chinstrap)
Strong cotton shorts
Long light cotton pants
Bullet proof gaiters
Dunlop Volley sandshoes — coat all seams with
  Spread-Sole
Socks — wool/cotton blend
Bathers (optional)
Light woollen sweater
Light Gore-Tex showerproof jacket
100 per cent UV protection sunglasses
Sunscreen
Rid insect repellent, or mosquito mesh

Accommodation

Ground sheet
3-Season Karrimat or Thermarest
Small torch (long life batteries)
Sleeping bag rated to 5 degrees C, (e.g. J & H
  Rock Ledge)
Silk inner sheet

Getting There

Air to Broome, bus to Derby
Hire vehicle (and driver) drive to King Leopold
  Ranges, arranging specific return pick-up time

Transport

Kimberley Discovery Tours c/o Derby Tourist
  Bureau (091) 911426
Silva type compass
Plastic pealess whistle
1:100,000 series topographical maps
5 mm diameter light climbing rope
Internal framed 60–80 litre backpack (Karrimor
  Condor series recommended)
Waterproof self-sealing inner bag — essential for
  gorge swimming
Extra waterproof pack liners
Smaller waterproof stuff sacks for clothing

Camping (Bivouacking)

Matches (in self-sealing plastic bags)
Swiss army knife
Cup, bowl, eating utensils
Aluminium billy
Food — worked out for each day and placed in
  self-sealing bags. It is desirable to include
  alternatives to Ryvita, such as johnnycakes or
  drop scones.

First aid kit
Toiletries, toilet paper and group trowel
Two 1 litre waterbottles and 5 litre water bag or
  wine cask bladder

Recreation

Light day pack
Slater, Slater & Slater, *Field Guide to Australian
  Birds,* Lansdowne-Rigby, Willoughby, NSW,
  1986
Conservation Commission of NT, *Plants of the
  Tropical Woodland*
Camera bodies in very waterproof bags
Lenses the lightest & widest (18 or 24 mm) &
  short telephoto (105 mm)
Tripod — light but stable
Slow speed film
Notebook & pen

Bushwalking Clubs

Contact through state associations

Further Reading

Burbridge, A., Keneally, F.K. & McKenzie, N.L.,
  Nature Conservation Reserve in the Kimberley, W.A.,
  Submission by the Department of Conservation
  & Land Management to the Kimberley Regional
  Planning Study, Perth, 1987
Easton, William R., *Report of the North Kimberley
  District of Western Australia*, Derby Library, 1921
Hart, J., *Walking Softly in the Wilderness*, Sierra
  Club Books, San Francisco, 1977
Idriess, I., *Man Tracks — With the Mounted Police in
  Australia's Wilds*, Angus & Robertson, Sydney,
  1940
Idriess, I., *Outlaws of the Leopolds*, Angus &
  Robertson, Sydney, 1952
Pallin, P., *Never Truly Lost,* NSW University
  Press, Kensington, NSW, 1987
Thompson, P., *Myles Dunphy Selected Writings*,
  Ballagirin, Sydney, 1986

CROSS COUNTRY SKIING

Langlaufing, nordic, cross country skiing, bushwalking on skis, whatever the title, moving through snowfields on skis has been around a long time. While there is no evidence to suggest Australian Aborigines travelled over snow, an ancient rock carving of a skier found near the Arctic Circle has been dated by archaeologists at approximately 4,000 years old. Scandinavia, of course, claims the origins of over-snow transport. In Hoting, Sweden, a petrified ski discovered in a peat bog was carbon dated at 2,500 BC.

Seventeenth century illustrations show Norwegian hunters on nordic skis, and in a way cross country skiing has traditionally been associated with a violent means of survival. Bloody battles were waged on skis during WWI and WWII. However, what began as a means of transport and developed into a tool for hunting and waging war, thankfully has now returned to being an exhilarating means of travelling.

Thankfully, Australia's history of cross country lacks officially organised wars fought on skinny boards, but just as the Vikings brought skiing to Scotland, cross country was introduced to this country by some of their descendants. Norwegian miners brought their knowledge with them when they came to Kiandra's goldfields in southern New South Wales. Lacking suitable skis, the locals removed palings from the town's cemetery fence, strapped them to their feet and Australian-style bushwalking on skis was born, though they called it "snow-shoeing".

By 28 July 1861, a *Sydney Morning Herald* reporter found that in Kiandra:

□ OPPOSITE *The Jagungal wilderness is a mosaic of alpine and sub-alpine landscapes.*

"Scores of young people are frequently engaged in climbing the lofty summits with snow shoes and then sliding down with a volancy that would do credit to some of our railway trains."

The most noted outdoor photographer of the era was Charles Kerry. Coping with a monster sized lump of glass and timber masquerading as a camera he captured images of brave lads and lasses riding their skis straight down slopes. A stout stick held between the legs was a brake, of sorts, and the whole crew looked a bunch of maniacal witches bent on self destruction. But they professed to enjoy such madness and formed the world's oldest snow skiing club outside of Norway.

Until the 1850s, transport skis consisted of one long ski with a smooth base used as a glider and one shorter wider ski with a fur base used as a kicker. Originally the activity was called "sheing" after the Norwegian word for the sound made by a piece of timber passing through soft snow. Nordic skiing on two skis of similar length began with the Norheims in Telemark, Norway. In Kiandra, after the cemetery palings ran out, the locals headed into the bush to craft solid skis from straight grained mountain ash. The skis were up to two and a half metres long with turned up tips. With constant use, grooves formed on the ski bases giving rise to their local name, "butterpats". There is a pair of butterpats, which were used by Kiandra postmen during the 1860s, in the Powerhouse Museum, Sydney.

On 19 August 1897, Charles Kerry led the first winter ascent of Mt Kosciusko (2,230 metres). It was a trip where "an all consuming thirst made our dried tongues cleave to the drier palate. 'A pound for a pint of water,' murmured someone in front. The only response was an advanced bid." Many journeys followed, yet it wasn't until 1927 that a Sydney gynaecologist Dr Schlink led the first of what is now the classic Australian ski tour from Kiandra to Kosciusko.

Cross country skiing, unlike downhill resort-based skiing, does not result in a destruction of the landscape or require the construction of permanent structures — it instils a respect and love for the wilderness. With development and the apparent "control" of the alpine environment

there's a danger that instead of regarding mountains with reverence, skiers have come to look upon them "as soaped poles in a beer-garden which you set yourselves to climb and slide down again with shrieks of delight".

Venturing into a snow covered back country on cross country skis is gentle and quiet, producing no angry motor-powered, bone jarring rattles. In fact the deeper into a wilderness you ski the quieter and more respectful you become. As Steve Colman, co-founder of adventure travel specialists Wilderness Expeditions (and an excellent back country, cross country skier) puts it, "Downhill skiing you are pretty

☐ *Although more difficult to learn than downhill skiing, cross country skiing does less damage to the environment.*

much enveloped by a security blanket of lifts, ski patrol and resort facilities. But once you move over that hill you start to rely on your own resources and those of your fellow skiers".

Cross country skiing demands personal fitness. It is rated as an almost perfect cardiovascular exercise. The upper body is used as much as the lower body. Cross country skiers can burn 5,000 kilojoules per hour continuously, rising to 8,750 kilojoules per hour during short bursts. With that sort of energy demand it's little wonder that in its purest form cross country skiing is not only a graceful art but also the province of finely-balanced Olympic fitness athletes. But, this doesn't preclude recreational skiers from taking it a little easier and gradually becoming snow fit.

So smooth and gentle is the action of cross country skiing that you can begin late in life. That doyen of the Australian bush, Paddy Pallin, took up skiing at the age of fifty-four and suffered a couple of broken bones for his trouble. However, there's no doubt that the learning curve is much less bumpy the younger you start.

Whenever you first clip on skinny skis the experience of cross country is the same as it was last century when Fritdjof Nanasen wrote after the first crossing of Greenland: "One's complete awareness is absorbed by the skis and surrounding nature. It is something which develops not only the body but also the soul...".

Thanks to the existence of alpine national parks and wilderness areas, the same challenges as years ago can be tackled in the largely unchanged landscape.

Cumbersome heavy planks and between-the-legs broomsticks are gone from Australian slopes, as are top hats, ties and dress coats. Modern lightweight materials and complex construction techniques have replaced mountain ash, and high tech waterproof fabric is firmly at home in the back country (see page 166).

But that most frequent of activities, falling down in the snow, is still as common as in the past. Learning to ski cross country is harder than learning downhill skiing — being loose heeled on skinny skis and tracking over naturally packed snow ensures that it remains so. Some people joke that if you can walk then you can cross country ski. This is true, but only for those talented, perfectly balanced people who can instantly tackle the slippery surface beneath the two metre long planks attached to the toes of their boots. The skiing action lies somewhere between skating and running.

Perhaps a more realistic attitude is to accept that in learning to cross country you are often going to fall down. This is not too much of a problem, since aside from when it has turned to bone jarring sheet ice, snow makes for soft landing areas, so tumbles are at best fun, and at worst bruising, though broken bones are possible. A couple of hundred soft snow sitzmarks, headplants, ground falls, rollovers, skicrosses and unplanned landings later, a whole new world is opened up for your confident exploration.

Between first putting on skinny skis and linking turns down the fall line are heaps of panic stops where you leave the landscape littered with bomb craters. Determination, a

☐ *Learning to read a topographic map is important to be able to navigate in the snow. Most snowcraft courses include navigation as an integral part of cross country skiing.*

☐ *OPPOSITE A small group of skiers on the summit of Mt Townsend. Venturing into the Kosciusko National Park on cross country skis fosters a deep respect for the wilderness.*

modicum of balance and good instructors, help to ease the learning curve. Begin with a lodge-based trip (preferably above the snowline) over at least five days with Australian Ski Federation instructors. As the skills of striding, turning and stopping improve, venture further afield. Trips are punctuated with heart-starting climbs to take in mountain panoramas, then enthusiastic downhill runs back to the lodge spurred on by the anticipation of hot showers, warm dry clothes and a satisfying meal.

Once you can move about confidently on skinny boards it's time to leave behind the cocooning security of a centrally heated lodge for the less secure shelter of a double skinned tent warmed only by body heat. Although venturing into a snow covered wilderness requires an ability to ski competently with a full backpack, today, taken sensibly,

snow camping is an adventure, not a survival expedition. In the correct winter wilderness location, purpose-built snow tents provide secure accommodation, especially if care is taken to choose a good and sheltered site. Before pitching the tent everyone turns into snow bound kangaroos, parallel skis jumping up and down to pack down the loose snow and create a level tent site. Ideally, if you can create a base as flat as a billiard table, the extra work will be amply rewarded with a good night's sleep. However if you rush the base flattening process and reckon near enough is good enough, then nights on the snow will be long and uncomfortable and punctuated with bouts of "swimming" back up into the tent on what will overnight become a slippery sloping patch of ice.

On snowcraft courses you learn to construct igloos (using cut blocks of hard packed snow) and snow caves (dug out of a suitable large drift of deep snow). Making either is time-consuming, though fun on a sunny day, and depends on finding the right snow conditions. All the effort is worth it however, since there's an extra fascination to spending an evening in the wilderness within the candlelit confines of a self-built snow structure. Although it takes a bit of convincing to be believed, you'll be toasty warm inside such a structure since snow acts as an insulator from the dropping temperatures outside and specially designed sleeping bags and self-inflating mattresses protect you from the cold. Becoming cold overnight is even more unlikely if you keep your head covered with the sleeping bag hood or a woollen beanie and wear minimum clothing in the bag. Though meals are more

basic than at a lodge, being base-camped in the snow more than compensates for any epicurean shortcomings.

The whole advantage of establishing yourself in a snow covered base camp is that the skiing starts just outside the tent flap. Day tours (carrying only an ultra light pack) take you into Australia's best backcountry skiing. They are fun, but snow camping trips also deal with a more serious side of winter travel, that of mountain navigation and learning minimal impact camping in this fragile alpine environment.

This is one location where, because of the scarcity of timber a campfire is usually not lit.

Being aware of snow safety and avoiding hypothermia (life-threatening cold) also increases your confidence in entering a winter wilderness.

My featured adventure is set deep in the Jagungal wilderness of Kosciusko National Park.

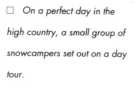

☐ *On a perfect day in the high country, a small group of snowcampers set out on a day tour.*

SKI TOUR TO THE "MOTHER OF THE WATERS"

Over our little cluster of dome tents it is snowing — dumping with enthusiasm. Big scads of the stuff are wafting to earth and laying a white mantle over the landscape. The landscape changes form as I watch — the dark leafed snow gums ghosting over and blending into the background, and the gurgling sounds of a nearby stream slowly becoming muffled by falling snow. Just on dusk and kilometres from anywhere, there's nothing better than being inside a snow tent — secure, warm and dry. I roll my down jacket into a pillow, pull tight the snow bag hood's drawstring and snuggle further into downy warmth. Sleep comes easily when my ears are caressed by snow gently plinking on the walls of the tent.

To arrive at this idyllic location deep in Kosciusko National Park took two days. We drove to Guthega power station, walked for an hour sharing the weight of a heavily packed sled, then skied almost constantly upward to our overnight campsite at White River. Next day a long backpack shuffle took us to our campsite near the Valentine River via a tricky crossing of Schlink Pass in almost zero visibility. The pass was named after Dr Schlink, a gynaecologist and an enthusiastic exponent of cross country touring, who toured the area in the 1920s. I'm sure the hills are just as steep as they were in his day, though thankfully our guide didn't administer the good doctor's suggested remedy for reviving tired skiers — Schlink somewhat harshly suggested

☐ Although it is possible to melt snow for drinking water, this is a time and fuel consuming task. It is preferable to find running water.

"swearing and rough language" and for more severe cases "the swallowing of several strychnine tablets . . . to carry the old stager home".

Our soft snow shuffling under the pressure of weighty backpacks was made just that tad harder with muscles unused to off track skiing conditions. Toning up fitness prior to a tough backpacking ski tour is always recommended and makes good sense, but somehow those pre-trip training schedules are easily pushed aside, so my joy of the first couple of days was tempered by frequent periods of a pounding heart, aching back and rasping breath.

Lugging a backpack on cross country skis means travelling with a

☐ FOLLOWING PAGE Heading for Mt Jagungal. Small groups set up a base camp, then, weather permitting, attempt an ascent of the mountain.

155

The trunks of snowgums always seem more vibrant amid the colours of winter.

raised centre of gravity and while uphill stretches are pure grunt and struggle, downhills are adventures in staying upright. Even while ensuring that on downhill runs one ski is pushed out in front of the other, my camera laden pack seemed to take a perverse pleasure in throwing me off balance at the most inopportune moments. Like a beached, overturned turtle I struggled from horizontal to vertical half a dozen times or more and it sapped my energy as fast as melting snow in a microwave. A vicious circle developed; the more tired I became the stiffer and more upright I skied and the more I fell over. At the site of the base camp, "ah", the simple joy of undoing my waist straps and dropping my leaden pack. The knowledge that this would be home for the next few days was enough to breathe new life into a tired body.

This morning, looking at tents wrapped in white, it seems that it must have snowed all night. As the sounds of black cockatoos act like an alarm clock, the sun gives a half hearted attempt to penetrate the clouds and our small group emerges to sit around the stove and eagerly watch it boil water for a morning cuppa.

Glimpses of sun encourage us to work out tired muscles with a few hours skiing. Finding a suitable crossing spot we rock hop Valentine River and head for a nearby ridge. I stop for a photograph just as the valley walls begin to close. The water sparkles in a patch of sunlight and my companions appear as pure black cutouts dancing across a white world. At the ridge top I gaze with enthusiasm across at the Grey Mare Range, but in seconds it is swallowed by an evil-looking low black cloud. Chasing us back to camp the cloud arrives before we do and turns our world into a dim, dark, slightly foreboding place. Snow is still dumping down that night but we have all shoehorned into a temporary communal tent where chatter, laughter and steaming dinners give everyone a friendly, cozy glow.

Not a lot is glowing next morning though, rather it's like the weather is glowering at us. Wind gusts flay the tents with driven snow and sinister clouds race across the sky. Hell, it's so cold, even my toes feel iced and they are encased in fibre pile tent booties.

Up and dressed, life seems friendlier. We do a single file meander up through a white dusted forest trying to avoid the big dollops of snow dumping down from overladen branches. A tailwind has us really motoring uphill with skis slipping over a snow more like beach sand than frozen water crystals. Light dies, taking with it all contrast. We are now deep within a world of softly bleached grey where all concepts of distance and speed have gone. Instinctively we close up ranks and begin to rely more heavily on our leader. Guided by local knowledge and wavering compass pointer, she takes us on through the white out.

Mawson's Hut emerges out of the gloom like something from the past. It was built in 1929 by Herb Mawson for a snow lessee, the New Zealand and Australia Land and Finance Co. Scattered throughout Kosciusko's mountains, some of these huts date back to mining days, a few date from early ski touring clubs and others from the days when wildflowers and native grasses were cattle fodder. Mountain huts once had a place, today they simply intrude into the purity of a wilderness experience. Unfortunately huts encourage ill-equipped winter wanderers, and through overcrowding are a source of pollution and disease. It feels good to return to our self-contained temporary camp, and to know that when we leave, no trace will remain for the next snow campers.

Next morning I awake encased and serene. Overnight the falling snow has cocooned my tent and all is silent.

A couple of bumps on the side walls brings miniature avalanches and the sounds of the Jagungal wilderness return — softly rustling snowgums, the chinking of small bush birds and the irreverent cries of crows, but no falling snow.

My fingers wrestle with a frozen tent zipper before it gives way to

reveal pure, unfiltered rays of sunlight. The sunlight's arrival hastens my exit.

Although sub-zero air caressing my toasty body quickens the dressing process, it is still a long business: a layer of thermal underwear, woollen shirt, double weave stretch pants, down vest, down jacket, two layers of woollen socks, three layers of gloves and a beanie. I emerge from the tent to a world where sunlight seems to strike the snow with an almost vicious brilliance — lots of

☐ A white-out is a frightening experience. Unable to see through the blizzarding snow, the landscape disappears and it becomes almost impossible to tell whether or not you are ascending, descending or stationary.

sunscreen today. Breakfast is consumed with vigour, as a feeling of urgency to be gone overwhelms us all. There's even a queue for loo paper.

Skis, planted in the snow overnight, have grown a layer of frost that is unmoved by the early sun. Stocks are likewise encrusted — the leather straps are as hard as steel.

Another rock-dancing river crossing, a smooth gentle valley ascent, fast quirky descents, a glide past Big Bend, a higher ascent of the ridge beyond, and there, shimmering in the distance, is the "Mother of the Waters", Mt Jagungal. This point dominates the landscape — and my mind. Long traversing tacks take us ever higher, but the Snow Seal (a waterproofing agent) I'd used to stop the snow from balling up my skis reduces their gripping ability. My ascent is a slow motion slip-sliding affair liberally peppered with falls and expletives.

Within last-push distance of the summit, I take off my skis and make temporary steps in the iced snow. Just under the lip of the summit an open air gallery of wind-created ice sculptures captures my imagination and lifts my spirits. It carries me up the last fifty metres to a rare place just 2,061 metres above sea level.

Standing silently on the peak, my gaze follows the unique white wilderness landscape, a place relatively unaltered and undamaged. Not all that many people have tasted this mountain's fresh clean winter air since a group of adventurous miners first tramped up here in 1898. And it is beautiful to contemplate that given correct management, for cross country ski tourers the challenges and rewards will always remain.

☐ Opposite *The summit of Mt Jagungal, known as Mother of the Waters, is a favourite destination for cross country ski-tourers.*

LOCATION GUIDE

The Jagungal wilderness is a 98,000 hectare jewel about fifty-eight kilometres long and thirty-five kilometres wide, within the crown of Kosciusko National Park. At 627,218 hectares, Kosciusko is the largest national park in New South Wales. It runs 225 kilometres from the Victorian border to mountainous country just west of the Australian Capital Territory. After many years of lobbying by Myles J. Dunphy and the National Parks and Primitive Areas Council (set up in 1934), this superb region was declared a state park in 1944.

Before its declaration as a state park, then a national park, Kosciusko had been suffering from the effects of uncontrolled sheep and cattle grazing. Scandalous land degradation and the deliberate draining of peat swamps was reported in the 1890s, but it took until 1969 before the hardhooved destroyers off this priceless high country were evicted. More than thirty years later the land, trees and wildflowers are still recovering and introduced weeds are still being eradicated.

From 1944 until 1970 the Snowy Mountains hydro-electric scheme was created, redirecting some eastward flowing rivers and turning them to the westward drier area of the state. In 1978 UNESCO recognised Kosciusko as a Biosphere Reserve.

The Jagungal wilderness is a mosaic of alpine and sub-alpine landscapes, a blaze of wildflowers in summer and a land of exquisite snowgums in winter. Snowgum (*Eucalyptus pauciflora*) is a beautifully coloured gum which is confined to locations above 1,400 metres and is the only tree growing at or above 1,830 metres. According to research by the Adelaide University, within the region there are stands of trees 250 years old with one tree at approximately 400 years of age. Sharing this special sub-alpine and alpine environment are the broad-toothed rat (*Mastacomys fuscus*) and the mountain pygmy possum (*Burramys parvus*). The former is a relict of the Ice Ages and the latter is so rare that it was known only as a fossil before 1966.

These creatures burrow under the snow where they rely on the small air layer between the snow and the ground to exist. They are thus extremely vulnerable to ground compacting caused by heavy oversnow vehicles.

Access to the Jagungal wilderness for ski tourers (and bushwalkers in summer) is via Kiandra from the north or from Guthega Power Station through White's River in the south. Key sentinel to the wilderness is Jagungal, or the Big Bogong. Bogong (*Agrotis infusa*) is a fat moth which was keenly sought by the Aborigines during their summer hunts in the high country. Mount Jagungal is also known as "Mother of the Waters" since it gives birth to the Geehi, Tumut and Valentine Rivers. Although it now hovers 2,061 metres above present sea level, the mountain is comprised of basalt, laid down as ancient submarine lava flows during the Ordovician period, more than 445,000,000 years ago. Also contained in this region are Mt Twynham (2,196 metres), Mt Townsend (2,210 metres), Dicky Cooper Bogong (2,003 metres) and Gungartan (2,068 metres) along with

☐ OPPOSITE *The snowgum (Eucalyptus pauciflora) grows at altitudes above 1,400 metres and within the Jagungal wilderness there are stands of trees more than 250 years old.*

the Kerries, the Brassy mountains, and the Northern Grey Mare Range.

A winter ascent of Jagungal is often a one-in-ten chance since mountain winter weather changes from brilliant sunshine to mind-numbing blizzard with alarming speed. The coldest temperature in the Kosciusko region was –22 degrees Celsius, recorded in 1947. According to Steve Colman, co-founder of Wilderness Expeditions, the prime cross country skiing time is August. By then the area has a good base of snow and is still covered by occasional fresh falls, with not too much risk of rainfall.

Rain is more likely in September. As Steve points out, "I can't think of much else that's worse when snowcamping. I really enjoy being out in high blizzard conditions when it's snowing and dry, but move the temperature up five degrees and it's unpleasant and far more dangerous.

Plus three or five degrees with heavy rain falling and a fifty knot nor' wester blowing is as extreme conditions as you can get anywhere in the world — pure survival stuff — it's horrible."

FUTURE PROBLEMS

The Jagungal wilderness is a place of early and excellent snowfall and is thus eyed with greedy interest by downhill ski resort entrepreneurs. In light snowfall years they would like to tow skiers behind oversnow vehicles or use helicopters to land skiers in remote locations — both would seriously degrade the wilderness values. It is often claimed that downhill skiing takes up only three per cent of Kosciusko, but this is twenty per cent of the park which is above the snowline (only fifteen per cent of the park lies above the snowline).

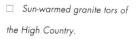
☐ Sun-warmed granite tors of the High Country.

Summer sees some illegal grazing, intrusion by four wheel drive vehicles and an invasion by bushwalkers — enough to cause track erosion in some places. Although there are some hydro works, several power transmission lines, a few tracks and roads (all closed in winter), and snow poles and huts, the Jagungal region is still regarded as a superb wilderness.

THE BASICS

The principle of skiing cross country, away from lifts and altered environments, is that given an application of one's energy, cross country skis will climb hills. As the lead ski slides forward unweighted it glides over the snow, as weight is transferred to this ski, the camber is flattened and its base "grips" the snow-enabling forward travel. The toes of cross country boots are held onto the skis by three pin bindings and the heels are loose so that they rise off the back ski as each forward step is made.

To achieve the required grip to move over the snow, early back country skiers attached animal skins to the base of their skis. This method is still used today in very steep country, though with strips of sticky-backed artificial mohair. Early skiers prepared the smooth bases of their skis with special waxes created from a witch's brew of Stockholm tar, beeswax, resin, kerosene and ground up gramophone records. Waxed skis are still used today with special waxes prepared for precise snow conditions and temperatures.

In Australia the great majority of skis are waxless, achieving their grip

through a specially patterned base first modelled on fishscales. Waxed and waxless skis come in a variety of widths and designs to suit many types of cross country.

Racing skis (forty-four millimetres wide) are very light, designed for skiing fast in specially prepared cut parallel tracks. Light touring skis (forty-eight millimetres) are designed for prepared tracks and day skiing on untracked snow. Touring and heavy touring skis (fifty-two to sixty-three millimetres) are stronger, stiffer and broader, which enables them to cope with much greater stress and to float over the surface of most snow. They often come with metal edges which help the ski to bite into icy slopes, are side cut (slightly narrower under the foot) to help in turns, and have a wider section at the front of the ski (the toe).

The correct length of skis can be judged by standing the skis on end and reaching up to the ski tip. If the ski tip is at the palm or wrist of your upstretched arm the ski length should be correct for your height. Skis should just hold their camber while the skier is standing evenly on both skis (you should be able to slide a sheet of paper under the base of the skis directly below the feet), though softer skis can help beginners, as they decrease velocity on down hill runs. Ski poles, when held vertically, should reach just to the armpit.

Graceful travel over flattish ground is achieved by a variety of means including double-poling (planting, then bringing both stocks through at the same time) and diagonal striding. This latter movement is a natural extension of walking where the body weight is moved forward by reaching forward with the right arm at the same time as the left leg comes forward and vice versa. With good balance and a smooth action, diagonal striding results in a very energy efficient glide and a graceful style of skiing. With shorter, quicker movements and confident weight transference, slight hills can be climbed this way too. For steeper slopes, to decrease

Given the right conditions snowgums can grow to enormous proportions.

climbing angles, ascents are usually tackled by zig zag traversing, like tacking upwind in a sailing boat. Ultra steep sections need side stepping with skis parallel to the fall line or are tackled by using a herringbone technique where ski tips are splayed out in a vee and knees brought closer together so that the skis edge deeply, biting into the snow.

Edge (moving the knees across to tilt the skis and thus use the edges to grip), pressure (where weight is applied, often to the heels) and rotate (where the skis are turned out or in) are the three words most frequently emanating from cross country ski

OPPOSITE Sunset in the Jagungal wilderness. Alpine weather can be fickle — a 48-hour blizzard followed this peaceful sunset.

instructors' lips (usually with a tinge of frustration).

Reversing the herringbone gives a snow-plough shape to the skis (tips of the skis close, tails wide and knees turned inwards) which allow gentle descents. While in the snow-plough, transferring weight to one side creates changes of direction towards the other. Of course it's always possible to descend by traversing across the hill, then stopping by gently lifting the ski tips till they are pointing up the hill, and then turning around and traversing back across until you get to flat ground. However as you gain confidence there's nothing quite so exhilarating (and frightening) as crouching into a tuck position and just zooming down the fall line. It looks even nicer to stop at the bottom of the run using a controlled turn or later still in steeper country being able to carve a series of beautifully arcing telemark turns weaving between the snow gums. The telemark dates back to the 1860s when it was used to finish off the run out after a skijump. Today it is one of the loveliest parts of cross country skiing, though also possibly the most frustrating to learn.

Although learning to ski will be done often with the temperature hovering around –5 to –10 degrees Celsius, the first thing noticed is heat! Cross country skiing is warm fun and venting is the answer to avoiding a steambath beneath your clothing. It is essential to dress in layers, beginning with thin thermal underwear, then building up with outer layers of wool and finishing off with a down vest, down jacket, gloves, woollen beanie and a thin shower-proof Gore-Tex wind shell. The whole outfit is only worn when

☐ *Part of the attraction of cross country skiing is peace and solitude — something easily destroyed by over-snow vehicles.*

standing around admiring the landscape. As soon as skiing is contemplated take off the thickest outer layer — unless there's a full blown blizzard on the rage. Even skiing across flat country will generate a surprising level of warmth, but grinding uphill climbing really causes pressure cooking. Sometimes it is a pain to take off clothing (when pack carrying for instance), so search for zippers — undo as many as decency allows, take off gloves and beanie, roll down socks and gaiters and slow down on the rate of ascent.

The objective is to avoid undue sweating. The reason for this is not so much because it is generally a fairly long time between showers, but because warm sweat rapidly turns to chilling water.

Once a summit is attained all your outer layers — particularly the wind shell — should be quickly zipped up again.

Descents are real ice formers, particularly if downward travel is punctuated with assorted snow dives. For that same reason it's a good idea to do up the windshell's hood before attaching the fall line.

CROSS COUNTRY SKIING, JAGUNGAL WILDERNESS – LUXURY CHECK LIST

Body Protection

2 sets of silk or thermal underwear
Long sleeved long tailed wool shirt
Cotton bandana
Double skin lycra XC ski pants (rainbow braces optional)
Wool pants or longjohns of wool or thermal synthetic (for night)
2 pair thin & thick long woollen socks
Fibre pile tent booties & spare woollen socks
Long snow gaiters (velcro fastened Gore-Tex)
Silk balaclava & inner gloves
Wool beanie & middle thickness gloves
Woollen sweater & down jacket, preferably with hood, & long enough to reach your thighs
Gore-Tex waterproof full length jacket with hood, overpants & mitts
Ski goggles & sun hat/visor & 100 per cent UV protection glacier style sunglasses

Accommodation

4-season double skinned tent with aluminium snow pegs
Sleeping bag rated to –15 degrees C (e.g. J & H Winterlite)
Silk inner sheet
Gore-Tex bivvy bag (keeps everything dry & uprates the sleeping bag)
4-season Karrimat and 3/4 Thermarest mattress
Torch & spare long life batteries

Getting There

Fly to Cooma, bus/hire car to snow
Mt Jagungal tour: Wilderness Expeditions, 8th Floor, 37 York Street, Sydney NSW 2000

Transport

Silva type compass
Plastic pealess whistle
Jagungal 1:50,000 topographical map
Nylon cord (>30 m)
Stiff soled ski boots (75 mm bindings)
Strong touring skis (preferably metal edged)
Aluminium stocks with large baskets
Plastic ski tip, spare basket, tape, & 5 minute epoxy (for repairs)
A fully adjustable internal framed 65–85 litre backpack with well padded waist strap & shoulder harness (e.g. Karrimor Condor series)
Waterproof pack liner
Smaller waterproof stuff sacks for clothing
Light day pack
One litre waterbottle

Camping

Matches (in self-sealing plastic bag)
Candle lantern and spare candles
Swiss army knife, cup, bowl, eating utensils, trangia stove (with kettle)
Methylated spirits (in more than one container)
Food (worked out for each day & placed in self-sealing bags)
Toilet paper (plus plastic bag to bring used paper back) & toiletries
Snow shovel

Recreation

Camera body (plus spare) & lenses
External battery system (fits in pocket to keep warm)
Shower cover for camera, slow speed film
Notebook & pen, paperback

Adventure Tour Operators

Wilderness Expeditions: 8th Floor, 37 York St, Sydney, NSW 2000. Tours run in Kosciusko National Park NSW, ranging from day trips to 10 day expeditions.
Bogong Jack Adventures: P.O. Box 209, Wangaratta, Vic. 3677. Nordic skiing & snow shoeing weekends, 5 & 8 day adventures. Comfortable lodge accommodation and/or camping, working from Mt Beauty.
World Expeditions: 377 Sussex St, Sydney, NSW 2000. Weekend, 5, 6 & 8 day trips in NSW & Vic.
Peregrine Adventures: 9th Floor, 343 Little Collins St, Melbourne, Vic. 3000. Weekend & 6 day tours in Vic. & NSW.

Further Reading

Australian Ski Yearbook, 1929, Ski Club of Australia, Sydney, 1929
Caldwell, J., The Cross Country Ski Book, The Stephen Greene Press, Vermont, 1981
Flower, Raymond, The History of Skiing and Other Winter Sports, Angus & Robertson, United Kingdom, 1976
Geehi Bushwalking Club, Snowy Mountains Walks, Geehi Club, Cooma, 1983
Hueneke, K., Kiandra to Kosciusko, Tabletop Press, Australia, 1987
Pallin, P., Never Truly Lost, NSW University Press, Kensington, 1987
Plan of Management Kosciusko National Park, National Parks & Wildlife Service, Sydney, 1982
Seisman, Peck, Brownlie, Ski Touring Australia, Algona Publications, Northcote, Vic. 1986

CANOEING

Canoeing in Australia began with the human occupation of this continent. Eons past, during times of greatly lowered ocean levels, a movement of people flowed down from Asia; these people could create a variety of canoes — initially bark boats and dugouts, then later single and double sailing outriggers. Their dispersion throughout the continent and across to Tasmania is well documented. In 1977, Birdsell in *Wangka: Austronesian Canoe Origins* reported, "The simplest of several types of bark boats is found in the interior of south east Australia where oldest human remains have been dated at greater than 30,000 years".

In 1802 French navigators Peron and Freycinet found the Aborigines at Port Jackson (Sydney) making use of canoes. During his journeys the explorer Leichhardt had noted that natives made small canoes from stringybark trees, and even in 1935, D.S. Davidson could find "hundreds of trees which have furnished bark for these canoes". As a result of wholesale clearing and the natural death of ancient trees, discovering a canoe tree is a rarity.

Scattered throughout the country's museums are preserved examples of finely crafted canoes, both dugout and tied bark constructions, but because the materials used quickly decay in the field and because of the loss of whole Aboriginal tribes following the white invasion, much canoe-making knowledge — though not all — has disappeared. The Yanguwa people of northern Australia call the canoe "na-wulkan", and they can still create lightweight bark boats using what is basically a cut, heat and stitch method.

Anthropologists wrote and sketched, artists painted

□ OPPOSITE *A winter dawn on the Noosa River in Cooloola National Park.*

This is without doubt the best means of accessing this wetland wilderness.

and photographs were taken, yet the images always portrayed Aborigines using canoes to hunt, fish and travel. I'd like to think that there were times when ancient Australian peoples set their canoes upon the water just for the pure joy of it and like Longfellow's Hiawatha "... floated on the river like a yellow leaf in autumn...".

Throughout the world, from crude craft, beautiful sleek modern canoes have been developed. Eskimos gave us kayaks with bone frames and hulls of stretched animal skins. North American Indians created birchbark canoes, some ten metres long, to travel the length and breadth of Canada. Trappers and fur traders followed, sometimes in gigantic canoes. Voyaging canoes in the Pacific region ranged from three to thirty metres long, and used wind and paddle power to cross oceans and carry migrants to begin new lives in distant lands.

And just as manufactured canvas replaced animal skins, hand crafted wooden canoes have been superseded — first by aluminium and now fibreglass and thermoplastics (see page 186). Canoeing as pure recreation is credited to John McGregor who built himself a canoe and began a canoeing club in England in the nineteenth century. But it is only during the last fifty years that Australians have taken to canoeing in a big way.

Little wonder, that its enchantment is seducing an ever-increasing audience: the hard-shelled hull glides easily, almost silently, with just a rhythmical dip, thrust and lift of a paddle blade entering and leaving the surface over which the craft is carried — the merest ripples

are the only trace of its passing. To canoe through a wetlands wilderness is to become uniquely part of it. There is no stink of fuel fumes surrounding the craft to smother the delicate aroma of the bush, no polluting oil slick to lay death on the water surface and no raking wake to cut into fragile river banks. Canoeing is both user and environment friendly.

Noted environment writer Sigurd F. Olson said, "The way of a canoe is the way of the wilderness and of freedom almost forgotten". Because of this, canoes are welcome on the gentlest of streams, quietest of rivers and the most pristine of lagoons — they only temporarily take up space where water and air meet. In the delicate management of a wetlands wilderness, making provision for canoe access requires no fuelling points, jetties or deep-dredged channels. Even garish speed limit markers are unnecessary — fatigue takes care of reckless fast paddling.

Paddling is essentially a loving, fluid exercise tinged with a little magic. The simple pivoting action creates easy progress. Smoothness and consistency are paramount since over-powering lunges of the blade just make for a haphazard, doglegged progression. Given a little balance and a modicum of stamina, paddling a canoe is easy to learn and a joy to perform.

The principles of paddling today continue in a direct line from ancient traditions. Certainly the materials for construction are different, but the means for movement — muscle power — remain identical, as does the principle of floating across the surface of the water.

It must, therefore, be something perverse in the human makeup which seeks to make things far more complex than they really need to be. There is absolutely nothing difficult or mysterious in flat water canoeing. In fact, it is this simple purity which makes the recreation so delightful; just four essential elements are required: still or slow moving water, a stable canoe, a single bladed paddle and you.

However, there are thousands of canoe designs. You can build craft that will catch the wildest waves, brave the biggest white water, float smoothly on ponds and safely cross the world's oceans. Almost as many paddle shapes clutter the world of canoeing. And it is quite possible to detail nearly thirty different paddle strokes (see page 186 for a few), including such gems as high telemarks, trail reverses and crossover reverses.

Two paddle strokes (forward and backward) are essential and a couple more (J stroke and draw stroke)

make cruising much less of a battle — a battle which shows itself in a mad-dash zigzagging progression along a straight stretch of river, usually peppered with liberal outbreaks of ringing abuse. The remaining of paddle strokes are really there so that mastering the art of paddling a canoe is a never-ending lifetime joy. Or perhaps it is a dangerous obsession as Florence Page Jacques, a canoe voyager, discovered, "I've become very fond of this companion of ours, which carries us along so resolutely. All the more so because one is so thwarted in an affection for a canoe."

Thwarted perhaps, but like sailing, every time you settle into the seat of a canoe you begin to learn something new. Ideally everyone should start off as a bow paddler. In that position you can't do too much damage, other than standing up and capsizing the craft. Plonked in the bow, you are mainly decorative additional power and are there to evenly weight the canoe. The stern paddler does much

☐ *This Canadian canoe easily copes with a full load of camping gear.*

more, in fact virtually all the steering. To be bow paddler with an experienced stern paddler instils an appreciation of a graceful stroke and effortless manoeuvring. It also provides a tantalising glimpse into the completely addictive qualities of water that's faster and wilder and whiter (see Rafting chapter).

Long distance flat water canoeing can, however, be a chastening experience in which pain levels are shared equally between bow and stern paddlers. As the hours mount and the kilometres pass, backs that ache, knees that cramp, shoulders that burn and hands that blister all provide little trials of endurance — as do those seemingly endless stretches of water when the wind is dead ahead, and it arrives pushing bottomless supplies of rain. This rain is collected ever so diligently by your canoe seat thus creating a large impromptu bucket of icy water easily capable of soaking through the best of wet weather gear.

Alas, even when the headwinds flutter and die, hovering above glassy pools are the stickiest flies and hungriest mosquitoes. Yet committed canoeists just grit their teeth, comment on how well the insects are surviving the greenhouse effect and paddle on.

These trials of canoeing are apparently timelessly universal. If you will pardon the sexist language of the age, as the *Nepean Times* of 11 November 1882 put it: "It is impossible for a man thus to endure suffering in this heroic spirit without becoming better and nobler ... he must necessarily be better fitted to meet the trial of ordinary life than is the man who has not been purified and strengthened by canoeing."

□ *Solo canoeing can lift the spirit, but it requires a good paddling technique.*

With this in mind my water gliding experience features the Upper Noosa River in Cooloola National Park, southern Queensland.

REFLECTIONS IN COOLOOLA

Like a giant hand, a squall scurries across Lake Cootharaba churning the water's surface as it goes. Chasing this rain comes a last glimpse of sunlight, enough to turn gloom into rainbow optimism. It briefly sets dappled clouds alight with warming colour but the light is then extinguished with the next shower. Darkness takes over as we slip past Kinaba. This information centre hovering over the water looks like a guarding ancient fortress strangely abandoned for the night. Beyond it, Fig Tree Lake is a faint shadow. The campsite is devoid of light and life. Beneath a quickly pitched tent, the little Trangia stove gives heat for a bowl of steaming soup and we snuggle into down sleeping bags warm and dry.

Canoeing in Cooloola National Park has begun.

☐ *The northern wings of Lake Cootharaba, south Queensland. Wind generated sand patterns can be seen through the shallow tannin stained water.*

Each time I wake during the night it seems the wind has just unleashed another rain-assisted onslaught on the trees surrounding our little tent. It is still hard at work when a grey sickly dawn coughs its way over the horizon. Tent down, gear ready to load, the sun emerges — and it rains even harder!

A wind-assisted passage has the canoe heading quickly over joggling waves toward the entrance of Como, a tear-drop shaped lake which lies beside the Noosa River. Taking a sharp right turn just before the lake, the canoe's bow finally bites into pure Upper Noosa River water — water that seems in a damn hurry to make it to the sea. Unseasonal rains have created a high river level and a much faster than normal run. This feels like we're canoeing uphill.

A couple of bends later the natural world of Cooloola is closing in. The river deepens and narrows. The breeze is smothered, and even the rain disappears. Instead of a river surface of a trillion ancient wrinkles, the canoe starts to glide over a flawless water surface. Close to the banks are the first glimpse of the Noosa's mirror images. Big-hearted *Banksia roburs*, their characteristic yellow stripe seeming to carve each leaf in halves, come down right to the very edge of the water. They provide startling patches of brilliance beside the fine stemmed reeds which, peculiarly, seem to create their own fine grey mist.

Around the next bend Noosa's surface seems bent midstream by a curved stump the shape of a tired swimmer's arm.

Coming down to meet the water are a myriad of melaleucas, their softly peeling barks like ancient scrolls. In the stillness of the water surface their reflection forms a curving bough which becomes a perfect circle and their limbs with their rippling bends create ovals. Not wishing to disturb any part of this lovely scene, we pause in our paddling and let the canoe glide slowly to a complete halt.

"Real" paddlers keen to notch up the kilometres can rip through this area called The Narrows in no time flat. But they miss the point. It's the journey, not the arrival, which is important in Cooloola canoeing.

Reluctantly, we recommence a slow, even stroke, trying our best not to create the reverberating drum beat which resounds when a paddle collides with the side of the canoe. In appreciation, a stunningly beautiful azure kingfisher occupying a low dead branch just above river level bobs his head as we approach. (They all do that anyway, but it's nice to imagine that the bird minds us less if we approach gently and quietly.) In a burst of blue and orange the little apparition powers upstream, stumpy body behind a huge beak looking for all the world like a gaily painted flying dart.

Rudely disturbing the peace, a raucous flock of rainbow lorikeets flap by. In a mad reckless hurry to get somewhere or other they screech their way through the forest crowns. Just as noisy, but content to occupy the imperious heights of prime waterfront angophoras, are the noisy friar birds, clucking and carolling as we pass. They and the honeyeaters and wattlebirds seem unconcerned by our presence, but a poor little pied cormorant has just managed to dry

its wings when we glide into view. Moments of indecision follow. We float nearer and nearer. It dithers and dithers till finally we are too close and it dives off the low perch back into the water again. Damned people!

Where other rivers show evidence of degraded, damaged banks and cleared catchments, turning a sludgy mud brown after downpours, the pristine Upper Noosa River merely goes a lighter shade of deep maroon. From the surface level the water seems black, stained indelibly by tannin to achieve its mirror-like reflective quality. But black is a false colour. Anything placed into the water shows a sweetly bronzed appearance, with the colour deepening in response to the depth of water.

The Narrows are well behind us as

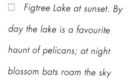

☐ *Figtree Lake at sunset. By day the lake is a favourite haunt of pelicans; at night blossom bats roam the sky*

Harry's Campsite hoves into view. If we'd arrived here in the 1870s the air would probably have been brown with dust and blue with swearing. This was the spot where giant rainforest trees were unloaded from bullock wagons, flying foxed across the river, then reloaded for further transport. Now the big trees are all just fading images in history books. For us Harry's is devoid of human activity. During school holiday time the place is a popular bush camping location.

Our campsite is set beneath a sanctuary of surrounding casuarinas, their fallen needles creating a carpet of soft brown. Inside our tent is comfort and security, yet in the stillness of the night death stalks outside. A whoosh of wings, a rustle of bushes, a cry, then the beat of wings. An owl is hunting.

The softness of the winter morning reveals a river bedecked with clinging white mist. Ah, there be dragons moving in the mist. No, just my companion enjoying a solo paddle. With almost eerie silence her silhouette emerges then disappears back into the mist again. Not a breath of moving air disturbs the river's dark surface and it shows a perfect reflection of river banks and emerging blue sky.

This hush is in evidence even after we have broken camp and are paddling a laden canoe upstream. By then the sun has burnt off any last traces of morning mist and decrees the wearing of broad brimmed hats. But, although lit by a colder, clearer light, there's still no wind and the reflections remain. In front of us the river seems created anew and the canoe seems suspended just faintly above the water surface. Our wake is

A lace monitor or sand goanna (Varanus varius) uses its beautifully designed claws to cling to the smooth bark of a scribbly gum.

a mere trace of ripples and a faint line of bubbles. Anyone coming behind us will be able to share this magical sight.

With the sheer joy of paddling on such a phenomenal morning the kilometres slip quickly past. Campsite 1 is soon behind us. (Above Harry's all the campsites are wilderness, bush locations numbered 1 to 15.) Our destination is campsite 2, another four kilometres upstream.

Our grey skinned tunnel tent looks so perfectly at home at this campsite that we leave it alone and head on foot for the Cooloola sandpatch. Judging by the number of sticky face encounters, our route is wending through what is apparently the most popular section of Cooloola for large web-building spiders. As the grade steepens melaleucas give way to lush green bushes aptly called foxtails because of their luxuriant brushy deep green fronds. Overseers of the bush here are the numerous stands of very old, very tall banksias. And dotted all over their branches are clusters of "old man" banksia cones, some producing life-like caricatures of our most disliked politicians.

After gently stepping around a

basking black snake with a startlingly
red underside we stroll out of the
bush into a bright white world of
sand. It's probably the same laconic
Australian style which first termed
some of the world's most lovely
rainforest as "scrub", that is
responsible for having named an
awesome mass of moving sand
located 600 metres above sea level a
"sandpatch". So large are the sand
masses of Cooloola that when Cook
sailed past in 1770, Sir Joseph Banks
wrote in his journal for 19 May,
"We could see through our glasses
that the sands which lay in great
patches of many acres each were
movable . . .".

These wind driven glaciers in
reverse are still drowning forests,
though because today is windless
they seem to be taking a break. From
the sharp angled leading edge of the
sandblow we can see Cooloola laid
out before us. To the south, massive
Lake Cootharaba dwarfs its sister
lakes Como and Cooloola. The latter
is all but unnoticed by those who
venture into this region. It is
completely surrounded by devilish
country, locally called wallum. The
region is home to banksias and the
rare ground parrot, but it quickly
becomes a quagmirish nightmare in
response to human attempts at
exploration.

A writhing line of deepest emerald
traces the progress of the Noosa
River. Our eyes follow its direction
up-river into the thinner, quieter,
upper reaches until it disappears into
the vagaries of the river's Western
Catchment. This integral part of the
national park was at first excluded
and planned as a pine forest. It was
only through a dogged struggle by
the Cooloola Committee that this

☐ Opposite *Sunset in Cooloola
National Park. The park covers
40,900 hectares and is
approximately 200 kilometres
north of Brisbane in south east
Queensland.*

area was finally spared from the bulldozer and included in Cooloola National Park (see page 182).

Even from the lofty heights of the sandpatch, our enjoyment of natural peace and beauty is rudely constricted by the flashing whirling blades of a helicopter as it follows the river only thirty metres or so above the tree tops. How appalling it is for anyone paddling deep in the raptures of wilderness to be buzzed

This sandblow is so huge that it was seen and noted by Sir Joseph Banks when he sailed up the coast with Captain James Cook in 1770.

by an aircraft. There is much to be said for preserving the airspace over wilderness areas.

Just on sunset at campsite 2 our airspace is beautifully cluttered by a sky full of golden clouds fringed with rich red. In cut-out black, silhouetted trees on the far bank look like thin black coals in a huge fire raging both in the sky and beneath the water surface in a perfect reflection. Its image of slowly fading brilliance keeps us from an appointment with ground parrots. Sometimes, just on dusk, the high pitched cries of these rare birds can be heard as they call across the wallum.

Next morning after days of not seeing other humans, the piercing drone of an outboard motor comes as an unpleasant first contact. Its sound is low for a while, then high, then back to low. The reason for such a range of noise becomes obvious as the boat flies around the corner near our almost hidden camp and then performs a high speed 360 degree turn — apparently just for the hell of it. It is a great shame that the Queensland National Parks and Wildlife Service must share the management of the Noosa River with the state Department of Harbours and Marine, otherwise it is likely that all power boats would be restricted to Harry's and not allowed further.

Unofficially, upstream of campsite 3 is for canoes only and as we journey past there's an almost perceptible sigh of relief. For anyone with a couple of weeks, many kilometres of still water paddling await from here following the meandering course of the Noosa until it meets up with a beautiful little stream called Teewah Creek at

An angophora sheds its bark.

what is regarded as the navigable headwaters. Given persistence and time, it is possible to negotiate the log jams to penetrate much further upstream.

Alas our journey this time takes us only to campsite 5 before we are begrudgingly forced to retrace our steps back to Fig Tree Lake. Before the rain returns we are blessed with a still Kodachrome sunset. Standing at the edge of the lake, just as unfed sandflies, mosquitos and leeches are fighting each other to get take away blood, the sky's fire dies to slate grey and the water turns to the colour and texture of molten lead. Into the grey come a thousand little shapes wheeling and dancing their way through the tree tops. It's the first wave of countless squadrons of blossom bats ready for a night of wild uninhibited feasting on native hibiscus.

LOCATION GUIDE

Cooloola National Park (40,900 hectares) is approximately 200 kilometres north of Brisbane in south east Queensland. Through it runs the Noosa River, which, upstream of the National Parks and Wildlife Service information centre at Kinaba, is a pristine waterway — probably the only one left in southern Queensland. Canoeing distances are not immense, but are enough to immerse you deep within this wetlands wilderness. Taken in slow style, a magical couple of weeks can be easily soaked up. One suggested trip would be Boreen Point to Kinaba (six kilometres), then to Fig Tree Point (three kilometres). Fig Tree Point around Fig Tree Lake and exploring the top end of Lake Cootharaba (ten kilometres). Fig Tree Point to Kin Kin Creek and back (fourteen kilometres). Fig Tree Point to Harry's Campsite, via Lake Como (ten kilometres). Harry's to campsite 2 (six kilometres) — campsite 2 is a good starting point for the walk to the Cooloola Sandpatch (eighteen kilometres round trip). Campsite 2 to 8 (nine kilometres). Campsite 8 to 15 (five kilometres). Trekking side trips can have you enjoying the Kin Kin rainforest, melaleuca swamps near Harry's, dry vineforest beside the Noosa River, high dunes on the sandpatch and wet-foot exploring up Teewah Creek.

Not that you'll be the first to wander Cooloola. According to archaeologist Dr Peter Lauer, Aborigines resided in the region as long ago as 300 AD, but from carbon dating they could have been present up to 40,000 years ago. To date 102 shell middens have been recorded in Cooloola, and were almost exclusively composed of eugaries (*Plebidonax deltoides*). Other anthropological relics include a number of gunyah and canoe trees and trees robbed of native bees' honey. Camping and ceremonial sites (bora rings) have been identified, but many of these have been disturbed or destroyed since European settlement. A number of other sites have been entombed by advancing sandblows. Many of the existing tracks follow ancient Kabi Kabi footpaths and the name "Cooloola" comes from the Aboriginal name for cypress pine.

Cooloola was declared a Forestry Reserve in 1881, but Cooloola the national park didn't just drop from the sky, it came after an arduous struggle. Queenslanders could see more value in this superb region being a national park than a high dune sandmining site, even if their Government couldn't. The granting of extensive sandmining leases prompted Dr Arthur Harrold and others to form the Cooloola Committee. Their campaign took countless hours of toil from hundreds of dedicated people. Petitions containing thousands of signatures were collected, letters bombarded newspapers, money was raised and paid advertisements were placed, media releases were written, time-consuming deputations lobbied ministers and the then Premier Joh Bjelke-Petersen, radio and television interviews were conducted, and aerial and ground tours of Cooloola were organised.

Finally, in December 1975, with the groundswell of public opinion firmly on-side, the Queensland Government gazetted Cooloola National Park. But this park lacked

OPPOSITE *This blackbutt* (Eucalyptus pilularis) *managed to escape the timber getters who began operating here in 1869. Sadly, few remain in the area.*

the Noosa's Western Catchment. Taxing the patience of even the most ardent of conservationists, another campaign ensued.

Finally in September 1983 the Western Catchment was added — it was more than twenty years since conservationists had begun to ask for a national park.

Cooloola National Park is one of a natural trilogy. When combined with the Great Sandy Strait (migratory home for immense numbers of birds and humpback whales), and Fraser Island (the world's largest sand island with more than forty perched freshwater lakes and superb stands of vineforest), the three areas make up the Great Sandy Region.

After stringent scientific, cultural and historical evaluation, a strong case was presented to both the Queensland and Commonwealth Governments to nominate the Great

Sandy Region for inclusion on the list of World Heritage properties.

Why this hasn't been done remains a mystery and it'll probably require a struggle similar to that encountered in the campaign to create Cooloola National Park.

As noted conservationist John Sinclair points out, "The Great Sandy Region is for sand dunes what the Great Barrier Reef is for coral reefs". The region contains the oldest age sequence of giant coastal sand dune systems yet recorded in the world: up to 400,000 years old. Yet the ecosystems of Cooloola range from these sandblows to dense rainforests. Essentially growing on sand are pockets of brush box (*Tristania conferta*), kauri pine (*Agathis robusta*), piccabeen palm (*Archontophoenix cunninghamiana*) and hoop pine (*Araucaria cunninghamii*). Remnants of rainforest also occur near Kin Kin Creek.

☐ A melaleuca forest at sunset in the wet season. Many such areas along the Queensland coast were dismissed as ugly and useless, fit only to be drained, filled and built on.

Tall forests adjoin rainforest areas and vary from pure blackbutt (*Eucalyptus pilularis*) forests to mixtures of blackbutt with tallowwood (*Eucalyptus microcorys*), red bloodwood (*Eucalyptus intermedia*), brush box (*Tristania conferta*), scribbly gum (*Eucalyptus signata*) and forest oak (*Casuarina torulosa*).

Within Cooloola, timber operations began in 1869 when a sawmill was established at Elanda Point on Lake Cootharaba. Little wonder the timber-getters came: one kauri called "Bell's tree" was said to have a butt girth of 25′ 3″ (7.6 metres), but that didn't save it. In 1873, Pettigrew and Sim constructed Queensland's first private railway to cart timber from Broutha Scrub to Poverty Point at the northern end of Cooloola. The rails were spotted gum set into slots in cypress pine sleepers. Remarkably, the remains of these rails can still be seen today. Unfortunately the same cannot be said for most of Cooloola's immense trees.

Cooloola's diverse ecosystems are reflected in the 750 species of flowering plants (including the very rare *Boronia keysii*) and ferns found in the region. It's interesting to note that 150 species are found only on the sandstone soils represented by the Western Catchment of the Noosa River, an area which would have been turned into a pine plantation monoculture had it not been for the efforts of the Cooloola Committee. Summer sees the Noosa Plains aflame with brilliant christmas bells.

Cooloola has more than 230 species of birds, is a flyway and stopover location for migratory wading birds and a vital habitat for the endangered ground parrot

☐ Boronias played an integral part in the preservation of Cooloola National Park since the very rare keysii variety are found in the park.

(*Pezoporus wallicus*). It is also a significant habitat for amphibian fauna requiring very acid waters including acid frogs, like the cooloola tree frog (*Litoria cooloolensis*) and the three-toed, reduced-limb skink (*Anomalopus aphioscincus*). The Upper Noosa River is a home for Australian bass (*Macquaria novemaculeatus*), a fish under pressure through loss of habitat. Cooloola has nineteen species of earthworm new to science — one, *Digaster keastii*, more than eighty centimetres long. There are more than 300 ant species, twenty species of termites, a giant subterranean cockroach and a cricket-like creature new to science, called *Cooloola propator*.

FUTURE PROBLEMS

Unfortunately, instead of being a pure haven for unpowered craft, the Upper Noosa River is subject to oil pollution from outboard motors and river bank erosion. With uncontrolled usage this will only get worse.

One month prior to the gazettal of the national park, Widgee Shire Council showed its environmental sensitivity by cutting a road and placing overhead power lines across the Noosa Plain to establish a pumping station on Teewah Creek (which is the main feeding stream into the Noosa River). Roads to service pumping stations and pipelines (there is another on Seary's Creek) increase the pressure on the highly erodable alluvial plains and stream banks.

Cooloola's high dunes act as a huge aquifer, and given the area's high annual rainfall, contain immense reserves of water. This area may be forced to provide water to meet the future urban needs of the Sunshine Coast and there is a danger that large-scale uncontrolled water extraction could interfere with water table levels over large parts of the catchment, particularly in the upper two-thirds of the Noosa.

THE BASICS

Canoe

Plastics and fibreglass are the dominant forces in modern canoes. Strength and ease of construction make them all but impossible to resist. However, despite a couple of thousand years of canoe design there are still some atrocious floating monsters produced by backyard operators. If you are purchasing a canoe, select from long-established manufacturers and get advice on suitable designs from canoe clubs (see page 189) before buying.

For flat water paddling you should seek a roomy boat 4.5 to 5.1 metres long, with good initial stability. This stability is achieved by a generous beam and a flatter, less rounded hull,

with a defined keel. The keel makes the boat slower to turn, but is of great assistance when travelling in straight lines — though to see some paddlers you would swear the keel of their boats formed the outline of a Z.

Entry and Exit

Board by placing both hands on the upper edges of the canoe (gunwales), keep low and place one foot in the centre, then sit down swiftly but smoothly. Canoes are not the place to stand on a soap box and discourse, for, aside from politicians, the rest of us find it damn hard to talk underwater. Exiting should be done when the canoe is parallel to the stream bank and steadied.

Paddling

Except for Olympic canoeists and masochists, paddling is a quiet, fluid action. There is little point in suffering terminal burnout in the first 500 metres of a ten kilometre paddle. So learn to paddle as my grandmother always suggested I should do everything — with less haste.

Forward stroke: the hand furthest from the side of the canoe on which you are paddling is over the top of the paddle, the other hand grasps the front of the shaft at least half way down from the top. Upon placing the blade of the paddle into the water the top arm is extended and the lower arm slightly bent at the elbow. The top hand rolls the upper end of the paddle forward only marginally — acting more as a pivot — while the lower arm draws the blade back through the water. Keep the paddle close to the side of the canoe and

draw the blade straight back parallel to the keel, not the side of the boat. With bow and stern paddlers both stroking on different sides this stroke should propel you forward in a straight line — forward yes, straight line, perhaps not. Heading in straight lines looks easy but it isn't at first. Both paddlers should make consistent strokes of a gentle rhythmical nature, not mad flurries of greatly varying speed and power. For the stern paddler whose job it is to steer, just as in sailing and soaring, the key is to take corrective action prior to losing direction completely. Work as a team and don't threaten violence on the bow paddler.

A jam stroke, holding the blade hard against the flow of the water, will slow the canoe. It's nice to use it when you are coming in to land on a rocky shore. A backward stroke does the same thing, but will eventually propel you backwards, turning bow paddler into a temporary stern paddler, thus it has lots more directional power and great potential for zig zags.

A J stroke is used by the stern paddler to keep the canoe tracking straight, or by solo paddlers to keep paddling on the one side. It begins the same as a forward stroke but midway through, the top wrist turns the blade away from the canoe side and the outward movement produces a slight sideways thrust and thus makes the J tail.

A draw stroke is used to move the canoe sideways. With the blade parallel to the keel you reach out square to the boat (abeam) and, keeping the shaft upright, dip the blade into the water and draw it back towards the side of the canoe, ending with the shaft vertical.

Body Damage

A sore lower back and bum can be minimised by a little padding on the canoe seat. Shoulder and back strain is reduced by paddling at your own comfortable pace while working as a team with your co-paddle and not spending the days trying to out-do each other with sheer power. Cramps and blisters can be avoided by not trying to do too much too soon. Allow heaps of time to do small distances on the first couple of days and take plenty of breaks to get ashore and have a walk. Long days of paddling may result in "paddlers wrist", a tendonitis of the wrist where the extensor tendons become inflamed. A rest day, ice and aspirin are best.

Dangers

Like any water based activity it is possible to drown while canoeing. Capsizes on smooth flat water are always caused by someone doing the wrong thing at the wrong time. On wild windy days, getting broadside to the waves is an excellent way of creating a capsize. Try to always run into or with the waves even if this means long detours. In such situations it is essential to wear a buoyancy vest and to have all gear well stowed.

Wilderness canoeing requires greater care especially when meeting wildlife. I can't go past the nicely underplayed advice offered by the South Australian Department of Recreation and Sport in their *River Murray Canoeing Guide*: "Quietly avoid snakes swimming in the water. Don't hit them with a paddle as this may flick them into the canoe and cause them to become aggressive."

Canoeing, Upper Noosa River – Luxury Check List

Body Protection

Long sleeved cotton shirt
Bandana
Broad brimmed hat (with chinstrap)
Strong cotton shorts
Long light cotton pants
Dunlop Volley sandshoes
Socks
Bathers (optional)
Woollen sweater
Gore-Tex waterproof full length jacket with
  hood & overpants
100 per cent UV protection sunglasses
Sunscreen
Rid insect repellent

Accommodation

Roomy tent, built-in floor & insect netting
3-season Karrimat, Thermarest or Lilo mattress
Candle/reading torch (spare long life batteries)
Sleeping bag rated to 0 degrees C (e.g. J & H
  Bushlite)
Silk inner sheet
Tent torch and spare long life batteries

Getting There

Air to Brisbane or Maroochy Airports, bus to
  Tewantin
Arrange pick up from canoe hire
Wilderness Camping Permit: Write to
  Queensland National Parks and Wildlife
  Service, Elanda via Tewantin, Qld 4565

Transport

Lake Cootharaba Boat Hire
Elanda Point Canoe Hire
Silva type compass
Plastic pealess whistle
Cooloola Coast 1:80,000 (drawn by Dennis
  Gittoes)
Nylon cord (>30m)
Internal framed 65–85 litre backpack (e.g.
  Karrimor Jaguar series)
Waterproof self-sealing inner bag
Extra waterproof pack liners
Smaller waterproof stuff sacks for clothing

Camping

Matches (in self-sealing plastic bags)
Candle lantern & spare candles
Swiss army knife
Cup, bowl, eating utensils
Trangia stove (with kettle)
Methylated spirits (in more than one container)
Aluminium billy (for fire)
Toasting fork
Food (worked out for each day & placed in self-
  sealing bags)
Lots of fresh vegetables (purchase prior to
  boarding canoe)
Toiletries, toilet paper & trowel (needed above
  campsite 3)
Two 1 litre waterbottles & 5 litre water bag or
  wine cask bladder (in times of peak usage boil
  all water taken from below campsite 3)

Recreation

Light day pack (wear long pants, local treks can
  be damaging to bare legs)
Slater, Slater & Slater, *Field Guide to Australian
  Birds,* Lansdowne-Rigby, Willoughby, NSW,
  1986
Flora & Fauna Checklists from National Parks &
  Wildlife Service, Kinaba Information Centre
Camera bodies in very waterproof container
Lenses, wide (18 or 24 mm) for river &
  telephoto (300 to 600 mm) for birds
Strong torch & flash unit for nocturnal visitors
Shower cover for camera
Sturdy tripod — for use in canoe & on land
Slow & fast speed film
Notebook & pen

Canoe Clubs

Contact through state associations
Australian Canoe Federation, 5th Floor,
  Sports House 157–161 Gloucester St,
  Sydney 02 272933.

Further Reading

Bearse, R., *The Canoe Camper's Handbook,*
  Winchester Press, New York, 1974
Davidson, D.S., "Chronology of Australian
  Watercraft", *Polynesian Society Journal,* Vol. 44,
  Department of Anthropology, University of
  Pennsylvania, New Plymouth, New Zealand,
  March, June, September and December 1935
Doran Jr., E. *Wangka: Austronesian Canoe Origins,*
  A & M University Press, Texas, 1981
Ferguson, S., *Canoeing for Beginners,* Reed, Sydney,
  1977
Olson, S.F. *The Lonely Land,* New York, 1961
Sinclair, J., *Discovering Cooloola,* Pacific Maps,
  Sydney, 1978

HORSE TRAIL RIDING

Horses and the ability to ride them have always been prized. In the business of war, tough unflagging horses have been worked to death: whether carrying jousting knights of the mythical King Arthur's Round Table, or combined to form cavalry.

Slightly less destructive uses were made of horses by the American Pony Express, and long before that, by Darius the Great of Persia, whose dominions were criss-crossed by an extensive network of postal roads — Susa to Sardis (2,400 kilometres) in six days. Long distance riding feats include some amazing journeys, e.g., the endurance ride of a Russian Cossack who rode the same horse for 8,800 kilometres in ninety-three days. He was knighted for the feat, but I think the horse should have received the award. In recent years an American rode from Dallas, Texas, to Fairbanks, Alaska, and back — 18,052 kilometres — in 195 days using seven well travelled horses.

Horse riding has been part of Australia's history since the white invasion. Drovers moved cattle for thousands of kilometres from one part of the country to another and, once squatters had pushed out beyond settled valleys, they utilised the high mountains to agist stock. Each year, as snows were melting, riders would saddle up to drive cattle onto the high plains for grazing. There they would camp in crude mountain huts scattered in secluded pockets, then descend to home properties. Before the snows of late autumn, riders would head back up into the mountains. In steep gullies and amid the snow gum forests riders would seek out the pasture-fattened cattle, muster them into holding yards then drive them down

☐ OPPOSITE *A cleft in the rocks aptly named Hell's Window.*

to the valleys. If winter blizzards arrived early and caught riders unprepared, it could be fatal.

Such stories provided grist for the poetic mill and good riding became synonymous with mountainous terrain. A love of equestrian things also became entangled with legends which told of bushrangers riding off into the sunset with someone else's gold. After bailing up the hapless coachman and passengers of Cobb & Co., or numerous other coaching companies, bushrangers frequently escaped poorly-trained mounted police simply because of their superior riding skills and greater bravado. Many constables really did take a pull at the frightening edge, deciding not to follow mad-cap downhill gallops. Tales of bushrangers stealing horses, daring riding and a thumbed-nose attitude at authority sat well with the writers and poets of the time. Banjo Paterson sums it up in his comment on good horses: "Those who can afford them, can't ride them. Those who can ride them, can't afford them."

Riding in Australia was based on a very formal English style and needed modification for local conditions. After extensive ringbarking left the bush littered with fallen dead trees,

☐ *Some of the aura and romance of the early Australian bush riders is maintained by bush riders today.*

as Gregory Mitchel details in *The Bush Horseman*: "Mustering... was like a steeple chase and stockmen developed a jumping style that aided both horse and rider... the skill lay... in maintaining control with the lightest possible touch."

In America, native Indians maintained that the only good thing brought by the white invaders was the horse — its strength and beauty adding to the landscape. In Australia, Banjo Paterson and other bush-balladeers managed the feat of setting malleable fiction into tablets of stone when they wrote of mountain riders performing amazing feats while chasing brumbies in the steepest landscape this country has to offer.

Myth and reality have grown even further apart over the years as the small size and fragility of our alpine landscape has brought conflict between its users. The true effect of the grazing industry's presence in the mountains was conveniently overlooked by bush poets, both old and new. While mountain riders of old may indeed have loved the high country, grazing was a scientifically-documented disaster. It has taken the Snowy Mountains more than thirty years to even halfway recover from the grazing begun there in the 1850s.

Without sheep and cattle, well managed, recreational horse riding can be compatible with mountain wilderness in a way motorbike trail riding cannot. Horse riding is quiet, physically demanding, requires no specially constructed trails and has the bonus of being superbly exhilarating. With mountain horses, good riding skills can lead to an unusual sharing of a wilderness experience. Just as well conditioned

A small group of riders ascend to the high plains. Horses can still be taken into some wilderness areas without causing environmental damage if their numbers are kept manageable and riders are responsible and employ low impact camping techniques.

human beings thrive on a physical challenge, so too can fit horses take to the mountains — provided that the rider doesn't sit on the horse like a sack of potatoes and give absolutely no assistance to the horse. Assistance frequently means lifting your weight off the saddle on very steep sections, and occasionally walking beside the horse. I believe horses enjoy hearing the laboured breathing of human beings.

Good riders are well balanced and light in the saddle — though attaining that state may require that a number of pain barriers be breached along the way. Even if you are gym fit, riding will antagonise different muscles. Your back will hurt if you don't sit properly and your knees will cave in, but gradually riding fitness will improve, along with riding skills. Accomplished riders are attuned to the horse, and the horse to them. Rider

requirements are transmitted to the horse gently without force or violence, and the horse's responses to quickly changing conditions are anticipated and acquiesced to by the rider.

Unfortunately, mountain horse riding creates two main problems, erosion and excreta. In truth, both are identical to the conditions encountered on heavily used bushwalking tracks and are a result of a lack of management, both in planning and execution. By allowing only small groups through an area at a time (both for bushwalking and horse riding), and by careful route selection and regular route rotation, minimal impact horse riding can be a viable part of the wilderness experience.

Surviving in one moving piece during a long wilderness ride is an interesting challenge requiring a high level of saddle fitness, a delicate touch and gentle riding. These are not unlike the requirements for completing an endurance ride. Horse marathons have blossomed since the middle '60s with the emergence of the Quilty 100 Mile Ride and later the Stockmen's Hall of Fame Endurance Ride (250 kilometres). Such events are run on extremely strict guidelines designed to protect the horses — riders have to cope as best they can. This makes an endurance ride a knife-edged compromise: if the riders go too slow they'll be eating dust, if they strive too hard they'll be vetted out.

All through such endurance rides the horses are checked by veterinarians. The vets initially look for lameness, cuts and abrasions, and then check the pulse rate. After a short break at each checkpoint unless a horse's heart rate returns to less than sixty beats per minute it is vetted out. Winning is a combination of training, guts, concentration and some luck. Fran Howlett, an accomplished rider from Queensland, describes an endurance event as: "... a matter of perseverance and dedication. There's nothing stylish about it ..." — which is a fair description of wilderness riding.

Because very few urban dwellers can afford the luxury of owning and regularly riding their own horses, the great majority of wilderness riding today is done using commercial outfitters. This has the advantage of allowing you to choose the degree of endurance you require of the horse, though to be perfectly honest, endurance is more a factor for the rider than for the horse. A well run professional outfitter uses well conditioned, fit horses which remain just as enthusiastic at the end of a challenging day as they are at the beginning.

To ensure you don't finish a tough ride slung over the saddle like a swag, ease into wilderness riding by tackling a few half day and full day saunters in someone's gently undulating pasture. Increase this gentle riding to overnight back country trips when your riding skills have developed, and your bum is saddle conditioned. Then your abilities might come close to matching your ego, and a wilderness ride can be contemplated with quiet confidence, rather than loud boasting.

Nothing dampens a new chum's brashness more quickly than the sobering demands of catching your horse to saddle it. The first little hurdle comes with picking "your" horse from the milling mob. Vaguely remembering you were riding "the brown one that farts" is not much good since unsaddled, five brown horses in the yard appear identical and none of them will own up to the perennial question of "Who farted?". And typically, no horse will give any response when you put the desperately stupid question "Which one of you is Jack?" Two solutions present themselves, either go back and linger over a cup of tea while waiting for all the others to choose their horses, or jam your pride under the Akubra and ask a wrangler to help.

Once your steed has been found, caught, brushed and saddled, next comes the delicate job of mounting. Those blessed creatures who are light and lithe simply spring from ground to saddle in a boring display of levitation. The rest of us must use devious means to go from standing to astride. This can range from ensuring that you are on the high side of sloping ground, to the somewhat embarrassing act of balancing on a fallen log.

Experience, or lack of it, is displayed in the degree of serenity and confidence accompanying the handling of horses. Bluffing fellow players in a high stakes card game is a snack compared to conning a horse. Like some extra-sensory power, unsureness zings through the sides of your legs to the tips of your fingers and down the reins to tap directly into the horse's brain. Few horses suffer fools gladly and once noted, the horse may decide to have a day of independent grazing, flirt with any other horse within nibbling range or decide today is the day for breaking speed records down semi-vertical scree. Such rides are misery. An experienced horse outfitter will judge your true ability to ensure that you are matched to a horse which will either slightly extend you or be patient with your stupidity.

When you have been matched with a horse that shares your temperament and skill, wilderness riding is a joy. With each day's riding a strong bond very quickly forms between horse and rider. Wilderness riding is not just sitting in the saddle and admiring the landscape — saddling, unsaddling, brushing, tethering, feeding and watering are usually your responsibility. This may feel like an overwhelming amount of work when your Cuban heels are dragging in the dirt after many hours in the saddle, but it isn't. In a way you are paying for the privilege of doing such work, but there's more to it than that. Rather than some chromed lump of

raucous technology, you are being carried through the wilderness by a living, breathing, hard-working creature.

Taking care of the needs of that animal is part of saying thanks for the effort.

Sharing sweat and endeavours makes a bond: willing the horse on as it struggles up slopes much steeper than you'd choose to walk, and then sharing the feeling of achievement on finally making it to the top — even though the horse has done most of the work. While you and the horse try to avoid wombat holes and fallen timber, pride changes to shared raw-nerved anxiety as the horse's four footed traction shifts and slides on the soft surfaces of mineshaft-like slopes.

Gentler slopes and flatter sections of terrain are where your adrenalin works overtime. Rising to the trot is essential to ensure the horse doesn't get a sore back. And it is essential for your own protection to stay alert while in the midst of lickety-split

☐ Riding ability, a willingness to give-it-a-go and understanding between a horse and its mount are all that is required to go trail riding.

canters and full-tilt gallops along narrow mountain trails — a minimal effort since they're a real buzz. Flashing along the track, the horse watches out for its feet, and you watch out for low slung branches. Learning to anticipate which way the horse will swerve is critical to staying in the saddle. Get it badly wrong and you may be temporarily gliding on thin air before making an all points landing.

Riding through trees at any speed requires that judgments be precise since there's little room for error. This was amply demonstrated on one occasion by my overconfident companion who thought he and the horse could just zoot under a horizontal branch. He was half right, the horse fitted through beautifully.

As on some other types of wilderness trips, individual riders soon become a cohesive group, with a solidarity born of common interest and shared experiences.

Balmy days of perfect sunshine are savoured by the group, but mountain weather is typified by fast changes. Cold, rain and, when riding late in the season, occasional sleet are taken as part of the experience. Some mornings are so cold that the horses can only bear the weight of saddles. They must be walked, sometimes for a couple of kilometres, before they are warmed up enough to be mounted. Once warm and especially when heading for home, they are super frisky.

My trail riding experience is set in Victoria's Alpine National Park.

☐ *Galloping a horse requires*
skill and nerve.

HIGH PLAINS RIDING

Apprehension hangs in the air like a mental fog. Prancing steeds catch the mood and help heighten it. They've been ready to go since 7 am and are fed to the teeth with standing about. Throughout this yard at Merrijigg, Victoria, horses are being introduced to riders, though the guides put it the other way around. Subtle assessments are being made about the way in which riders respond to the horses and handle the gear. Ideally everyone should end up on a mount that reflects their real, as opposed to their imaginary, riding skills — they don't, but things will be smoothed out one way or another.

Amid the saddling yard confusion, Jack Lovick, a doyen of mountain riders, moves about with a mischievous sparkle in his eyes. Sidling up close to the rump of a tentatively-mounted, twittery grey gelding he takes a good swipe. The horse's wild-eyed reaction as it shoots across the yard is almost as frantic as the rider's hang-on-for-dear-life response. "Who wants to ride the bucking horse?" Jack calls in delight. A deep silence lies in the dust: no one volunteers.

At the call of "Mount up!" I place bum in saddle for the first time in a number of years. It doesn't feel too familiar. The first half hour is make or break. I wait with some trepidation in a small group at the bottom of a long grassy hill watching the previous group ascend — at full gallop. Our turn arrives and we are away under the assessing eyes of our guides. My horse "Honey", a bay mare, is far keener than I am to get up this hill in record time, but I have little say in the matter. My heart rate

has overtaken the cadence of her legs by a good margin when we top the crest and there's no respite since the next test is log jumping. It's hard to fake log jumping, you're either there or you're not. The horse must be really sure of your desire and of its ability — propping at the crux is not pleasant. On my turn I make damn sure to convince Honey of her intentions and she clears the log by about the distance which gapes between the saddle and my rear end.

We head into long sloping forest country and a soft misty drizzle. Colourful modern garb is quickly cloaked in the brown-green of classic horse rider wet weather wear, the Driza-Bone. Our appearance as riders changes, present becomes the past as we ride into timeless bush. My hired coat is so threadbare I'm sure it is one of A.B. Paterson's cast offs.

In the mist, Honey walks as frustratingly slowly as a laconic Queenslander coming home from the pub, but she does tackle the steep slippery track with confident ease. Crossing over Red Hill, on a ridge that leads to Mt Timbertop, we start to descend, following Stockyard Creek on its journey to the Howqua River. Honey has a calmness about her which deadens any distrust on my part. A kilometre or so from Howqua Hills she spies a lugubrious mud puddle spanning the track. Unconcerned I urge her to follow the confident crossing of the horse in front, but get in response two reluctant steps and on feeling the mud rising, one almighty leap into the air. Like a heat seeking missile I'm launched into deep space, re-entering earth's atmosphere with a full body splashdown in the mud.

☐ *Horses can add beauty to the landscape.*

Honey, unburdened by my weight, makes it easily to hard ground. As we clip into camp, the sudden appearance of the sun ensures a good mud set — my skin should glow tomorrow, that is if I ever manage to get off the grey coating.

Howqua Hills is primitive with a thrown-together kind of Australian architecture typical of transient sites. Just up the track were Mountain Chief and the Great Rand, real here-today-gone-tomorrow gold mines. In *Cattlemen and Huts of the High Plains*, Harry Stephenson says that following the doubtful returns from these mines, "...there was talk of a swindle. A bank manager who had advanced

money to the promoters... committed suicide and the populace quickly 'folded their tents and stole away'."

I slip away on foot early next morning. Toting camera and tripod, I ease into a misty world which wraps trees in gossamer grey and gives the grazing horses a wild appearance. In the early morning they are unburdened but it's only temporary since they are easily tempted with a "free" breakfast, the real price of which is a bit and bridle.

As I return the cook is stoking the fire. She heads off looking for supplies, leaving last night's metal cups lined up before the fire. With flickering flames in the background it has the makings of an agreeable image. One extra cup would balance the composition. I find one half empty leftover, ditch the contents and set it in my picture. The cook returns in time for the camera shutter clatter, but soon drowns it with an indignant blast in my ear as she demands to know who pitched her fresh hot coffee!

White toast, fried bacon and saffron yolked eggs, with billy tea drowned in creamy milk — an old fashioned breaking of the fast. It is a wonder the pioneers ever lasted past the age of twenty-five before their arteries choked them to death. Perhaps all the exercise kept them going — like catching horses in the morning, persuading acceptance of the bit and tossing a saddle what seems like three metres into the air.

To the now familiar cry of "Mount up!" I crank myself into the saddle, only to find every one of yesterday's rub points has become today's combined pain centre. But we are away, moving easily as a group up the first hill of the day and gently down the other side to Sheepyard Flat. "Flat" for a bunch of keen horses and riders translates into a bit of a run. It is fun, adrenalin pumping action but fraught with hidden dangers. A piece of something bright catches the eye of the horse in front and it props, causing my mount to clamp on the anchors just as I'm rising out of the saddle. I land on the saddle pommel with a resounding thud, resulting in an inwardly suppressed scream.

The pain haze clears a few minutes later and I'm almost capable of resuming rational conversation with the rider beside me when we hit the Howqua River. The banks are shaded by groves of casuarinas and acacias with a skinny tunnel track running through them. In this section of its life the river resembles the writhings of a snake, and provides us with a bundle of river crossings: sparkling waters over smooth-glossed river boulders where horses' hooves unleash flying spray. After the first couple of sedate crossings the pace picks up and turns into follow the leader at a trot and a canter. With one hand on the reins and the other on my hat I'm on the look out for ill-placed trees and low branches looming out of the bush and zooming by at an uncomfortably close range.

Changes in direction are

☐ *A misty dawn in the mountains.*

☐ *Crossing a creek requires a surefooted horse.*

brought about by thought transference and subtle shifts in weight. The horse and I generally seem to agree which side of obstructions is preferable, but we are having some problems in deciding just how much clearance to give the tree trunks. Honey seems loath to allow for the fact that I am aboard, and my legs set down at either side of her body don't take too kindly to being scraped off by unyielding trees.

Dancing along a narrow track flanked by closely knit trees allows me no choice but to jump fallen logs. And the chance to brush up on my log jumping technique adds an extra element of fun. Twenty-seven crossings, a zillion logs and a squillion close shaves later, we canter into a lunch stop at Richie's Hut. It's time to recount near

misses and to hear about other riders' painful mistakes. Thinking about the way the horses can judge distances makes me remember a story by Pop Doherty recorded in *If Only I'd Listened to Grandpa*. "I had a creamy horse once and I was packing sheep skins on him. He went to go through two trees but he poked his head through and stopped. Then he backed up and went around: he'd got smart."

Breaking away from the river we forsake the comforts of the valley for the hills. It is steep climbing. I stand in the stirrups keeping my weight forward and use a handful of mane to maintain stability. My legs are screaming and I'm not even walking. Honey's breath is laboured, but her steps are strong; even so I decide to give her a break by using my own feet to ascend. "Hell, this is hard work," comes a wheezy rasp from a passing rider. He finds out just how tough once off the saddle and walking. In six hot kilometres we've gained 1,100 metres and, taking a spell at Bluff Hut, I find a new delight in lying horizontal on a sweet patch of long grass.

On the way up we have caught only glimpses of the surrounding countryside. It is only at 1,680 metres, at the top of Mt Lovick, that I begin to really take in my first long looks at the high country. These peaks are not the steep, jagged, bare mountaintops of European alps, but instead are ancient time-rounded peaks cloaked in a textured tapestry of eucalyptus green. As an old timer Frank Smythe wrote, "The hills of home may be low in stature, but they reach very near to Heaven".

Heading off the mountain, our guides led us to the edge of what I, and my horse, feel is a precipice, — so much for the "low in stature" comment, I'm with the "celluloid" Clancy when even he took a pull. For once Honey is happy to stand still while I photograph other riders making the descent. In fact this location was chosen for its steepness in the first "The Man From Snowy River" film. But, as we are actually riding what the film portrayed as "wild brumbies", I reason that they have already been down here, so my hardest task is to encourage Honey to remember she has done it before and and to keep her pointed straight downhill — skewing sideways would mean a roll and a fall. At the bottom I turn and am a little amazed to

have made it down this slope without becoming the pickled onions in a horse and rock burger.

At 6.30 pm, after forty-three long kilometres, Lovick's Hut is a welcome sight. This beaten up old stockman's hut is bush memorabilia, and an earthen dam nearby yields water for rinsing the horses. After an immense camp oven roast dinner I roll out my swag (Gore-Tex bivvy bag encasing a down sleeping bag) at the base of a friendly tree, preferring the stars to a stuffy cabin's ceiling. Even though the horses find this strange cocoon a curiosity to be sniffed, they move carefully and avoid trampling me.

My bag cocoon is itself encased in a layer of frost by next morning. The air is fresh and energising as I stroll to a nearby forest of woollybutts whose red brown base bark is still wet from morning mist. The first rays of sun turn the whole scene an alluring gold — even the smooth blue-grey high trunks and branches. These are wonderful trees; if left alone

☐ *A few minutes off the saddle is pure bliss — the horse also appreciates a break.*

☐ FOLLOWING PAGE *Riders cling to the skirts of a huge sky. It is little wonder that the bush poets of the 1800s and conservationists today have written so lovingly of the high country.*

201

and not axed they can attain more than sixty metres in height.

A careful inspection of all the horses results in some being rested for the day, Honey included. Her replacement is a brown gelding named Trigger, ostensibly about the same height as Honey. Now if that is so, then I must have shrunk overnight in the crisp mountain air since raising my foot high enough to contact the stirrup seems impossible. I'm not alone in this quandary — it seems that logs and stumps as mounting aids are all the go round here.

A pencil thin lass of more than sixty years canters smoothly past exclaiming how wonderful it is to be alive on such a morning. Trigger fires himself into joining her thus eliminating my concern at how painful it is going to be to ride today. Day three, I'm reliably informed is make or break, so for me it is a blessing that the terrain's attractions are so all-consuming.

Our route clings to a fine spur and is punctuated by steep pinch-gut climbing along ridges laid bare by the harshness of the weather. We pick our way twixt rock and airy drops, skirt wild fields of native flowers and thread through stands of one of my favourite

trees, the snowgum. Their gnarled, twisted form seems harsher in the summer sun, even if their colours are a little less intense than when seen framed in new snow.

On an in-between ridge I pause, stand and need a double swivel to take in a full panorama of blue-tinged mountain peaks reaching into the horizon. The climbing continues. Above Trigger's ears I see a thin line of riders reduced to miniature silhouettes clinging to the skirts of a huge sky. Ridge after ridge and mountain after mountain recede until the fine blue mist claims them. Up here the air is nippy and rarefied to the point of being almost flimsy. Little wonder the bush poets of the 1800s and conservationists today have written so lovingly of the high country. Ascending the edges of Mt Magdala (1,720 metres), I gingerly ease past a cleft in the rocks which frames a frightening descent. This is aptly named Hell's Window and was formed by the scouring of ice chutes a million years ago. It was a scene for one of the classic descent sequences in the first "The Man From Snowy River" film. Imagining the skill and daring to attempt such a ride makes my admiration for mountain riders grow anew.

Descending, out of the narrow steep rockfields and into an open sphagnum moss plain, I end thirty-three kilometres of wonderful riding in a gentle rollicking canter. I join other riders unsaddling their horses and leading them to a nearby stream where we use our buckets and hats to pour water over the sweaty animals before setting them free for the night.

☐ *A small pocket of Victorian Alps.*

Watching them — their manes flying in the wind through a gigantic sky — reminds me of their wilder past.

Animated campfire discussion is eventually insufficient to keep me awake so I bid the stayers good night and mosey off in the direction of my bivvy bag. At least I think I do. I'm sure I chose a site nestled between two gums looking out on the plain. Funny, I must have wandered off course. I backtrack and take what I'm sure is the right direction. Then the truth dawns on me. Those sneaky buggers, loving practical jokes,

have "borrowed" it. Sure enough they are bright eyed around the fire enjoying my predicament. I catch the gnomes trying to get my bivvy back in place.

An icy wind rips through the gums all night and it's a cold dawn. My first thought is for the rekindling of the fire; my second, for collecting the horses. A couple of guides canter off, vanish for a few minutes, then reappear guiding a free-spirited running mob. It's a grand sight.

After a slow jumbly claiming of saddles and gear we are away. Descending and sliding down dry, rocky ridges through dusty clouds and standing in the saddle, raked back against the decline, a series of switchbacks zigzag us down to a tinkling stream. Water snakes through what would once have been a delightful gully, but is now owned by rampant blackberries which draw blood on unprotected arms and faces as we pass. This place is symptomatic of an environment badly out of kilter thanks to previous clearing and grazing.

Emerging from the forest, everyone leaps forward en masse to race across the valley. On the uneven ground this gallop is madness, but it is also heady fun and ends only when we're stopped by the sparkling waters of the Wonnangatta River. Iced stream bathing is just the ticket for my aching muscles. Over lunch the unseen gnomes strike again. When approaching her horse after the call of mount up, one of the girls pauses, knowing something is amiss. It takes a few seconds for it to sink in that her saddle is on back to front.

Thank God for rest days — an indulgent time for fireside yarnspinning and dry bush humour — and not having to set bum on saddle!

The old Wonnangatta homestead is a few stones amid a bevy of memories and the graveyard sits small and alone in an expanse of returning bushland. In some ways history's tales of hardship and struggle, murder and revenge seem to mirror what was done in the name of progress to the high country in Victoria. Once pillaging gives way to sympathetic

management this wilderness may regain its former hold.

Saddling up, I find Jack Lovick is his usual lethal self, loosening off a saddle or two and attempting his rump slapping humour, but most of us are aware of him now and take care not to become a victim of his pranks. He still has the last laugh. Insisting everyone isn't riding well enough, he instigates a morning heart-starter — that we follow the leader in and out of the blackberries at a canter, and follow this with a mad dashing gallop across the valley floor.

Climbing out of Wonnangatta valley we take a route not travelled for a long while. Our progress is by guesswork, and for a while I joke that it's navigation by dog — as the dog seems to be the only one who really knows the way. Ascending with us is a wind, a wind which, when we reach an exposed ridge, becomes a roaring, possessed thing lashing the trees around us. Back in protected flatter country I forget that we are so high. That is until my horse and I come face to face with Brice's Gorge, a steep sided, razor-edged drop where Trigger declines all entreaty to go closer for a better look.

Lunching on the sparkling top of a long-drop waterfall is exciting enough but sharing it with a gregarious snake adds to the thrill. For light relief a few of the group discover that walking with smooth-soled riding boots on wet rocks equals a quick fall and a wet arse. It seems safer to be back on the horses, but this is self-deception. When we pause beside a pool of water to admire the snowgums, one of the horses decides to have a roll — with the rider still aboard. The rider escapes with no time to spare. Minutes later, as we weave through thick scrub, the smacking caress from a branch reverberates through the air. It generates a wonderful black eye.

A ride across open peat country appears harmless, but this too is illusory. Disregarding the maxim of following the leader, one rider attempts to take a short cut. A narrow stream's apparently firm bank is actually an overlaying mat of grass and air which supports neither horse nor rider. The horse falls into a narrow walled peat bog creek and is stuck. The guides assemble more quickly than blowflies on a corpse, expeditiously saving what could have developed into a serious problem.

While I am captivated by the unfolding drama, my horse has seen it all before and sidles up to the stream. I'm only brought back to reality when Trigger sums up the distance and decides to jump, leaving me in mid-air to fend for myself.

By late afternoon we are retracing hoof prints back to Lovick's Hut, and must continue to do so for a short period next morning. Our ascent to the Bluff is through what is for us new territory, but our enjoyment of the beauty of this route is tempered by a gusting wind. Cresting the peak, we curve around and into sheltering snowgums but on the way through this maze-like forest one rider misjudges a broken branch and crashes into it; copious quantities of blood and a broken cheek bone result. First aid controls the damage, and bandaging the broken bone enables us to begin a nasty little route called Charlie's Spur. It's steep and loose. A couple of horses fall, sharing some skin loss with their riders, then another rider is tossed, breaking a wrist. My bandana becomes an elevating sling.

☐ Jack Lovick is well respected among mountain people. His sparkling eyes give an inkling of a devilish sense of humour.

By the time I make to the cooling waters of Jamieson River I am feeling pleased to be only carrying sore knees and a creaking back. Horses tread the river for a while before we dismount to lunch at an idyllic spot near the junction of Clear Creek. After a dust-settling swim, the afternoon ride leads us to Upper Jamieson Hut. This little slab constructed piece of history resides in a wonderful locale of steep peaks, tall bluegums and a palm-fringed stream. It is a perfect spot for my last night camping with the horses under the stars.

LOCATION GUIDE

Palaeozoic sedimentary sandstone, shale and mudstone formed 570 to 440 million years ago make up much of the Victorian Alps. They were laid with infinite slowness on the bottom of huge oceans, but the igneous rhyolites and basalt were generated quickly from molten magma, later followed by metamorphic granite, slate and quartzite. Covering roughly 15,000 square kilometres, the Victorian Alps (1,500 to 1,986 metres in height) represent two fifths of the total Australian land area over 1,500 metres but cover barely one fifteenth of the state. Within that, the Victorian Alpine National Park (declared in December 1989) covers a total of 646,000 hectares and is made up of Bogong, Wonnangatta-Moroka, Cobberas-Tingary National Parks and Wabongo Plateau State Park and other public lands.

The Victorian high country may be a small area, but it is rich in flora with over 1,300 species of native plants, including just less than 100 orchids and nearly sixty endemic species. In the higher altitudes harsh living conditions are reflected by the ground-hugging nature of many of the plants, but on the lower slopes, of between 800 and 1,500 metres, magnificent forests thrive. Woollybutts (stringybarks) tower to sixty metres, but the reigning champion is the mountain ash, *Eucalyptus regnans*, which attains more than ninety metres in height, making it the world's tallest hardwood.

Of more than 180 species of birds found in the High Country, the yellow-tailed black cockatoo is probably the most raucous, the

currawong the most audacious, the flame robin the most brilliant and the powerful owl the least seen. Nearly forty species of native mammals can be found, including the common wombat, the eastern grey kangaroo, the tiger quoll, the rare brushtailed rock wallaby and the leadbeater's possum.

Utilising the warmth of kangaroo and possum skin coats and the protection of snug bark huts, local Aborigines were perfectly at home in the frequently cold, wet climate of the Victorian high country. Though the perishable items have long since passed, stone axes, stone woodworking tools, spear barbs, bone needles, stone skin scrapers and other implements remain as evidence of their presence. Also in evidence are numerous explorers' accounts of the gathering of many Aborigines during the time when the Bogong moths congregated. The moths packed into fissures and chasms in rocks in immense numbers — so many in fact that it was a time of feasting.

The tranquillity of Aboriginal nomadic life changed forever with the arrival of squatters. Harry Nankin wrote that "Jim Brown and Jack Wells drove cattle from drought affected Pelican Plains . . . to the lush summer herbage of the Bogong High Plains in 1851–1852. From that time on it became common practice . . .". This activity developed into heavy overgrazing and burning which damaged the ground hugging vegetation and, according to Dick Johnson, "Without the insulation of the plant cover the soil suffered breakup . . . wind and rain battered the soils, washing away the material between the tussocks . . . the rate of

☐ OPPOSITE *Tree ferns form the backdrop for this beautiful scene on the Jamieson River.*

erosion . . . far exceeded the natural regrowth''. Burning and sheep grazing were banned in 1947 and cattle grazing is to be phased out in some areas by 1991.

Even though the high country forms a small proportion of Victoria, only a tiny percentage enjoys any legislated protection from the ravages of ringbark axes, chainsaws, bovine hooves and the bulldozer. The Victorian Alps should have been made part of a continuous line of alpine parks stretching to the Australian Capital Territory when Kosciusko National Park was formed. Geographically the landscape does just that, but politically the connection was a long time coming within Victoria.

Enjoyment, rather than exploitation, of the high country began in European eyes with the landscape painters at the beginning of the nineteenth century. Walking the alps for recreation commenced late in the same century with the establishment of the Bright Alpine Club and later the Melbourne Amateur Walking and Touring Club. Moves for protection for conservation date back to the 1880s and resulted in small isolated reserves. The National Parks and Primitive Areas Council proposed a joint New South Wales/Victorian Alpine Park in the mid 1930s which, from the New South Wales side, eventually resulted in Kosciusko National Park. From Victoria nothing happened. Up to the mid-1950s still nothing moved. Harry Rankin puts this down to the then Premier Sir Henry Bolte, whom he saw as '' . . . a man unequivocally developmentalist in outlook''.

The Victorian National Parks Association was formed in 1952 and since then has struggled gamely against a number of pro-logging, mining, grazing and ski resort, development-oriented, state governments. An example of the difficulties it has faced was when the Victorian Government allowed logging in 1960 within the then proposed Wonnangatta National Park. Since then there has been a long frustrating struggle which has seen the loss of some marvellous country and the formation, albeit bedgrudgingly, of five separate parks in 1981. This formation however, did nothing for the concept of a joined Alpine National Park until a contiguous park was belatedly declared on 2 December 1989.

THE BASICS

Saddle

The traditional Australian stock saddle is built by hand and many knowledgeable riders claim it to be the best in the world, for both horse and rider. It evolved from European style riding saddles which resemble today's show saddles. By 1911 it had evolved to a stockman's saddle which retailed for five pounds and by 1950 had developed into a broken neck poley which allowed the rider to sit right behind the pommel — the rider was no longer in fear of being tipped over the pads on a rough horse.

Riding

To survive a week or two on horseback it is essential that you be comfortable on a horse whether it is walking, trotting, cantering or

☐ *Meandering across the landscape on horseback can be a satisfying recreation.*

galloping. Pre-ride training, which really means riding, is vital. An hour or two is better than nothing, but a series of day rides, particularly in hilly country, is excellent preparation.

Soreness

You can minimise saddle soreness by wearing well fitting suitable clothing. This doesn't mean a complete dressage wardrobe — stretch jeans are nearly as good as jodhpurs. After you saddle up, make sure the stirrups are short enough to allow you to rise easily out of the saddle. The key to decreasing pain is to ride lightly. Rising quickly to the trot instead of sitting and bouncing against the horse's back helps immensely, but more importantly it's much better for the horse. On a long, hard ride simulating a dead dog can cripple a horse. To prevent chafing, nothing matches the smoothness of wearing pantyhose under stretch jeans. For men there is the slight drawback of being ribbed unmercifully when trying to put them on in the morning and unfurl them at night. Hand chafing can be minimised by using light leather

riding gloves, or if you're not a traditionalist bicycling gloves work just as well.

Atmosphere

In the thinned air of the high country, sunburn and heatstroke are a distinct possibility. A broad brimmed hat is essential, but it must not blow off during a fast gallop. Not only is it a pain to go back on a retrieval mission, but its spiralling fall can spook the horse behind, creating a nasty accident. A group of riders tends to generate irritating dust and exacerbates eyestrain. Wear sunglasses with 100 per cent UV protection, preferably ones that hook around the ears securely and have an extra safety strap. Wraparound, "glacier" style glasses with leather side-pocket blinkers lessens the amount of dust coming in contact with your eyes.

Feet

Leather soled, block-heeled riding boots not only look good, they are a help in locating stirrups. Unfortunately, they seem to have a mind of their own and a special liking for slippery rocks and wet grass once you are off the horse.

Dangers

Dangers are mostly to do with coming unstuck — soft landing spots are infinitely preferable. Also, horses like to roll occasionally and they take no account of branches above their head height. Self-protection is keyed to being aware of what the horse's options are at any given moment, and seeing that it chooses the one least damaging to you.

☐ FOLLOWING PAGE *High in the Victorian Alps a small group of riders gingerly negotiate a descent that is much steeper on horseback than it appears.*

HORSE TRAIL RIDING, WONNANGATTA VALLEY — LUXURY CHECK LIST

Body protection

Long sleeved cotton shirt
Bandana
Broad brimmed hat (with chinstrap)
Stretch jeans or jodhpurs
Pantyhose
Riding boots
Socks
Bathers (optional)
Woollen sweater
Driza-Bone full length jacket
100 per cent UV protection sunglasses with
  leather side screens
Sunscreen
Rid insect repellent

Accommodation

Classic heavy bedroll swag or light modern
  equivalent (J & H Hollow Log bivvy bag &
  Dandelion sleeping bag, silk inner liner, on a
  Karrimat or Thermarest)
Candle/reading torch (spare long life batteries)

Getting There

Air to Melbourne, bus to Merrijig

Transport

Lovick's Mountain Trail Safaris, Merrijig,
  Vic. 3723
Silva type compass
Plastic pealess whistle
Maps: Watersheds of the King, Howqua &
  Jamieson Rivers; Macalister River Watershed,
1:70,000, both by the Victorian Mountain
  Tramping Club
Internal framed 65 litre backpack (e.g. Karrimor
  Jaguar series) — carried in backup vehicle
Waterproof self-sealing inner bag
Extra waterproof pack liners
Smaller waterproof stuff sacks for clothing

Recreation

Slater, Slater & Slater, *Field Guide to Australian
  Birds*, Lansdowne-Rigby, Willoughby, NSW,
  1986
Camera bodies in padded holder, inside saddle
  bags
Lenses, wide (24 mm or 35 mm) for horses &
  riders & short telephoto (85 mm to 105 mm)
  for mountain landscapes
Slow & fast speed film
Notebook & pen

Further Reading

Flood, J., *The Moth Hunters: Aboriginal Prehistory of
  the Australian Alps,* Canberra, 1980
Johnson, D., *Alps at the Crossroads — The quest
  for an Alpine National Park in Victoria*, Victorian
  National Parks Association, Melbourne,
  December 1974
McAdoo, M., *If Only I'd Listened to Grandpa*,
  Lansdowne, Sydney, 1980
Mitchell, G., *The Bush Horseman*, Reed, Sydney,
  1981
Nankin, H., *Victoria's Alps*, ACF Collins, Sydney,
  1983
Stephenson, H., *Cattlemen and Huts of the High
  Plain*, Harry Stephenson, Armadale, 1980

☐ *Riding into the Wonnangatta Valley.*

SAILING

Harnessed wind power as a means of transport has its origins in the earliest crude floating devices of primitive humans. On a raft, a couple of people standing backs to the wind presented enough surface area to catch a stiff breeze and set the craft going in the right direction, but skins, woven matting and cloth proved more efficient, especially when suspended by masts and rigging. This in turn led to the exciting outrigger sailing canoes which are still used in the South Pacific.

Like lumbering giant moths, Europeans sailed square riggers to "discover" Terra Australis, and then established a penal colony and trading system. But the craft were military and commercial since, not surprisingly for an outpost populated with unhappy convicts, private boat building was a criminal offence. Though he was on official business you could say that Matthew Flinders was the first to sail in Australia, undertaking his first voyage on 26 October 1795. His boat, *Tom Thumb*, was an open boat a tad more than 2.4 metres in length with a 1.5 metre beam, and in it Flinders, Bass and a boy sailed out through the heads of Sydney Harbour and down the coast to Botany Bay.

Flinders made nine voyages in six vessels, including a circumnavigation of Australia in the *Investigator*, but to me, sailing for pure adventure is typified in the singlehanded sailors. John Rob Roy MacGregor was credited with beginning the tradition in 1867 with a lone sail from London to Paris. In 1876 Alfred Johnson first crossed the Atlantic in a gaff rigged dory six metres long, and an American, Bernard Gilfoy, was the first singlehander to sail across the Pacific. His boat, *Pacific*, was 5.4 metres in length. Captain Joshua

□ OPPOSITE *The yacht Marielle dances along under a freshening southerly in South Australian waters.*

Slocum's three year global solo circumnavigation of 46,000 nautical miles ending in 1898 was an astounding achievement.

In his tracks came Robin Knox-Johnson's first non-stop trip in 1969, and in June 1988, Australian Kay Cottee became the first woman to sail solo non-stop around the world.

The weekend after Joshua Slocum sailed *Spray* into Sydney in 1896, the harbour was a joyous jumble of private sailing craft. At that time it was said that there were more sailors in Sydney than in any other city of the world. Slocum wrote, perhaps in slight exaggeration, "... everybody owned a boat. If a boy in Australia has not the means to buy him a boat he builds one, and it is usually one not to be ashamed of.... The typical Sydney boat is a handy sloop of great

☐ *A cracking breeze, a full head of sails and the open sea beckons.*

beam and enormous sail-carrying power; but a capsize is not uncommon, for they carry sail like Vikings.''

Bruce Stannard, in a wonderfully evocative book *Blue Water Bushmen*, gives 28 April 1827 as the beginning of sailboat racing with a wager among two British men-o'war. By the middle of the nineteenth century Sydney Harbour "... swarmed with every size of open boat ... twenty-four footers often carried twenty men — great chunks of 'live ballast' squashed triple banked on the gunwales ... there was no buoyancy, when the boat turned turtle, it often went straight to the bottom''. This speed-at-any-cost was a carryover from the theories of emigrant-ship captains who insisted that every possible piece of cloth be carried aloft, even in the most frightening of gales. Today, for some sailors deeply infected with sailing mania, nothing has changed.

Whether ancient or modern craft, sailing is wind-power harnessed by a technology as old as civilisation and controlled by ancient learned skills. Sailing gives us the chance to directly interact with the basic factors of nature. It's a collaboration of wind, sea, tide, current, sun and stars, where every factor changes in isolation, and in relation to each other. Each time you go sailing there are new skills to learn and new challenges to face.

And sailing is for all stages of life. Hardly out of the pram, youngsters can begin their capsizes in diminutive dinghies, which are relatively as demanding as the big toys — those space-age 5.4 metre boats which wing at a frightening pace from bay to bay. At an age when land-locked

people are complaining of aging bodies, many sailors are only just hitting their prime. Joshua Slocum was fifty-one years of age when he began the first solo circumnavigation of the world. H. W. Tilman, who was still adventure sailing into his eighties put it clearly when he wrote "strenuousness is the immortal path and sloth the way of death''.

Of course sailing might seem like the pathway to death next morning if you tackle a strenuous dinghy class when very unfit. Two-time Laser World Champion and Australian National Champion, Glenn Bourke, casually notes that his training schedule is very simple — he does 300 sit ups a day and sails every weekend. Not everyone would relish so many sit ups, yet sail for a few hectic hours on board a twitchy Laser and you will log up almost that many. Stretch out the boat length and width, put a cosy cabin on top and a keel under for self-righting and a sailor's need for fitness moves into being able to generate wind power on winches and being nimble on foredecks. As well as testing each individual's resistance to sea sickness (see page 232), spending many hours at sea on board a continually moving platform forces almost constant muscle work. Over a long period this results in a total body workout.

However, it is easy to destroy all the positive, life-enhancing values of sailing: by turning on a motor the spell will be broken. The strong calming stillness of water lapping the hull will be destroyed by the often vile noise and the exhaust emission.

The world has moved on since the real Robinson Crusoe (Alexander Selkirk) resided on Juan Fernandez Island. Long gone are the days when

□ *Though the hulls and sails now owe more to computers than natural materials, the challenge of sailing in the wilderness remains.*

an assistant could be sent with a template into the bush surrounding the boatbuilder's yard to find naturally bent timbers; and when it was possible to have your choice from a vast array of time-aged straight grained timbers from which to fashion broad planks. Most of the great boatbuilding timbers have been logged to the verge of extinction. Cruising yacht hulls are now more likely to be made of steel or aluminium fashioned by an arc welder, fibreglass sprayed in moulds or even to emerge from a masterly mix of chicken wire and concrete.

Sails were once made of japara cotton and red canvas and were bent on oregon (douglas fir) masts and spars which were held aloft by a staggering array of galvanised wires and running backstays. They were controlled, with difficulty, by muscle power and woven hemp sheets (ropes) running through head-cracking solid wooden blocks. Today the sails are computer-cut and made of exotic synthetics, which crackle like oversized brown paperbags, are run up superstrong masts with power crunching self-tailing winches and are held aloft by a bare minimum of stainless steel rigging. Where once the order to reduce sail sent a small army of fleet-footed and seemingly expendable sailors aloft to tempt fate high above the heaving deck, sails can be reefed today without stepping out of the cockpit.

In the early days of ocean travel, just seeing another sailing ship was such a treat that each would change course, drop sails and pass the time of day. Today the airwaves are full of single side-band radio chat and commercial ships are just colour blips on each other's radar screens. For cruising yachties, however, there is always time to yarn.

On his three year voyage Slocum navigated around the world with outstanding accuracy using an old tin clock — purchased for a dollar because the glass was broken. He even had to revive the clock by boiling it in oil. Today, it is possible to consult a computer which uses the cross bearings of three or four satellites for an accurate position fix. Old-time navigation by dead reckoning and hand-held sextant to plot a triangle, called a navigator's cocked hat, on a marine chart is left to the cruising sailor. Many Australian charts are still based on the work that Flinders did at the beginning of the nineteenth century.

Flinders circumnavigated the continent spending many months from his home port. The safety of the *Investigator* was in his hands — or not, as was the case on one voyage in 1802 when seven shipmates drowned at Cape Catastrophe. Today EPIRB (Emergency Position Indicating Radio Beacon) with four satellites provide a three to six hour detect and locate time around Australia. EPIRB provides a mantle of safety but it does nothing to keep a holed boat afloat or a gale driven yacht off a lee shore. Sailing today still relies on human beings who do make errors of judgment. Tiredness, inexperience or unfounded overconfidence can contribute to a swift end. An adventurous spirit, infinite patience, a meticulous nature, a respect for the sea and a modicum of luck are all still needed to go wilderness sailing. The true challenges of sailing are undiminished.

Following in the wake of Flinder's ship the *Investigator*, my sailing experience rediscovers the Sir Joseph Banks Group of Islands in South Australia.

OF SAILING AND SEA LIONS

On a heading of 090 degrees a soft breeze tinkles in over the starboard quarter and the mainland slips into the horizon. On 060 degrees we harden sail a little, pick up speed and attract the bow-kissing attentions of a pod of dolphins. Smoothly and with a sense of effortless decorum they take turns in diving deep, rolling over to display a white belly then looking up at the bow slicing into the sea above them. A slightly quicker thrust of the boat brings each dolphin to the surface for a whooshing exhale, a gulp of air and a new dive.

Even under the influence of a

☐ *Young Australian sea lions*
(Neophoca cinerea) *bask in*
the sunshine on English Island.

fifteen knot easterly putting the bone at her teeth — as the old timers used to refer to the white bow wave of a sailing ship which is moving fast — the dolphins show our boat, *Marielle*, a clean set of tails. Their ancestors probably did the same with Flinders' ship the *Investigator* when he tracked across the same patch of salt water in 1802. Where Flinders was making for the island he christened Kirkby (after a village in his home county), we are looking for English Island.

Describing English Island as an unpretentious place, rather overplays this tiny little collection of rocks and hardy vegetation. While humans might not immediately see the potential for long term habitation, a small colony of Australian sea lions find it alluring. At an estimated total population of less than five thousand, these are the rarest sea lions in the world. They'd be extinct if the brutal "sealing" days of the last century hadn't stopped.

Dropping *Marielle's* anchor near to the island elicits some begrudging interest from shore, but it is only when a dinghy filled with the crew heads towards land that the more energetic of the sea lions scuttle into the water then swim out for a close look at these strange pale creatures with long front flippers and even longer back appendages. By the goggle-eyed stares and excited barks of the sea lions it certainly seems they think we are a comical looking species. Others seem to have been struck down with warm rock lassitude and can't be bothered getting up for a look, no matter how strange and wondrous the sight.

As I inch to within lens-filling range of these comely creatures I can understand how, in their innocent curiosity, they showed little resistance to early sealers who came to brutally club them to death. Any fear that the present generation holds lingering ill will towards humans is dissipated as I meander about the island enjoying my interaction with the sea lions — aside from the shared frights of nearly stepping on a few inland sleepers. Stalking close to the boulders I come upon a female sea lion suckling her pup, and provided I don't stand up, but just lie on a big tor high above them I don't cause any disturbance. She opens an eye, checks me out, then goes back to dozing. The bub just keeps on drinking.

Leaving this colony to enjoy life, a sprightly breeze and judicious downwind tacking has us nosing into Moreton Bay on nightfall. But the encroaching darkness does nothing to discourage the wind which is still singing a lusty lullaby in the yacht's rigging as I snuggle into my bunk in the forward cabin. By daylight the breeze still reigns.

Standing atop the coach-house I see Reevesby, the largest island in the group, stretching off to the south. Once the sun lifts a few hand spans from the horizon, it reveals we are moored in a classic blue-water and white-sand arcing bay. Looking back from the top of a sand dune on shore, *Marielle*, a twelve metre boat, is reduced to a mere white punctuation mark in a two-tone blue page of sky and sea.

Walking on this part of the island, I am fascinated by the proliferation of shells and their multifarious shapes, sizes, textures and colours which litter the sand. At the back of the sand dunes is a broad concave depression which, from a distance,

☐ Blyth Island, one of the prettiest islands in the Sir Joseph Banks Group of Islands.

looks like an Aboriginal shell midden. Close up, it's an avian graveyard. Delicate bird bones devoid of sinew and feather have become a jumbled conglomerate of bleached white.

A trumpeting sky of clouds watches our departure. Under full sail and with a freshening eighteen knot southerly the boat heels so far its lee rail descends into kissing range of the sea, but the experience must be too much, for it develops a definite likeness for huffily rounding up into the breeze. Even though the boat is a bit overcanvassed, it's a great feeling to be at the helm as it does an inspired shake, rattle and roll, dancing to the beat of a short sharp chop. The spray kicks back up and over the bow to turn the foredeck into a glistening slippery floor.

Although we are pushing *Marielle* along at maximum speed, we aren't racing, so on the tacks I hold it back up into the breeze to let the winch grinder have an easy time of hardening the sheets. Steering on the leeward side, I can see the luff of the headsail and keep the tell tales streaming on both sides of the sail. It's a bit harder to see where I'm going from down here, but that's not too critical, since I'm on the only boat in our full compass of ocean stretching into the horizon.

Home Bay feels welcomingly quiet. We take the dinghy ashore and clump up the National Park's boardwalk to view the ruins of an old homestead. As well as this eyesore, introduced weeds and leftover farm machinery are reminders of an earlier time in Reevesby Island's history when, before it became a national park, it was a grazing run. It will be gratifying when the weeds are eradicated, the machinery dissolves in a pile of rust and the buildings turn to dust.

On what today is the windward side of Reevesby, Haystack Bay is wildly frothed. Wind and wave sculptured icons of sea weed decorate the beach. We tuck the *Marielle* into the far southern corner of the Bay. This position provides us with enough shelter to enable us to stop and enjoy some beautiful scenery: blossoming multicoloured native plants, and the seaside rock formations. On the western side of the island orange lichen creates the appearance of rusting rocks, but here the lichen is pure white producing an eye-captivating illusion of snow.

A large Pacific gull lands nearby catching my attention. It starts to walk directly towards the camera, then begrudgingly steps into the water and paddles, passing by in an arc of safety. Back on shore it strides, if a gull can stride, up to an innocuous ordinary seagull telling it in no uncertain terms to get lost. Clear of competition the bully goes

☐ *Not only is it exhilarating to be at the helm of a well-founded boat in a good breeze, but it takes your mind off becoming seasick.*

dabbling. A pause, a quick dunk and it comes up with a struggling crab — held firmly between two clamped shut halves of beak. Selecting a spot on the beach the Pacific gull makes short, crunching work of its supper and ingests the whole crab, most of the shell included.

Heading out next morning I almost make the mistake of crunching *Marielle's* hull on the reef between Reevesby and Lusby Islands where the water is a little on the thin side. With Dalby Island abeam we put in a starboard tack towards Blyth Island, a delicate sandy little cay sitting like a strange white oasis in a green desert. It proves too sandy to approach from this direction and shallow water forces us to tack again and head for Langton, a flat-topped

island where the vegetation all looks like it has a crew cut.

Flinders couldn't see all the islands when he viewed and named the Sir Joseph Banks Group, so Langton was often confused with nearby Roxby Island until 1965. On shore I lose sense of time exploring a network of caves being carved out of the island and giant tors decaying with infinite slowness under the attention of fungus. Hazy cloud turns the sky into a giant, soft reflector which helps my film to cope with the subtle brightness and shade of the niches and cracks in these powerful looking rocks. Thankfully no modern day spray-can carrying Neanderthal has been here to deface this beauty with a brain dead message.

Boulder-wandering also gives us

a few surprised introductions to little green rock parrots. The parrots materialise at the sound of feet on the surface of the rocks then once we have landed on another beach rock seem to disappear again. Overhead, gulls protest the intrusion, while underfoot, white splattered rocks indicate the local cormorant population's favourite sun perches. Little niches give way to broad slabs of rock inclined into pitched battle with the sea. Even on an exposed little dimple of an island, this south western side exhibits a wild, harsh quality where any vegetation has a massive struggle for life.

True hedonistic sun-lovers that they are, the sea lions reside on a warm sandy beach on the north west tip of Langton Island. But they are quite ready to give up the beach for a chance to swim with an alien. Walking about on land, I can feel a certain superiority of movement to sea lions, but underwater, in comparison to their effortless water ballet, I'm a bumbling dodo — perhaps even an amusing one, certainly to them, since encumbered by diving gear I represent a creature for fascinated examination.

Joining me on the sea bottom the sea lions rest on a mat of sea grass and set their big, puppy-like eyes to wide-open mode. I lie there trying not to cloud the water while estimating the distance from me to a young sea lion who looks particularly delicate and appealing — about two metres long. It has my complete attention. My Nikonos clicks away happily until my attention span is cut lightning

short. I feel a sharp tug on one fin. Sharing the cold clear waters of this locality are some very large sharks and my imagination is working overtime as I spin around (a forced lumber might be a better description of my panicky turn). Relief swamps fear when I see that my "shark" is merely another sea lion examining my twin "tail" by giving one fin a tug with its teeth. My looking at it does nothing to

dampen its enthusiasm, for the sea lion moves down the fin to gently mouth around my heel. I am curled up into a squat position only a metre away, and can see the size of its teeth. My heel could easily be turned into mince meat, but my nibbling friend handles me with gentle care.

I leave it to continue the examination and turn back to see that my previous subject has been replaced by a very large male. It doesn't have quite the open, puppy-like manner of the female, in fact all the other sea lions move out of its way. I lie on the bottom again in what I'd like to think is a non-threatening manner. Weighing more than half a tonne this animal could demolish me and not even raise its heart rate, but

☐ FOLLOWING PAGE *The Australian sea lion (Neophoca cinerea). Bulls can grow to 3.5 metres and weigh up to 300 kilograms, while cows can grow to two metres and 100 kilograms.*

there is no animosity, it is untroubled by my presence and just does a slow circuit in a controlled authoritative manner to satisfy its curiosity, then moves on.

I swim on towards a group of milling sea lions. I turn and try to frame three young ones who are "standing" in the water quietly pushing out a little stream of air bubbles — probably not a bad mimicry of what I am doing. I've almost got their antics on film when the camera lurches. Turning my head, I see my fin-nibbling friend has come along for the ride, this time taking a liking to the bright purple underwater strobe attached to my camera. As I watch only a few inches away, it takes the back of it into its mouth and delicately feels the plastic. From eyeball to eyeball range its teeth are even bigger. I'm not too sure of sea lion etiquette so I wait expectantly for it to finish. It seems quite a long while before I breathe again.

Out of film and low on air I fin slowly back to *Marielle*. Behind me the underwater circus troop jump and play. They're still at it as we up anchor and run downwind towards Roxby Island, where a jibe has us on course for Blyth Island. Skirting an unexpectedly long finger of reef we nose cautiously in to the leeward side of the island. Crystal clear water has the bottom seeming even closer to *Marielle's* keel than it really is, so we err on the side of caution. A longer trip to shore in the dinghy is much preferred to putting the yacht on the hard.

At a distance, Blyth has all the classical lines of a cliched tropical island, minus only the palm trees, but they are no real loss. Close up the island retains its beauty. We run the dinghy up beside a huddle of lazy tors — to my eyes they resemble a cluster of basking sea lions. And there's a bonus. It's always a wonderful experience to set foot on a beach and find no footprints, just a myriad of intriguing tracks: wandering lines of three pointed prints, mysterious scrapes and infinitesimal pinpricks of an animal that has made an epic journey of a few metres. On a meandering circumnavigation of this perfect little circle of white, wind-rippled sand, our feet make tracks that hopefully the next big tide will erase.

Even in the late afternoon sun the grains of sand sparkle with harsh intensity. But my attention lifts skyward: a chilly seabreeze is in full flight and a flock of Pacific gulls is using its constant lift to glide above the beach. Their skill is evident for nary a feather moves and they seem to be almost stuck against the deep blue sky. As a further backdrop a half moon hangs behind them. However, it proves an elusive combination and I am unsuccessful in my attempt to bring it all together in the viewfinder of my camera.

Almost back to the dinghy we troop along a little more quickly and stumble right into a little pod of very surprised sea lions. They skip across the rocks and dive into the sea, but once they are safe they turn from their flight and paddle back for a closer look at us.

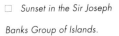

By 9:30 pm we are ready to head back to the mainland. A big lush moon dominates our world coating everything in silver, but the breeze picks up enough to almost brush the silver from the sea surface. We put a reef in the main and even under reduced sail *Marielle* romps along in a rising sea. *Marielle* rides up with some waves, leaps over others and buries itself in a few. The latter break over the deck with such spray-flying enthusiasm that they threaten to truly test the wet weather gear. Below decks is a mad, tossing-about world only fit for those lucky souls with iron clad stomachs and sea legs of stainless steel. Not being one of the fortunate ones I take the helm, keep in the world of fresh air and try to concentrate on sailing the boat rather than thinking about becoming seasick.

Moonlight reflecting off the luff of the mainsail is bright enough for me to see whether or not I am sailing too close to the wind. Fortunately, on the course we want there's a spread of three bright stars in the shrouds, so with these as impromptu guiding lights, we sail into the night. To our lee the islands of the Sir Joseph Banks Group are mere hints of black against a soft grey sky. We are just one boat alone under the night sky, with only our navigation lights to signal our presence.

LOCATION GUIDE

The Sir Joseph Banks Group of Islands lies approximately fifty kilometres east-nor-east of Port Lincoln at the bottom of Spencer Gulf. There are twenty islands in the group, seventeen of them incorporated into a conservation park. They are mostly low-set islands, flat, domed or undulating and vegetated with a small range of hardy shrubs. With the exception of Blyth, a sand island, most of the islands in the group are limestone on a bed of granite covered with brown sandy soil. Many have exceptionally beautiful white sand beaches and Reevesby, now the largest island in the group, is believed to have once been three separate islands. There are no creeks or natural reservoirs of fresh water on any of the islands. During the peak of the last glaciation, the islands would have been connected to the mainland, but by about 8,500 years ago rising sea levels had cut them off.

Native terrestrial animals are dominated by reptiles. The black tiger snake (*Notechis ater niger*) and the death adder (*Acanthopus antarticus*) are prolific on most islands. As with most snakes, if you don't go looking for them, or try handling them, the likelihood of being bitten is remote. The death adder in particular should not be handled as it can reach around to bite anything — even reaching as far as the end of its tail. Twelve species of lizard have been recorded on the group — Gould's goanna was introduced in the 1920s and 1950s as a snake control measure.

Sixty-nine species of birds utilise the islands of the group, with twenty-two known to breed there.

Among them Cape Barren geese (*Cereopsis novae-hollandiae*) excited the most interest when they were nearly brought to extinction by hunting and loss of habitat. Favouring the low shrubs and rocky edges is the brownish-olive rock parrot (*Neophema petrophila*) while on the island fringes are large flocks of little black cormorant (*Phalacrocorax sulcirostris*) and pairs of pied oyster catcher (*Haematopus longirostris*). Little penguins (*Eudlyptula minor*) turn many of the islands into mine fields of burrows and can be seen coming ashore at night. Silver gulls (*Larus novaehollandiae*) and Pacific gulls (*L. Pacificus*) make a wonderful sight soaring into the afternoon sea breeze.

The Australian sea lion (*Neophoca cinereus*) breeds on many islands in the group. Bulls grow to 3.5 metres and weigh up to 300 kilograms, cows grow to two metres and 100 kilograms. Given that their total world population is only 5,000 there is not a great deal known about them. There would be even less known if the sealing trade which killed them for their hides and oil had kept going much longer. Sea lions are thought to eat fish, squid, crayfish and penguins and are frequently found to have from half a dozen to three dozen stones in their stomachs — from walnut to tennis ball size. The simplest way to tell seals and sea lions apart is to watch their movement over land. Seals drag themselves along while the sea lions are able to turn their rear flipper forward to waddle or wriggle (with great speed when necessary).

There are seventy-five species of fish in the waters of the Sir Joseph Banks Group including white pointer sharks — none of which is protected

□ OPPOSITE *Reevesby Island, one of twenty in the Sir Joseph Banks Group of Islands. Seventeen of the islands are incorporated into a conservation park.*

by the islands classification as a conservation park. Dolphins are also common, though thankfully they are rarely killed nowadays.

Matthew Flinders sighted the Sir Joseph Banks Group on 26 February 1802. On 6 March 1802 he landed on Kirkby Island to get bearings of the islands, and named all the islands he could see (fourteen) after villages in Lincolnshire. The brutal trade of sealing started in about 1798 and by 1806 there were signs that the sea lion populations were diminishing. By 1860 sealing had all but died out, as had the sea lions. The last organised killing in South Australia was on Kangaroo Island in 1880. In the 1830s grazing runs were established; guano mining persisted from 1898 to 1905; and an attempt was even made to farm chinchilla rabbits.

Flora and Fauna Reserve status was conferred in 1966, riders over leases followed and then the presently constituted Sir Joseph

Banks Group Conservation Park came into being in 1974. Spilsby is privately owned. After a history of short-sighted exploitation, the islands are slowly regaining their original wilderness values. Their chances of keeping these values rely almost solely on their remoteness. Status as a conservation park takes little account of wilderness — it is in fact hard to find the word used in any South Australian National Parks and Wildlife Service, Department of Environment and Planning document. Access to the islands is virtually unrestricted and unpoliced though camping is only allowed on Reevesby Island. The graveyards of bottles on the sea bottom near popular anchorages are mute testament to the slack attitude of many visitors.

And while land dwelling animals are respected, the archaic notion that it is okay to kill the marine life in the waters fringing the islands, persists.

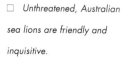

☐ Unthreatened, Australian sea lions are friendly and inquisitive.

THE BASICS

Propulsion

Since it is invisible, wind is inferred from visible indicators and felt rather than seen; its pressure on the cheek and a fluttering flag indicate both its strength and direction. Ruffled water "darkies" or "cat's paws" moving towards you indicate stronger wind is about to hit. And smooth patches can be pockets of light wind, "holes", which the boat can fall into and are roundly cursed by racing sailors. Rather than being pushed along by wind, a sailing yacht moves into air of lower density. This is achieved because sails slow the air on their inner side and speed it up on their outer side, thus creating a pressure difference.

Direction

Essentially a sailing boat takes its direction from the wind direction. The boat "runs" when travelling downwind (180 degrees off the wind), "reaches" when travelling across the wind (ninety degrees to the wind) and "works" or "beats" when travelling upwind (forty-five degrees off the wind). When the boat is headed too close to the wind the leading edge of the sails (the luff) flutters. Continuing up even closer to the wind will make the boat stall, the sails flap and the boat will be caught "in irons". In catamarans this is an often-experienced state. Ideally when on a work or reach, the tell-tales (light pieces of material on either sides of the sails) should both be streaming towards the back of the boat. When on a work a "knock" is a disliked change in wind direction which forces you further away from your chosen direction. A "lift" is a helping change in wind direction.

Heading upwind on a work means "coming about" or "tacking". That is, pushing the tiller across and so bringing the bow from one side of the wind through the eye of the wind and pointing to the other side. In the middle of the tack the jib is released, the back of the sail (leech) goes around the mast and as it fills with wind from the new tack it is tightened up on the other side. Jibing is the same thing but done when running downwind and results in the boom coming across very quickly — sometimes just when you are not expecting it to do so. In dinghy sailing unplanned jibes are frequently the cause of a capsize.

Boat Bits

Because in the square rigger days it was often life and death to grab the right bit of the boat at the right time, there are six squillion specially named "things" on sailing boats. Learning them all is a great way to extend your vocabulary and to confuse non-nautical friends, but it is not desperately important today.

However, there are a number of essential names to be familiar with: Bow and stern — are respectively the front end (sharp) and back end (sometimes blunt) of the boat. Port and starboard — are respectively the left and right hand sides of the boat — when you are standing on the boat facing the bow. Mast and boom — are respectively the upright pole, usually aluminium (or poles in the case of a ketch, schooner or yawl), and a smaller diameter pole set at right angles to it and laid out aft.

Jib and main — are respectively the front and back sails of a sloop (single masted boat).

Topping lift — is a useful wire or rope that keeps the aft end of the boom up out of head hitting range when the mainsail is down.

Sheets — are actually ropes, but the anchor can be attached by a rope and/or a length of chain.

The bitter end — is the end of the anchor rope which should be firmly attached to the boat. The skipper becomes extremely bitter if you chuck over the anchor and the end of the rope is not attached to the boat.

Jib sheet and main sheet — control the tension of the sails.

Halyards — raise and lower the sails.

Stays (forestay, backstay, shrouds) — are standing rigging which keeps the mast up.

Winch — is used to assist muscle power to raise sails or create tension in the sails.

The head — is the toilet usually operated by hand pump and prayer.

Dinghy — is a small twitchy little boat out of which it is extremely easy to fall.

Figure of eight — is a simple easy-to-learn knot which is put on the end of sheets.

Sea Sickness

Sea sickness is the most terrible thing in the entire world. At its worst the sufferers would gladly choose death by a thousand cuts of a blunt breadknife, but only if they can get off the boat first. Prevention depends on individual makeup — I prefer to take the tiller and stay there as long as possible, only going below decks if my life depends on it. Less drastic measures are ear patches, wrist bracelets and motion sickness tablets. Trial and error is the only way to find out which works for you.

Dangers

On board a yacht there are many and varied ways to damage yourself if you lumber carelessly about the boat. Broken ankles are easily achieved as are torn ligaments and concussion. Drowning is also a distinct chance — male members of the crew emptying their bladders over the stern at night find that this is an excellent way of leaving ship without anyone else noticing. If only one member of the crew is experienced he or she should organise a person-overboard drill i.e. throw a bright, floating object over the side and then go below while the crew discover the fun and excitement of turning the boat around to retrieve the surrogate person. Choose an inexpensive item rather than a lifejacket since the chances are pretty high that it will either be lost forever or end in a mangled heap after suffering blows while being run down two or three times.

During the course of many years sailing on yachts I've been crowned by swinging booms, stepped backwards and fallen straight down an open hatch, been smacked in the face by a luffing jib, jammed fingers in a cleat, been rope-burned by a fast moving sheet and broken a toe on a deck fitting. In dinghies and catamarans I have often spent so much time upside down that the safety boat skipper at my sailing club has suggested I put the boat numbers on the hull rather than on the sails. Despite all this, I'm still in one functioning piece and seriously addicted to sailing.

☐ OPPOSITE *Cutting smoothly through the water a yacht makes very little impression on the ocean. In closed or restricted circulation water-ways, however, there is a need for holding tanks to be fitted to all boats with overnight accom-modation so that no waste water or raw sewage is dumped overboard.*

SAILING THE SIR JOSEPH BANKS GROUP OF ISLANDS — LUXURY CHECK LIST

Body Protection

Long sleeved cotton shirt
Bandana
Broad brimmed hat (with chinstrap)
Strong cotton shorts
Long light cotton pants
Dunlop Volley sandshoes for rockhopping
Socks
Bathers (optional)
Woollen sweater
Gore-Tex waterproof full length jacket with hood
100 per cent UV protection sunglasses
Sunscreen
Rid insect repellent

Accommodation

Sleeping on board yacht

Getting There

Air to Adelaide, air to Port Lincoln
Permit needed only if camping on Reevesby Island: Write to SA National Parks & Wildlife Service, P.O. Box 866, Port Lincoln SA 5606

Transport

Hire Bare Boat: Port Lincoln Yacht Charter, P.O. Box 929, Port Lincoln SA 5606
Sailing tour to Sir Joseph Banks Group (ex-Adelaide): Osprey Wildlife Expeditions, 27B Strathalbyn Rd, Aldgate SA 5154
Charts: AUS 776 South Australia, Williams Island to Winceby Island, 1:150,000 at Latitude 27 degrees 15 minutes
A photocopy of Matthew Flinders' original chart

Recreation

Light day pack
Gaiters & strong boots give some protection against snakes
Slater, Slater & Slater, *Field Guide to Australian Birds,* Lansdowne-Rigby, Willoughby, NSW, 1986
Flora & Fauna Checklists from SA National Parks & Wildlife Service
Camera bodies in very waterproof container
Lenses, wide (24 mm & 35 mm) & telephoto (105 mm to 300 mm) for sea lions & birds
Nikonos & Aqua Sea 140 underwater strobe
Wet suit & snorkelling outfit (Scuba hire is available in Port Lincoln)
Slow & fast speed film
Notebook & pen

Further Reading

Heaton, P., *The Singlehanders,* Michael Joseph Pty Ltd, London, 1976
Slocum, J., *Sailing Alone Around the World,* FA Thorpe Ltd, Anstey, Leicestershire, 1900
Stannard, B., *The Blue Water Bushmen,* Angus & Robertson, Sydney, 1981
Tilman, H.W., *Adventures Under Sail, Selected Writings,* (Edited by L. Perves), Victor Gollancz Ltd, London, 1982

SEA KAYAKING

Eskimos had a need for a durable boat, one strong and resilient enough to tackle Arctic waters but light to handle, and swift enough for hunting and fishing. Opportune driftwood, animal bones, stretched seal skins and sinews came together under adroit human hands to produce the kayak and the umiak. The umiak was an open boat which was often rowed or sailed. Surviving photographs and early sketches of kayaking Eskimos show them sitting amidships in craft often less than 0.6 metres wide and 5.4 metres long, paddling with either single or double-bladed paddles. There were many kayak designs, including the Greenland version which Jay Evans records: "The deck... was often quite flat to accommodate an inflated bladder and line attached to a hunting spear...". So that the Eskimo paddler could protect against being swamped they would simply "... fasten a waterproof parka around the rim of the cockpit". Other Eskimo kayaks used a larger cockpit designed for two paddlers sitting back to back. No sealing skirt was used when hunting walrus because the hunter quite often became the hunted and a quick exit was essential for a longer life.

As explorers from many nations entered the Arctic regions the original kayak designs were taken back and adapted for local conditions. Jorgen Samson states: "Kayaks were first seen by Europeans when Greenland and Canada were discovered about the year 890. About 1450 some Greenland kayaks were shipped to Denmark and Norway." Ralph Frese reports that in 1859 the father of modern canoeing and kayaking, John MacGregor, "visited his cousins in Ottawa — canoed in a dugout, a birchbark and an India rubber canoe...

□ Opposite *Making it out through the shore breakers in a sea kayak is a matter of good timing and lots of luck.*

and noted skin kayaks''. Using modifications of the Alaskan craft MacGregor first toured Europe then wrote about his voyages in a manner which popularised canoeing and kayaking. He followed this up by designing folding boats and craft which could be packed in sections. Frese also notes that in 1867, "George Waters of Troy, New York, conceived the idea of laminating paper over a form to build a boat".

Seven years later Nathaniel Bishop travelled 4,000 kilometres in such a craft.

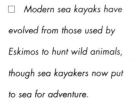

☐ *Modern sea kayaks have evolved from those used by Eskimos to hunt wild animals, though sea kayakers now put to sea for adventure.*

The value of a seaworthy, manoeuvrable and compact craft given to stealth was not lost on various bickering nations and their use as war craft was mooted very early and actually used effectively during World War II. Kayaks were used in the *Krait* raids on Singapore and also during the Falkland war by the British to avoid Exocet missiles. The Australian submarine force is now equipped with Amphibian sea kayaks.

More benevolent uses were found for sea kayaks in 1907, when a tailor from Germany, Johan Klepper,

designed the first folding kayak. Sea kayaking journeys since then have been nothing short of amazing. Peter Pool from Trek Outdoor Australia wrote of Karl Schotts' two years of paddling from 1923: "He paddled down the Suez Canal, crossed the Indian Ocean to India, then... around India to Singapore." Atlantic Ocean crossings were achieved by Captain Romer in 1928 and Hannes Lindemann in 1956. In 1977 kayaks rounded Cape Horn. In the previous year the author of what many regard as the definitive book on sea kayaking, Derek C. Hutchinson, led a sea kayak expedition in the North Sea. Ed Gillet paddled sixty-three days solo from the West Coast of the United States to Hawaii. Australian journeys in the 1980s have been many, including Rodney Dredge's trip from Brisbane to New Guinea and the 1986/88, 12,000 nautical mile voyage around Australia by Mark Darby and Michelle Thesse.

As it passes over the water surface a sea kayak leaves no lasting mark, generates no pollution, and disturbs no other living creature. Sea kayakers travel under their own muscle power, reading the weather and the sea. To the sea kayaker the same stretch of water becomes different each time it is paddled — each day produces a completely new situation.

Setting out on a sea kayaking voyage might seem to some akin to a shipwrecked sailor putting a note in a bottle and pitching it into the sea — it might never reach land. Set against a backdrop of burgeoning ocean swells and wave-lashed coastlines, sea kayaks do appear slim, frail, diminutive craft, but today, they are stable and seaworthy.

Yet as safe as kayaks are, it is the paddler's skills that are vital in dealing with the fickle, unpredictable, and at times dangerous moods of the sea. Sea kayakers need commonsense and good judgment, well developed paddling techniques, a knowledge of the sea and the marine environment and competence in self-rescue. They develop these skills by joining others — first on sheltered trips then on trips gradually increasing in difficulty. Three boats is a bare minimum for exposed coastal paddling.

In either single or twin kayaks, paddlers use light, twin-bladed, offset paddles (see page 252) in a smooth flowing action which makes the nautical miles pass under the hull in a surprisingly short time. Setting a rhythm and establishing an easy pace takes practice, but once established even dreaded headwinds and a rising short chop can be tackled in an efficient manner. Efficient yes, dry no. Lovers of staying dry should not try sea kayaking — and particularly should not try punching into choppy waters as the front paddler in a twin kayak. You'll be frequently wet, and occasionally cold — except in tropical waters. But spray, and the occasional dollop of green water, is a small hardship to endure.

Even with a good paddling rhythm sea kayaking is physically demanding, especially on the lower back, shoulders and arms, but it is far more so if you are not properly braced. Aside from a few sore muscles and a wet bum, for the beginner, the rocking action of the turning wrist can produce a kind of repetitive strain injury termed "paddler's wrist". Doing anything

other than paddling for a day or two is the only cure.

A combination of ancient, time-proven design skills paired with modern materials and advanced safety concepts gives sea kayaks exceptional strength, flotation and sea kindliness.

Though based on original Eskimo craft, the development of more stable designs which incorporated waterproof bulkheads, accessible through watertight hatches, and hand operated bilge pumps, have dramatically increased the sea-going abilities of the craft. Put simply, narrow kayaks are unstable, wide ones are stable, but the shape and characteristics of the hull are also significant. Great initial stability is fine in a pond, but can be dangerous at sea. For example, a five metre wide, flat-bottomed barge is very unlikely to fall over but is impossible to padde; pencil thin, round-bottomed boats go like rockets but unless perfectly balanced tend to spend most time upside down.

Modern sea kayak designers seek to achieve a workable compromise between stability and manoeuvrability, designing craft which will part the waves with a sharply pointed bow, have a flatter forward section to give lift and a broad midsection for stability. Rather than just sitting in them, kayaks are "worn" by their paddlers. In something akin to the driver's seat of a Formula 1 racing car, the paddler squeezes into a snug cockpit. Legs are supported at the sides by knee pads and feet make firm contact with a footrest. Rear paddlers in a two seater have their feet in two rudder pedals. The lower back is held by firm webbing or padding. Rather than slopping about in a vacuum, any body movement of the paddler is immediately reflected in a change of the kayak's attitude.

Around the cockpit is a coaming about twenty-five millimetres wide over which an elasticised skirt or spray cover is fitted. It is held up on the body by an over-the-shoulder strap. It is not as fetching a garment as one could imagine, but it is very necessary for stopping litres of water dumping into the boat. Making sure the top chest elastic fits firmly is a good idea — if it doesn't you will have the memorable experience of a dollop of chilled sea water slipping inside the spray cover and landing on your lap.

Launchings and landings in a sea kayak are about as much fun as two consenting humans can have in public and stay legal. At the very least they are memorable events. Getting aboard, fixing the spray skirt, pushing off and paddling out through the surf is fine in theory, but fraught with fickle tricks of nature. The Murphy's Law of sea kayaking says that any spray skirt will refuse to be fitted upon seeing an approaching rogue wave. It also says that choosing a safe place above the large waves to get into the boat and fit the skirt will ensure that no future wave comes near you. Conversely, being three paces too far into the water before boarding guarantees that the largest set of waves will arise from nowhere to bounce you about like a lump of waterlogged driftwood.

Once out through the surf and in clearer water, paddling a sea kayak is either a joy or a pain in the arse. Using offset paddles (one at right angles to the other) can be very relaxing provided it suits your

dexterity — either right handed or left handed. Right handed paddlers use the right wrist to turn the shaft as the left blade is about to enter the water; vice versa for left handers. Becoming composed is a matter of being well braced in the boat and finding a cadence which suits.

As paddlers, some people resemble duck dabblers. They attack the job like noisy threshing machines with a high dipping rate and a very shallow stroke. This is a wonderful stroke for bow paddlers in a twin kayak wishing to create a continual shower for the stern paddler (who becomes sterner as the shower soaks through to the skin). Other kayakers utilise the benefits of a longer paddle, stroking at a slower rate but making each paddle blade do more while it is in the water. I find this style less tiring and quieter and it generates less flying water. For compatibility between paddlers it is essential that both use the same style — in that way the cadence established by the bow paddler can be synchronised by the (happy) stern paddler.

The strokes used for sea kayaking are the same as those used for conventional kayaking but usually only the forward, backward, draw and sweep strokes are needed. The main difference is that timing your strokes with the approaching waves becomes very important to achieve smooth paddling when a heavy sea is running. When side-on to breaking waves sea kayakers lean into each wave, rather than the opposite which is taught in white-water kayaking.

Waves are the most exhilarating and frightening part of sea kayaking. Hitting the crest of a wave then sliding down into the trough and watching the next one slide towards you is wonderful stuff. The big ocean swells are seas generated from a long way off which smooth out into long, regular, definite wave lengths. Unfortunately they are also interspersed with locally generated seas which have sharp irregular crests that can often spill forward forming whitecaps. Paddling close to

the seaward sides of headlands and islands brings you in contact with deflected waves, that is, waves which have bounced back. Being at the point of contact between incoming and outgoing waves, called a haystack, is not the place to be in a sea kayak.

As waves shallow near shore their speed decreases but their height increases and they eventually topple over. This is fine for beach landings when the waves break at a gentle slope, but the real excitement is generated by a dumping shorebreak

in which all the wave's energy is released at once. A steep sloping beach or offshore wind can create dangerous conditions for sea kayaks. When behind waves, dumpers can be distinguished by a white smoke of spray wisping away from their crests close to the shore. The recommended method for tackling dumpers is to wait for the largest set to pass then paddle in right on the back of the last. The trick is to pick which is the last big one.

On a sea kayaking trip in South West Tasmania we made the right choices, some of the time.

SOUTH WEST SEA KAYAKING

As we slip astern of the Celery Top Islands, a warm sun lights on the dispersing clouds. They take any vestige of breeze with them and leave us paddling on the highly-polished, bronze water. The bronze comes from tannin which leeches out of thousands of little streams whose waters slide down from surrounding mountains and slip into Bathurst Harbour. As we skim along, the doubled image of one of these mountains, Rugby, is reflected in the waters borne from its slopes. And as blades flash in time with each pair of paddlers, another set of paddlers keeps exactly the same time from beneath the water surface.

By morning tea-time a delicate arc of glowing sand called Balmoral Beach emerges from behind a little headland; we have travelled seven and a half kilometres in an hour and a half. The speed of these boats is amazing. The morning plans of a camp inside Bathurst Channel are blown away as we nose out into Port Davey and encounter our first

□ *Beach launchings can be wet affairs, even with the assistance of a couple of helpers.*

239

sluggish ocean swells after they have sneaked past the Breaksea Islands. Perfect conditions encourage us to have an island lunch. Close inspection reveals a problem — finding a landing place on the jagged shore.

Grant and I land by using the swell to lift us onto a comforting bed of kelp. Fine, but now what? What looked like an ideal place to pull the boat out is an impossible jumble of hull-cutting rock and the swells are lifting the boat and swirling it like a toy. From shore I balance on kelp the size of small trees and attempt to heave the bow around. It jams and I take one step too many; half a metre of water becomes twenty. A backwash whooshes me out to sea like a bobbing cork, then the next one returns me to beside the bow. In the interim before the next swell, I can finish lifting the bow over the rock it's jammed on and the nasty grinding sound coming out of the stern ceases. No, it is not Grant's teeth, just the rudder. Our companions find an easier exit path and we join them, suitably chastened.

Breaksea has long been in the possession of thousands of shearwaters. Not that there's much to see, all their homes are underground. Climbing to a vantage point on the island, we are careful not to cause cave-ins or to frighten the chicks. But this is the least of their worries since these mutton birds, as shearwaters are known locally, have a bit of a hard trot. They are still killed and eaten by Tasmanians, and since 1989 have been trying to cope with an international ecological disaster. Each year short-tailed shearwaters migrate 24,000 kilometres to Alaska,

site of the *Exxon Valdez's* 50.9 million litre oil spill.

Thankfully, the only white froth despoiling the Southern Ocean blue that I can see from a knife-edged vantage point is caused by large swells exploding against the seaward side of Breaksea. We feel their power once back in the kayaks and heading across open water towards Norman Cove. The last of twenty-four kilometres of paddling has begun as we start to get a lift from shore-bound waves rattling past us on a collision course with the beach. An adrenalin surge has us paddling fast and nudging in behind a generously proportioned wave as it arrives on the beach. We get up and out of the boat, and we run it up on hard sand and out of range of the froth of the waves behind us. Coming in behind us, Anne and Bob get a touch too enthusiastic, pick a large wave, catch it, broach, almost disappear in a sea of white foam as it breaks over them, then emerge again still upright and are swept up the beach sideways — to grins, relief and laughter all round.

High tide at Norman Cove leaves not much but bleached rock showing above the water, so we snuggle down into six little patches of comfy rocks for a night under the stars. Comfortable rocks are the ones left over when the uncomfortable ones have been removed. Choosing which is which is the problem. During the night I wake and am sure the cymbal sounds of the surf are letting forth with renewed vigour heralding big morning rollers but it is just my overworked imagination. From my bivvy bag the dawn reveals still-benevolent lapping waves lazily falling onshore.

☐ OPPOSITE *A superb undersea garden mirrors a time-worn, pinnacle of rock that faces out into an uncharacteristically smooth Great Southern Ocean.*

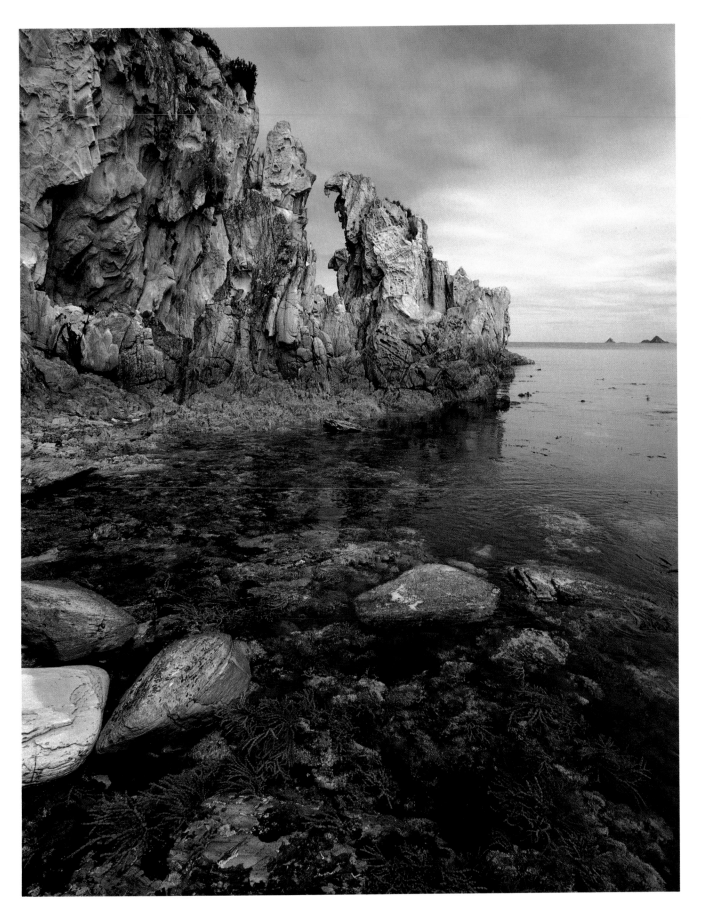

Of course, after photographing the others making good escapes through an easy slop, Grant and I pick a nice set of rollers to contest and emerge with a boat half full of water. We bail and pump and the boat is soon dry(ish). Heading to Big Caroline Rock via Swainson Islands we take a roller coaster short cut, knifing through a small gap under the uplifting attention of a back wave. The closer we come to Big Caroline the bigger it grows and the smaller we shrink. Sitting out alone facing into the roaring forties it is one jumbo sized rock. Massive ocean swells are simply shrugged off. This is fine for Caroline but exciting for us as the swells push and prod our little kayak like a new baby at a christening party.

As we paddle past, Hilliard Head is also knocking back swells like a committed drinker sinking stubbies. It's a mad crazy drunken world where the kayaks plunge and dip and dance. At last we can hang a left, enter calmer conditions and let the swells become stern waves. The good books on sea kayaking always treat stern waves kindly since they are

wonderful boosts to the ego; speed gains are spectacular when running forward wave-assisted. But it helps to conserve energy if you ease your paddles in the troughs since that's where you get the greatest drag.

In this hiccoughing fashion the kilometres zip past. All too soon we are at that terrible point of indecision again — out the back of breaking waves. We engage in a period of cerebral dithering under the guise of wave-watching. It's a long paddle and it's not getting any shorter while we sit here. A gaggle of big waves departs and so do we, finding a slot to sit in. Unfortunately the slot is moving faster than we are and looking back the waves loom even larger. Foam, spray and adrenalin are a heady mixture, inciting us to maniacal paddling. It works and we land on a hard surface. Unfortunately, we've landed not on the beach, but on a kelp covered rock — deep too, I discover, upon leaping over the side to drag us in.

Bob and Anne again supply the most exciting finish with a double broach this time, but unsportingly refuse the chance to do a complete 360 degree rollover for my spray-covered camera. Mike and Lisa do their usual accomplished landing. Our campsite is 100 metres away on a smooth grassy bank above a little creek in a shelter of blossoms. And it would appear we have arrived just in the nick of time. Waiting to welcome us is an army of march flies desperate for lunch, and a camouflaged squadron of mossies awaiting dinner.

How perfect is the weather's timing. A dry night, a sunny morn, and it begins to sprinkle just as I am shoehorning my last bit of gear

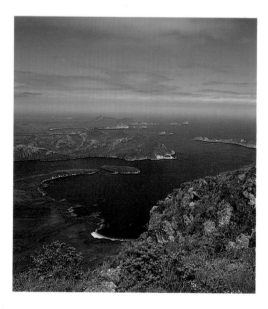

☐ From the summit of Mt Stokes looking out into Port Davey, Tasmania. The Breaksea Islands can be seen to the right.

242

into the forward hatch. After having performed this ritual each morning, I've found the right objects to fill in those curiously-shaped, sealed compartments in a sea kayak. All goes well until the last item. Just how can a sleeping bag grow overnight? Maybe I'm just getting weaker from paddling.

This morning Grant and I try yet another start technique; rear paddler holds boat, bow paddler in, boat grounds, rear in, skirt on, push off, away! Hell, it works, I think, as we do our interpretation of a Maori war party at full speed. Things are going well through the froth and the biggest wave in the group is just thinking about breaking as we drive up its face, and my end of the boat is completely airborne as we fly out the other side, landing with an excited yell, upright and relatively dry. Now, that is the way to do a beach take off.

We do all of half a kilometre before detouring to photograph a basking fur seal. I'm repacking the land camera when a series of loud booms echoes across the water. Everyone looks up and towards Sugarloaf Rock — in the direction of the sounds. As we draw close in to the island a white cray boat begins to move slowly away. Puzzling over the sounds, we paddle away from Stevens Bay across an oily sea. Low cloud and a misty sea combine to bathe us in a soft milky light.

From Wendar Island we can see sea lions on Sugarloaf. With memories of having dived with these wonderful creatures last month, I paddle over enthusiastically. I'm sure they'll be fascinated by weird looking creatures in long thin boats only a few centimetres off the sea. They see us all right, and make a frantic scramble to hit the water. But there is no surfacing about the boats, no playing, no big-eyed stares, just blank water. Yet some have stayed on the rocks. Edging closer I see why. The blood is still glistening fresh from the bullet holes in their hides. Other flattened carcasses indicate previous killings. And in the water is the floating body of a sea lion. We ease over to it, lay alongside and realising it is tagged, remove its tag. (It proves to be from Seal Rocks in New South Wales.) Cray pot floats are also nearby. Resisting the desire to sink the lot, we jot down the details and paddle on silently, stunned by what we have witnessed. I find it hard to believe anyone could murder the rarest sea lions in the world.

Rain settles in, and it comes complete with a headwind and a short soaking chop. The sea kayak becomes infected with gloom and feels like a leaden barge. These are fourteen of the hardest kilometres I've ever paddled and after more than five hours paddling my legs feel like marshmallow straws as I get out of the boat.

Next morning we hold a rafted consensus meeting. With conditions overcast but clearing on the horizon, we decide to head for South East Bight via open sea. There's nothing in the west for many thousands of nautical miles and the much travelled swells knock into Pt St Vincent with venom. The Saint gives as good as it gets, and the sea is a maelstrom of punch drunk waves through which our three sea kayaks attempt to bob and weave.

After what seems like a month of being chucked up and down,

and with North Head abeam, I'm as green as the sea. It's touch and go whether I will just slip over the side and put myself out of my misery, but ten minutes beyond North Head lies a different world: a smooth turquoise world fringed with a forest of kelp. The craggy, reef-fringed rocky beach never looked better. And there's a bundle of driftwood to make an impromptu kayak landing ramp. Again on solid ground, we can snooze, swim, play with the fish, view the crays, capture natural beauty on film, indulge in a long lunch. This is indeed heaven on earth.

Two kilometres further on we find an easy-to-land-on beach complete with its own natural breakwall of rock and kelp. We go for broke and surf to shore. The campsite is at the back of the sandy beach beside a softly singing stream, with only a few squillion beach fleas for company.

Dusk falls softly and gradually. First it shows a delicate sliver of new moon, but pure darkness reveals the faintest round image of the full moon to come. Once tucked into my sleeping bag I lie there wrapped in the night sky listening to effervescent surf expiring on the sand. I am asleep before the moon is fully up.

The shore break dances to the tune of the ocean, and this morning it is a riotous beat. The western sky has strong streaks of cloud charging across the blue, heralding the arrival of strong winds. Yesterday's low tide surf has grown ominously large. Just standing on the beach looking at it is very bad for my nerves.

☐ The unusually tranquil waters of Port Davey.

This morning everyone is dragging their feet, not willing to hasten the time for departure.

Leaving aside their reputations for spectaculars, Anne and Bob are first away perfectly picking a break between monsters. Minutes pass then Lisa and Mike streak out through a couple of large chunks of white water. They increase their paddling rate to frantic when a wave about half the length of the boat starts to stand up in front of them. It's only by the finest of margins that they lift up the wall and break out the other side. Fine, two boats out and one to go.

The pattern seems to be half a dozen monsters then a break of smaller waves. Grant and I ride out the first half dozen standing still in the froth, then we decide to go in what should be the quieter set. Fifteen metres later things are not looking good. Up rises a nasty looking green wall. As I realise its intentions the look on my face would probably be worth framing. The wave breaks on the tip of the bow and hits me with the force of a small freight train. I'd fondly imagined being able to bend forward and go through the wave in the style of body surfing, but being locked into a kayak makes this impossible. The body of water simply unfolds me with a snap and flattens me back along the cockpit coaming and deck.

I'm still in shock at the force of

☐ FOLLOWING PAGE The waters of the wild south west coast of Tasmania abound with small crayfish and other fish that can be fed by hand.

☐ *Driving up the face of an almost-breaking wave without a second to spare.*

the first wave when number two runs us down. Dead in the water is a good description of our readiness for this experience. I call out to Grant to make sure he hasn't been swept out of the boat, not realising that seated in the bow I'm taking most of the weight of water. His exact reply is lost in the washing machine action of wave number three, which attempts to slew us into a pre-rollover attitude. This prompts us into a frightened paddling action and we are lined up just in time for waves four and five. The quieter set follows. Now we can rip out, up and over, to finally claim that sanctity of pre-broken water.

"What kept you?" comes the query from our companions as we paddle our water-filled kayak up to them. They only saw us pushing off — followed by an increasingly ominous space of time with no sight of our kayak. Pumping and

bailing, we fill in the details of an experience neither of us is keen to repeat.

The actual height of ocean swells is difficult to estimate from the cockpit of a kayak. Consensus brings it to about five metres. This sounds a lot to me, but all the swells look big. Some are so tall that they literally take my breath away. It is hard not to exaggerate how tall. When we are at the bottom of each trough the island we are travelling toward, West Pyramid, is completely swallowed.

We decide that the Southern Ocean is not the place to be with a westerly gale just over the horizon. We set course for North Head and find it a place of white violence. Ocean swells have set about the task of reducing it to rubble. Rough Bay is living up to its name and the back washes are wildly confusing, tossing us about in a completely offhand manner.

Even from a distance I can see Pt St Vincent has a point break large enough for the most fanatical big board Hawaiian surfer. Never mind the aesthetics, it scares the hell out of me.

We detour out further seaward to ensure we clear the breaking rollers, but even then, as soon as we turn, massive swells (harmless to us) seem to drive us towards the breaking water. It's just a trick of distance and angles but even so, as we rip past the danger zone, each time a roller the size of a small block of flats breaks it sounds like an exploding depth charge has been released just off the stern quarter. I'm discovering that pure fright is the fastest temporary cure for sea-sickness yet devised. Whaler's Point is the last of the big swells, so feeling a little cocky, Grant and I surf through a short cut inner gap. Success, relief at being in more sheltered waters, and tiredness combine into overconfidence. Fifty metres off the beach, which is to be our camp for tonight, we decide to catch a wave to end an amazing day. We have no problem catching it.

What we don't realise is that the wind is off shore and makes this roller stand to attention. Up goes the stern and down goes the bow. As the bow and I do a deep-six dive, it's like the worst fear of a submariner — being left on deck as the sub dives. In what seems like fascinatingly slow motion, the bow disappears and is replaced by a sheet of moving green water. It rises up its only obstruction, me, obliterating my world. A broach pulls us hard left, the stern goes even higher and we perform the easy half of an Eskimo roll. I'm still in the kayak, upside down only ten metres out from the beach unwilling to let my leaden camera gear take a dive to the bottom. I lean up to get a breath at the same time as Grant, who has come out of the stern, stands up in the shoulder deep water and pushes the kayak upright. The wave recedes and two sodden paddlers slide a barge-like kayak up the beach. It is hardly a textbook ending.

☐ *Just near our campsite at the exit to Bathurst Channel, an icy fresh water stream glows with deceptive warmth in the afternoon light.*

LOCATION GUIDE

Bathurst Harbour, Port Davey and the surrounding coastline lie within Tasmania's South West National Park. During past glaciations this area has experienced dramatic sea level changes. Bathurst Harbour is a drowned valley. The present coastline is rugged and exposed, featuring high cliffs, arches, blowholes, sea caves and wave-cut platforms. Given headland protection, beaches have evolved. The oldest Precambrian rocks (mainly quartzites, phyllites and schists) form the backbone of the south west.

Wet and cool, the climate of the region has much in common with parts of South America and New Zealand. Within the park are alpine environments, rainforest, eucalypt forest, scrub, heath, moorland and grassland communities. Unfortunately many species of timber are killed by fire. Bushfires have been started for most of the last 30,000 years by Aborigines, but of late, prospectors, timber getters, fishermen, and occasionally bushwalkers have caused immensely damaging fires.

The region has few introduced species and burrowing freshwater crayfish and marsupials are reminders of the ancient super-continent Gondwana. Six of the thirty-seven mammal species are endemic to Tasmania, as are fifteen of the 150 bird species. There are twenty-one species of freshwater fish. Off shore islands, being remote and severe environments, are home to elephant seals, New Zealand fur seals, Australian sea lions and Australian fur seals. They are also important habitats for seabirds including shearwaters, fairy penguins, diving petrels, albatross, Australian gannet and fairy prions.

Many middens, dated at between one and four thousand years old are evidence of Aboriginal re-occupation of the south west. By the time Europeans arrived the region was inhabited by the Port Davey tribe of about 300 to 400 people. The port was "discovered" by James Kelly in 1815, though Matthew Flinders noted the entrance in 1789 when on a voyage in the *Norfolk*. Seeking huon pine, minerals and whales, the Europeans entered the region in the 1800s. A settlement of more than fifty people was established inside Port Davey at Settlement Point and a whaling settlement was once in Bramble Cove. By 1927 there were no inhabitants. Port Davey State Reserve of 512 hectares was declared in 1951, Lake Pedder National Park (23,877 hectares) came in 1955, and in 1968 it was extended by 168,192 hectares and became known as the South West National Park. The present park covers an area of 442,240 hectares and was included on the World Heritage List as part of the Tasmanian Wilderness nomination in 1989.

THE BASICS

Designs

Originating from Eskimo craft, the early sea kayaks were characterised by a strong sheerline (curvature of the gunwale line) which gave good sea riding characteristics and a lot of rocker (curvature of the keel line) which resulted in excellent turning

□ OPPOSITE *Bathurst Harbour, Port Davey and the surrounding coastline lie within Tasmania's South West National Park. Wet and cool, the climate of the region has much in common with parts of South America and New Zealand.*

abilities but called on great skill to keep the kayak upright. This also prompted the development of numerous versions of the Eskimo roll — a means to re-right an upturned kayak while staying in the cockpit.

Paddling

The paddle should be gripped so that your hands are slightly wider apart than the width of your shoulders. Your hands will keep warmer closer together, but in a high wind need to be placed further apart. In a twin kayak the front paddler has the hardest job due to a number of factors including the kayak's shape and the height of the paddling position, so it is advisable to swap around occasionally with the rear paddler. It is also nice to be able to direct where you are going — steering is done by the rear paddler via foot pedals connected to the rudder. Paddle blades with a more rounded tip allow the blade to enter

and leave the water with minimum resistance.

Clothing

Weather conditions dictate just how much warm clothing to wear. Some days require only bathers, tee shirt, fingerless gloves, broad hat and suncreen, and others demand thermal underwear, longjohn (sleeveless), wetsuit, wool socks and wetsuit booties, neoprene gloves, wool jumper and woollen hat.

Tides

Two high water tides and two low water tides occur each lunar day (twenty-four hours and fifty minutes approximately). Shortly after a new moon or a full moon, tides are highest high waters and lowest low waters (spring tides). About nine days after a new moon or a full moon are the neap tides — lowest high waters and highest low waters.

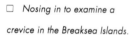

☐ *Nosing in to examine a crevice in the Breaksea Islands.*

SEA KAYAKING, SOUTH WEST TASMANIA — LUXURY CHECK LIST

Body Protection

Long sleeved wool & cotton shirts
Bandana
Broad brimmed hat (with chinstrap)
Strong cotton shorts
Long light cotton pants
Wool pants
Dunlop Volley sandshoes
Longjohn wetsuit (3 mm)
Wetsuit booties and woollen socks
Wetsuit gloves & fingerless sailing gloves
Bathers
Woollen sweaters
Gore-Tex waterproof full length jacket with
  hood and overpants
100 per cent UV protection sunglasses
Sunscreen
Rid insect repellent

Accommodation

Roomy tent, built in floor and insect netting
3 season Karrimat, Thermarest or Lilo mattress
Candle/reading torch (spare long life batteries)
Sleeping bag rated to 0 degrees C (e.g. J & H
  Bushlite)
Silk inner sheet

Getting There

Air to Hobart
Light plane to Melaleuca airstrip: Par Avion
  Airways.

Transport

Sea kayak hire (at either end of season):
  Open Spaces, 28 Criterion St, Hobart
Eight Day South West Sea Kayaking Tour:
  Open Spaces, address as above
Silva type compass
Plastic pealess whistle
Topgraphical Maps: Old River and Port Davey;
  Tasmania 1:100,000 series published by the
  Department of Lands Hobart
Nylon cord (>30 m)
Waterproof self-sealing inner bag
Extra waterproof pack liners
Smaller waterproof stuff sacks for clothing

Camping

Matches (in self-sealing plastic bags)
Candle lantern & spare candles
Swiss army knife
Cup, bowl, eating utensils
Trangia stove (with kettle)
Methylated spirits (in more than one container)
Food (worked out for each day and placed in self-
  sealing bags)
Toiletries, toilet paper and trowel
1 litre waterbottle & a 5 litre water bag or wine
  cask bladder for each person

Recreation

Light day pack (wear long pants, local treks
  can be damaging to bare legs)
Slater, Slater & Slater, *Field Guide to Australian
  Birds,* Lansdowne-Rigby, Willoughby, NSW,
  1986.
Flora & Fauna Checklists from Tasmanian
  National Parks & Wildlife Service
Nikonos amphibious camera with float
Camera bodies in very waterproof container
Lenses, wide (18 or 24 mm) for landscapes &
  telephoto (105 to 200 mm) for mountainscapes
Strong torch & flash unit for nocturnal visitors
Shower cover for camera
Sturdy tripod (keep out of salt water)
Slow & fast speed film
Notebook & pen

Sea Kayaking Clubs

Tasmanian Sea Canoeing Club:
  P.O. Box 599F, Hobart, Tas 7001
NSW Sea Kayakers: NSW Canoe Federation,
  3rd Floor, Sports House, 157–161 Gloucester
  Street, Sydney

Further Reading

Evans, J., *The Kayaking Book,* Stephen Greene
  Press, Lexington, Mass., 1983
Commonwealth Department of the Arts, Sport,
  the Environment, Tourism & Territories, & the
  Government of the State of Tasmania,
  *Nomination of the Tasmanian Wilderness by the
  Government of Australia for Inclusion in the World
  Heritage List,* September 1989.
Hutchinson, D.C., *Sea Canoeing,* Adam Charles
  Black, London, 1984
Norman, D., *All-Purpose Guide to Paddling,*
  Dean Norman, United States, 1976.
Pool, P., "Sea Kayaking — A Growing Sport",
  Paddle Power Magazine, Vol 1, No. 9, Sydney
  1988.
Skilling, B., *Complete Canoeing,* Kaye & Ward,
  London, 1973.

ACKNOWLEDGMENTS

This book has arrived instantly after a fifteen year apprenticeship of freelance writing and photography. In that time my articles appeared in a variety of Australian magazines and newspapers — mostly under the by-line of Leigh & Barbara Hemmings. I'd like to thank Barbara for sharing many of those years and acknowledge her assistance in my long learning curve in the craft of freelancing. I'd like to thank Shelley Cartledge for her invaluable encouragement, precise editing skills, and firm belief that the deadline could be met. Also, my thanks go to all State tourism authorities, but in particular to Tourism Tasmania, the Western Australian Tourism Commission, the South Australian Tourism Commission and Victour. I'd also like to thank the professional adventure tour guides with whom I've had the good fortune to travel, and the many fellow adventurers whose company I have enjoyed around the camp fire.

INDEX